IMAGES
of America

SCOTT COUNTY CEMETERIES

On the Cover: Pictured is the Koehler Mausoleum at Oakdale Cemetery in Davenport, Iowa. (Courtesy of the authors.)

IMAGES *of America*

SCOTT COUNTY CEMETERIES

John Brassard Sr.
and John Brassard Jr.

ARCADIA PUBLISHING

ISBN 978-0-7385-8315-0

Published by Arcadia Publishing
Charleston, South Carolina

Printed in the United States of America

Library of Congress Control Number: 2011933818

For all general information, please contact Arcadia Publishing:
Telephone 843-853-2070
Fax 843-853-0044
E-mail sales@arcadiapublishing.com
For customer service and orders:
Toll-Free 1-888-313-2665

Visit us on the Internet at www.arcadiapublishing.com

This book is dedicated to all those tens of thousands whose lives we still know nothing about

Contents

Acknowledgments		6
Introduction		7
1.	Private Mausoleums	9
2.	Mayors	23
3.	Doctors	41
4.	Lawyers and Politicians	51
5.	Businessmen and Farmers	59
6.	Killings, Murders, and Suicides	91
7.	Others	95
8.	Davenport as They Knew It	117

ACKNOWLEDGMENTS

The material contained in this book is based on facts received from newspaper articles, interviews, memoirs, and records of the period. More specifically, some of the books used were the *1882 History of Scott County*, *The Portrait and Biographical History of Scott County* (1895), *Downers History of Davenport and Scott County* (1910), *The History of Davenport and Scott County* (written by August Richter, 1917), and microfilms of newspapers and court records found in the Richardson-Sloane Special Collections of the Davenport Public Library.

We would like to give thanks to Deb Williams of Oakdale Cemetery and the librarians of the Davenport Public Library for their assistance. This book would not have been made possible without them. All photographs of gravesites are by the authors. Photographs of the 1866 Pioneer Settlers Association of Scott County were taken by the authors and are courtesy of Oakdale Cemetery. All other images are courtesy of the Richardson-Sloane Special Collections of the Davenport Public Library.

Introduction

Cemeteries are a place to remember our dead, and through them, our past. Our loved ones pass away, and we inter them in peaceful places so that they may enjoy their well-earned rest after experiencing their lives. We erect monuments to them, both grand and humble, so that their memory, at least some way, stands the test of time with the potential to be known by future generations.

In that regard, the people in early Davenport, Iowa, were no different than we are today. In 1856, a group of people decided to found a new cemetery at what was then an area north of the city. Called Oakdale, it originally had 40 acres with some 3,000 lots on it.

On a grassy hill in that cemetery, a white tombstone has stood for more than 100 years. It is between two to three feet tall and made from white limestone. The wear and tear of time and weather is evident upon it. This is the final resting place of J.M.D. Burrows, one of the original founders of Oakdale and, at one time, one of the wealthiest men in the city.

He came to the area in the late 1830s from Cincinnati, originally arriving in what was then the town of Stephenson, long since renamed Rock Island. Burrows went back east, settled his affairs and gathered his family, and returned to live in Davenport. He originally intended to be a farmer, but he decided against it and went into the merchant trade. Needing stock, he returned to Cincinnati and obtained a part of his initial stock of goods from his cousin, who was one of the largest grocers in that city at that time.

In 1839, Burrows's wife became gravely ill. A doctor by the name of E.S. Barrows treated her and improved her condition after two other doctors had failed. He became the Burrows' family physician after that point and remained so for several years.

Eventually, Barrows would move to Davenport and build a house that still stands at the corner of Sixth Street and Pershing Avenue. He also had a prestigious and successful medical practice. When Doctor Barrows decided to retire, he gave away his library of medical books to another local doctor. Of course, Barrows decided to bestow this gift upon his colleague by loading the books into his buggy, going to the physician's office, and throwing the books at his office door.

In the last days of his life, Doctor Barrows broke his hip after falling in his kitchen and died a relatively short time later. His remains lie in Oakdale Cemetery in a special coffin designed to deter body snatching, located a short distance west of his former patient.

J.M.D. Burrows earned a great deal of money and was very successful. He built a mansion for his family on a bluff overlooking the Mississippi that he named Clifton. When the Panic of 1857 happened (an economic crisis of the times), the repercussions of it bankrupted Burrows. He tried to recover his losses by investing in one mill initially and then another, but both burnt down.

Burrows became a shadow of his former self. He grew vegetables and sold them in a cart that he pushed around Davenport. Burrows would also go to the Koch meat processing plant and get pork products to sell. His wife and all of his children died before him. When his time came, he was laid to rest in Oakdale Cemetery, the cemetery he had helped to create.

In the north end of Davenport, in Mount Calvary Cemetery, is the grave of Antoine LeClaire and his wife, Marguerite. LeClaire was of French and Native American descent and spoke French, Spanish, English, and several different Native American languages. After the infamous Black Hawk War, he was awarded a large amount of land. LeClaire, with the help of others, turned it into the city of Davenport.

LeClaire was an enormously wealthy man. He funded the building of the first Catholic Church in Davenport, a small brick structure in downtown Davenport where St. Anthony's Catholic Church stands now. LeClaire also gave money for the building of several other churches of various denominations in the area.

LeClaire's first home in what would become Davenport was called the Claim House, as it was a stipulation of the Black Hawk Treaty that in order to receive the land awarded to him, he needed to build a home on the site of where the treaty was signed. This was in the area of Fifth Street and Fifth Avenue in Davenport. LeClaire did so, and then several years later, he donated the house to serve as the first railroad depot in Iowa.

His third and final home was a mansion set on a bluff overlooking the Mississippi River, built in the 1850s. During his life, Native Americans would come to the house and camp in the surrounding yard. LeClaire was a gracious host that was very well liked and respected by the natives. Even after his death, Native Americans continued to visit Marguerite LeClaire.

Of course, their headstones say nothing about these events. They say nothing of these people's dreams, ambitions, successes, and failures, but headstones do let us know that these people existed. Headstones provide us their identities and give hope that someone will remember them, even if it is only their names.

Through the following pages, we will glimpse into the lives of some of these people who helped shaped the world around them during the eras in which they lived. Some of these people were prominent citizens who were wealthy and were involved in politics, influencing society and the area through their professions. Others are remembered for tragic circumstances that arose or even ended their lives. No matter what the reason, all of these individuals have stories to tell. Please come with us as we explore their stories and see history through their eyes.

One

Private Mausoleums

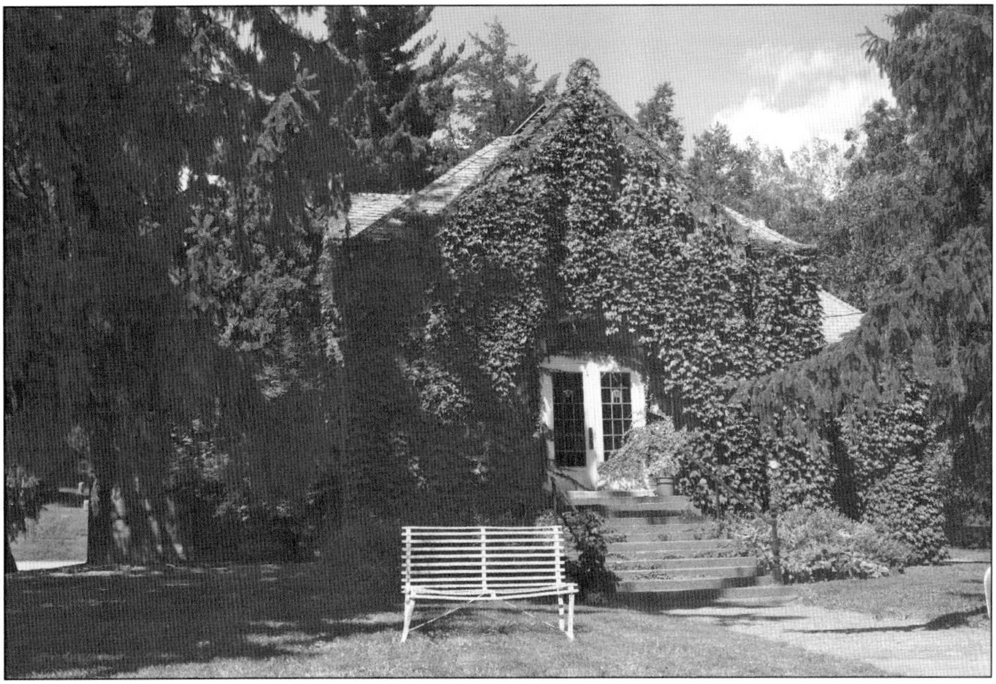

The Davenport Crematorium originally opened in 1891 in Fairmont Cemetery in the west end of Davenport, Iowa. The first person cremated there was Otto Kocher in March 1891. Kocher had worked as a clerk at J.H.C. Petersen's department store in downtown Davenport. His cremation was the first in the state of Iowa. The Davenport Crematorium is the ninth oldest crematorium still in existence in the United States.

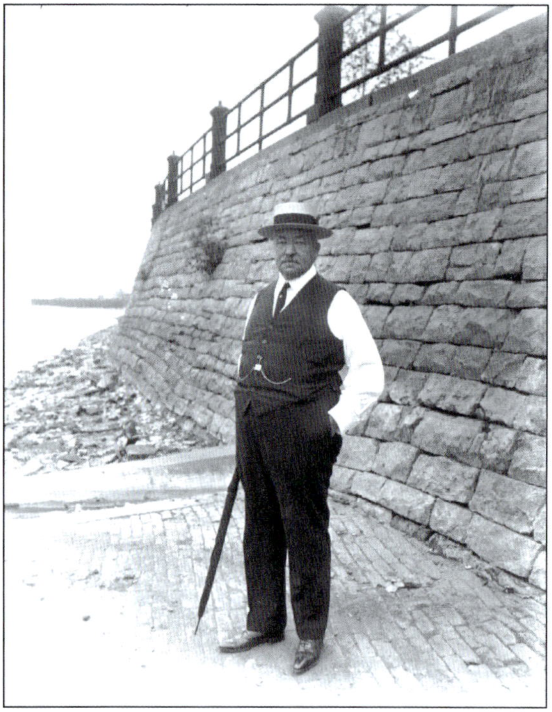

W.D. Petersen, one of the sons of J.H.C Petersen, was known as "the Father of the Levee." He had lobbied for the improvement of the levee after a trip to Europe where he had observed the development of German river city waterfronts and what it had done for those city economies. He donated large sums of his own money, inspiring the city council.

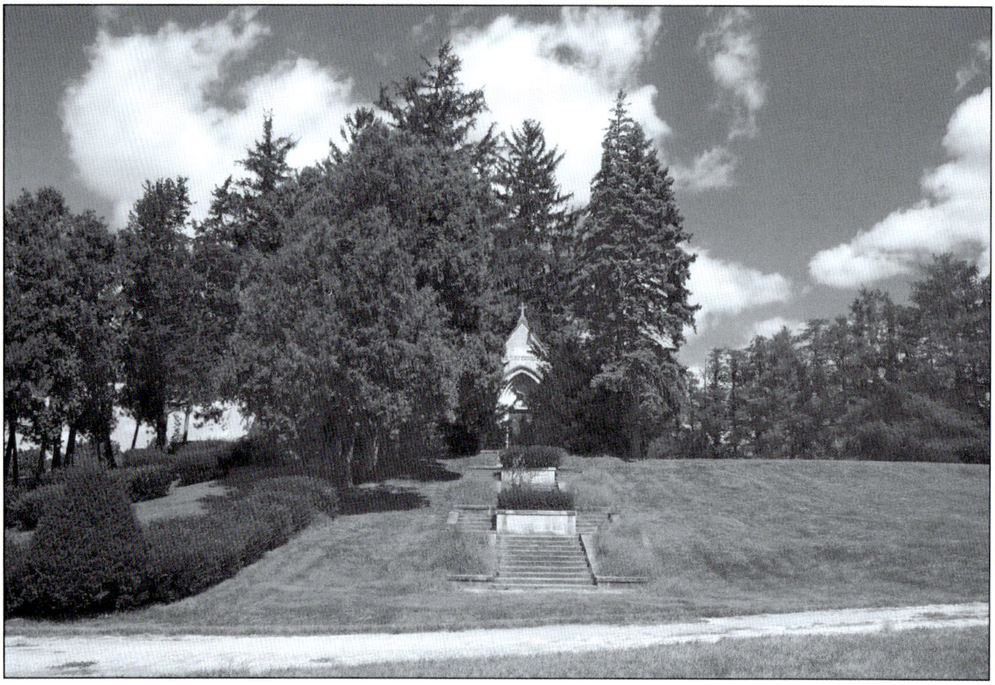

When his daughter Wilma died of heart complications, W.D. Petersen built the band shell at the levee in her memory for $50,000. He had this mausoleum constructed as his wife's memorial for $60,000 from 13-ton limestone blocks and marble imported from Greece, from the same quarries that supplied the temples and monuments there. He died from arteriosclerosis in Altadena, California, in 1928 and left an estate valued at $1,000,000.

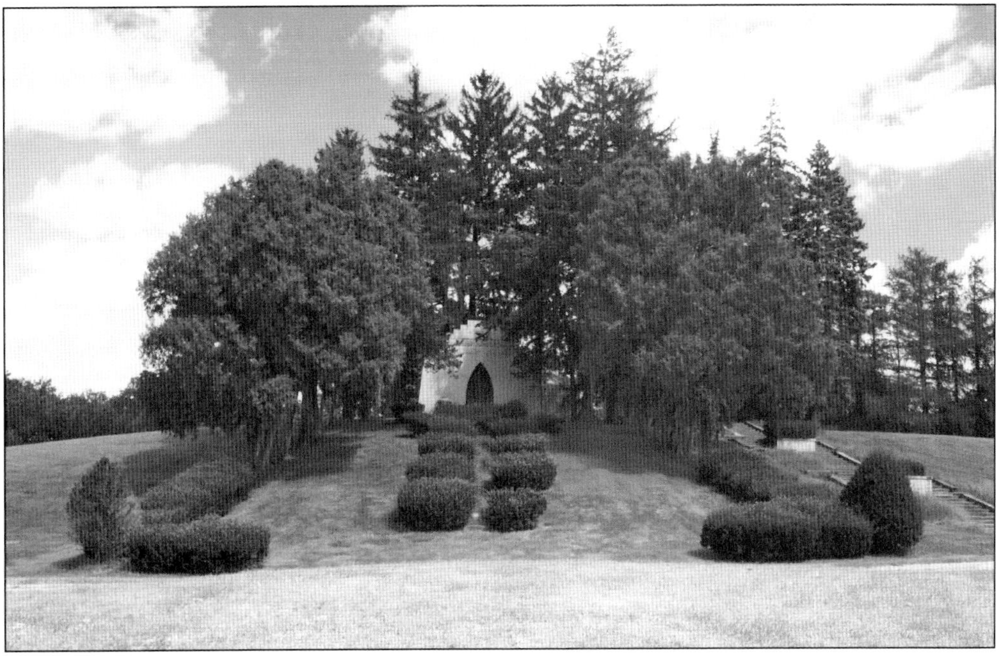

Hugo A. Koehler, a former resident of Davenport, died in St. Louis, Missouri, after an extended illness. He joined his brothers, Oscar and Henry, in the formation of the American Brewing Company in St. Louis. After the death of his brother Henry, he served as president of the company and later became president of the Independent Brewing Company in St. Louis.

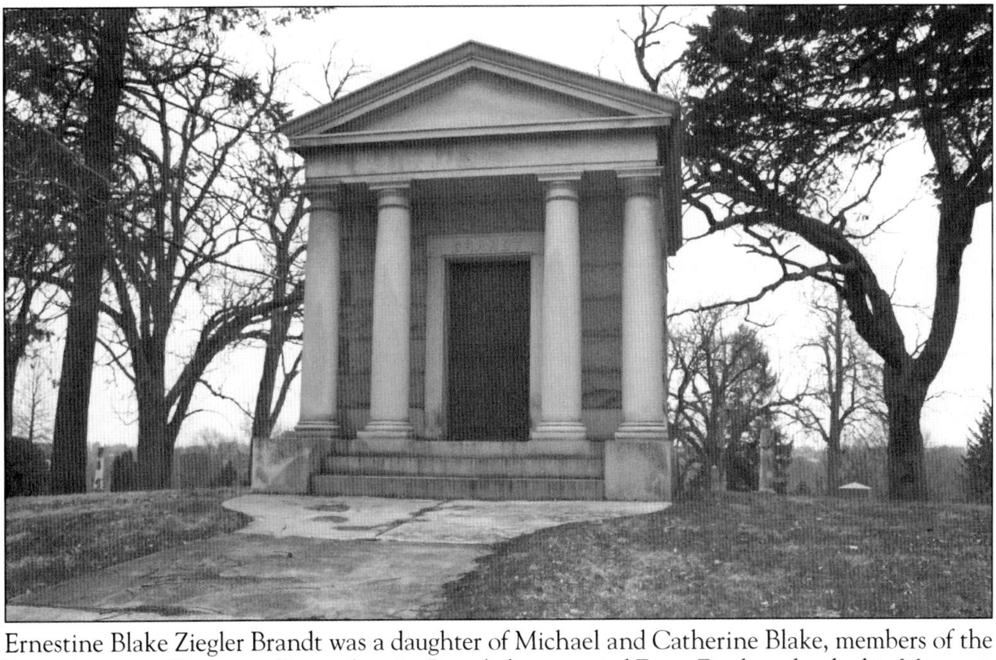

Ernestine Blake Ziegler Brandt was a daughter of Michael and Catherine Blake, members of the Rapp Society in Economy, Pennsylvania. Brandt first married Franz Ziegler, who died in Missouri. Their youngest son, William, was the Royal Baking Powder magnate, a mayor of New York City, and funded the Ziegler Polar expeditions in the early 1900s. He also erected the New Era church in Sweetland Township.

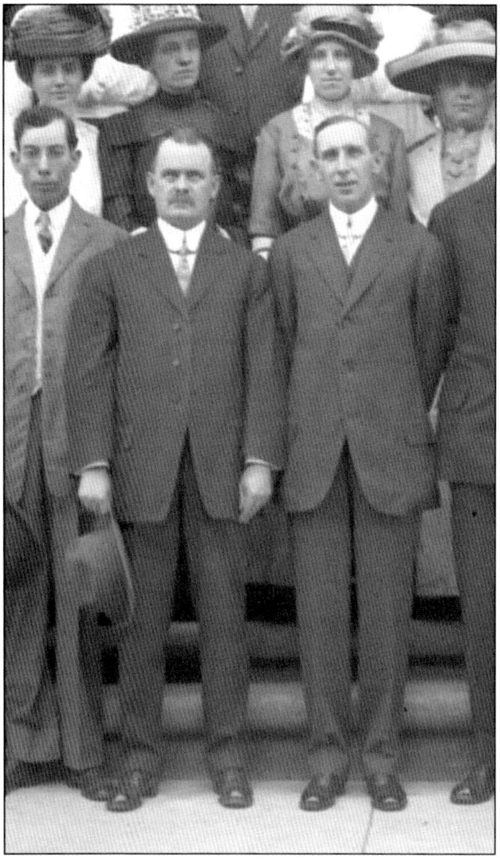

Singleton Gardiner (on left) was the superintendent of the Prudential Insurance Company in Davenport. On the night of January 11, 1926, the Gardiners, along with their maid, Sophie Inkman, and Charles Frey, a colleague of Gardiner's (on right), were unable to stop their vehicle on an icy patch of road and collided with a train as they approached Moline. Their Franklin Sedan was thrown into the air, and the gas tank exploded.

Singleton Gardiner died in the crash from heavy burns to his head and neck, but the others survived, thanks in large part to two men who came to their rescue. The injured were put on the train and taken to Moline. On the way to the hospital, the ambulance driving Charles Frey hit another car. Frey died at the hospital later. Gardiner lived at 1327 Arlington Avenue in Davenport.

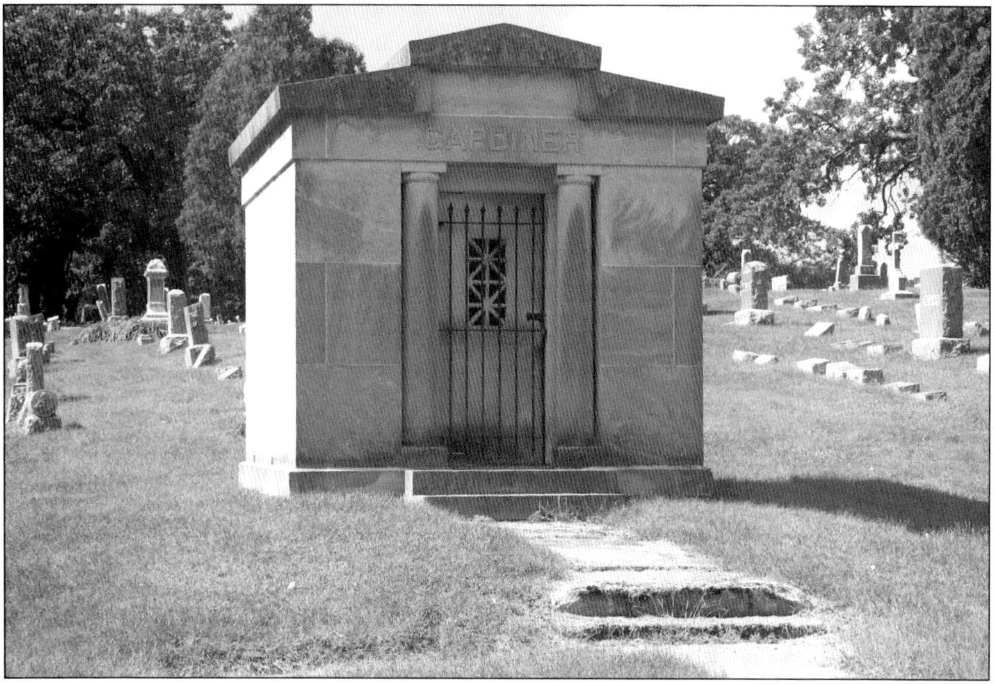

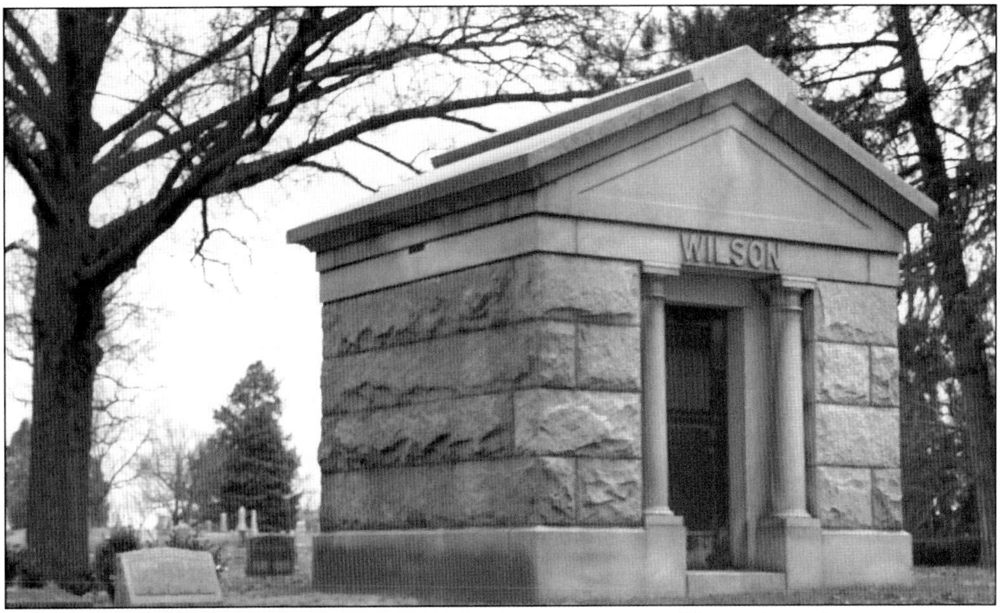

William Hamilton Wilson began practicing law in Davenport in 1871 and was the senior partner of the firm Wilson, Grilk & Wilson. A native of western Pennsylvania, he attended Washington & Jefferson College in Washington, Pennsylvania. His son Charles H. joined the firm in 1905.

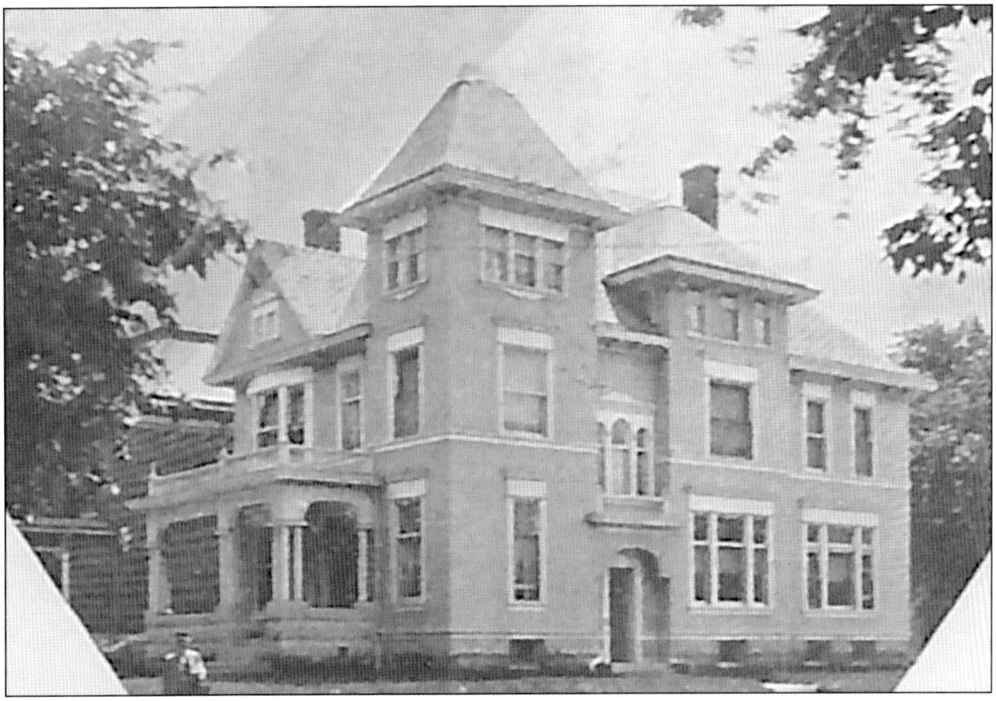

It has been said of William Hamilton Wilson that he "has probably saved more money to his clients through wise settlement of cases out of court than he has made for them in litigation." He was the president of the Davenport Loan, Building & Savings Association and a director and attorney for the Davenport Savings Bank. William died from a sudden heart attack at his home at 1430 Brady Street.

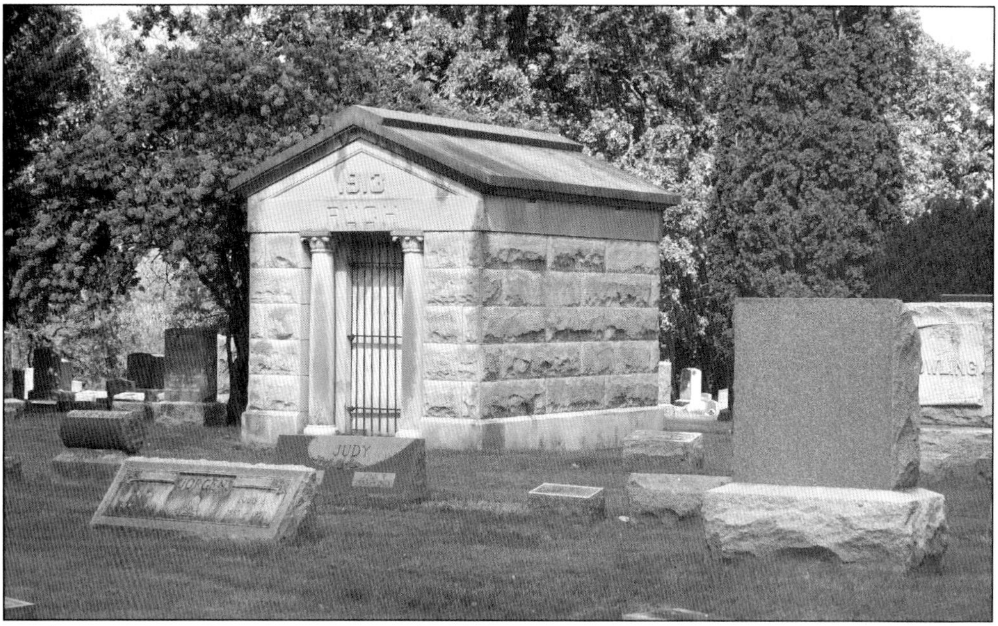

Balthaser Ruch was born in 1828 in Pittsburgh, Pennsylvania. He boated coal on the Ohio River, then mined coal in California for four years. Ruch later came to Davenport, living at 120 West Twelfth Street. He engaged in pork packing and made bricks with his brother John in Northwest Davenport. He manufactured 1,000,000 bricks annually.

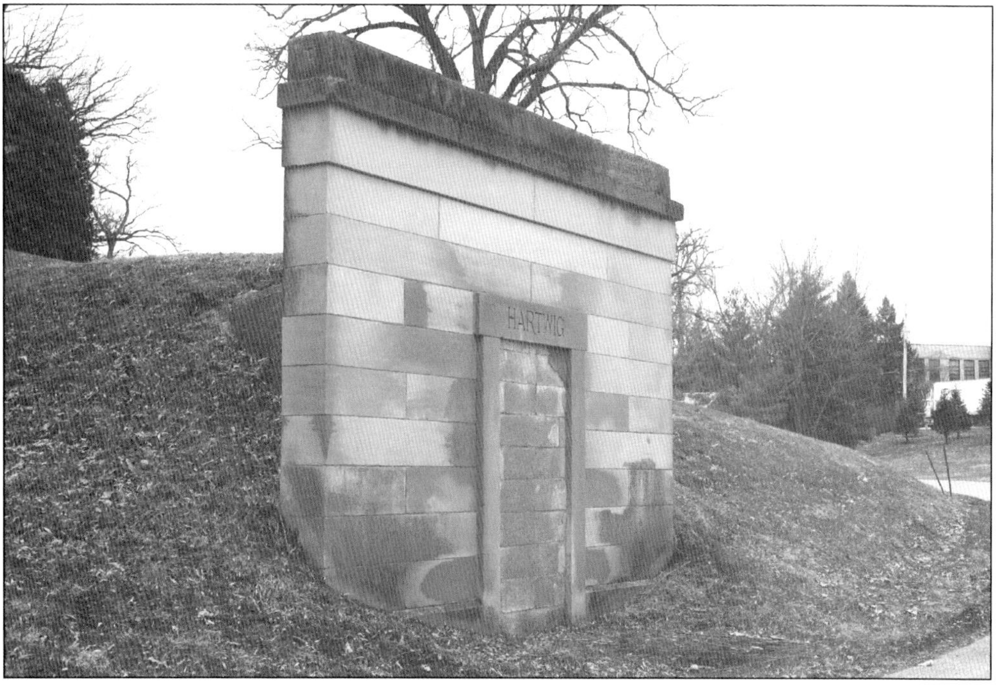

Caroline Hartwig, a former Union army nurse in the Civil War and the mother of a well-known local mortician, Albert Hartwig, died at age 91 of a stroke in her home at 428 1/2 West Second Street. Born in Germany, she was the wife of James H.V. Hartwig, who was the first proprietor of the Pennsylvania Hotel and later built the Western Hotel in 1863.

Joseph W. Bettendorf was born on October 10, 1864, the son of a schoolteacher. Bettendorf was a machinist and also worked as an assembly foreman. In 1886, he moved to Davenport where he and his brother William built the Bettendorf Metal Wheel Company. Later, the brothers would move their company to nearby Gilbertsville, which was later renamed Bettendorf in their honor.

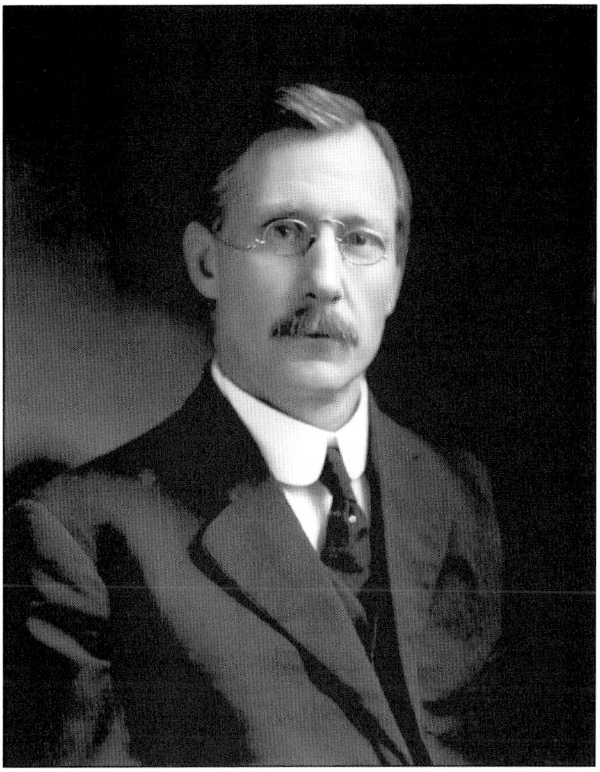

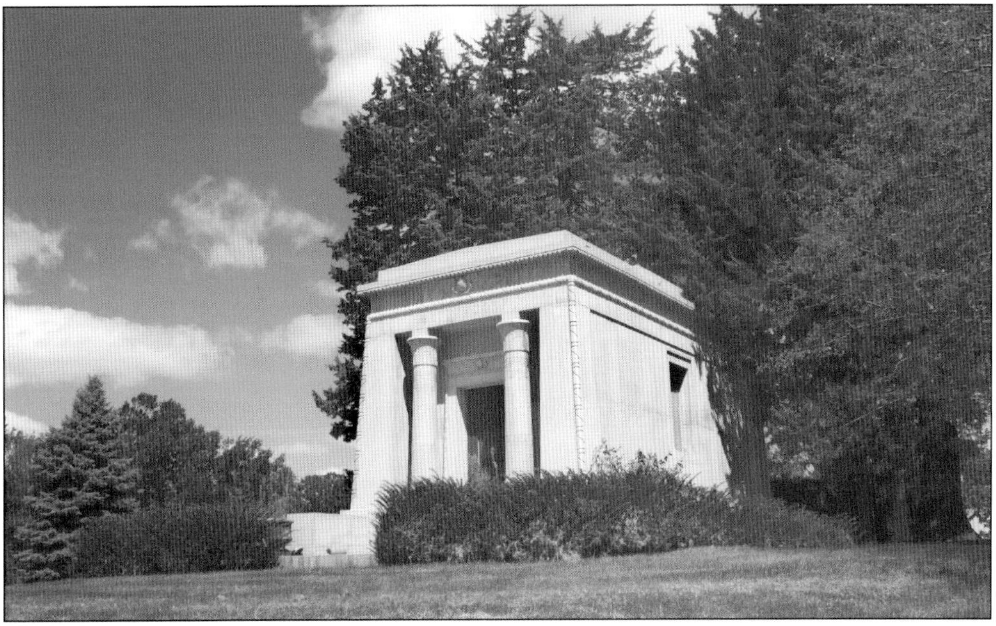

In 1890, Joseph W. Bettendorf went to Springfield, Ohio, to work and returned to Davenport three years later. He and his brother William went into business together, eventually building the Bettendorf Company in nearby Gilbert. They became extremely wealthy and erected mansions in Gilbert. Joseph died at his mansion from a coronary thrombosis in 1933. His estate was worth an estimated $738,596.

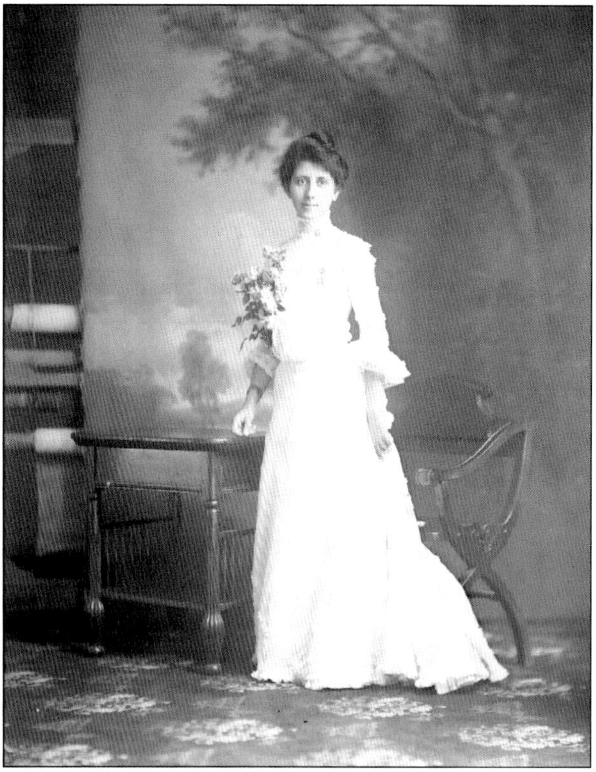

Selma Schricker was known as a lover of flowers. Born on October 13, 1880, to Lorenzo Schricker, the lumber magnate, Selma was a charitable woman who took pride in her lovely flower garden. She had imported a number of foreign flowers and plants to her garden. She died from cancer at her home on 1430 Clay Street when she was only 50 years old.

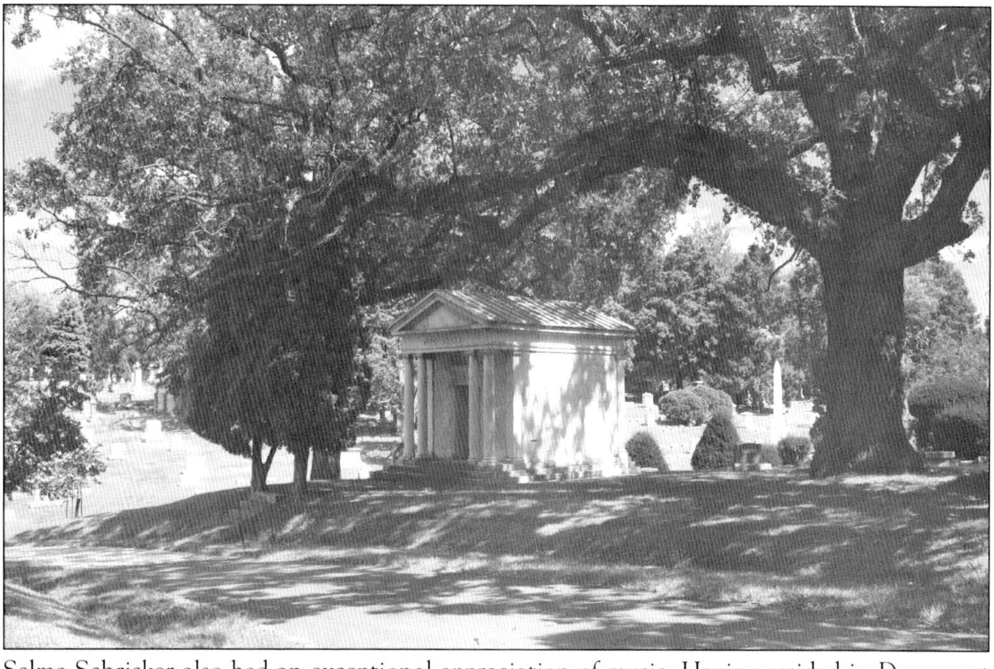

Selma Schricker also had an exceptional appreciation of music. Having resided in Davenport her entire life, she was educated in the area's public schools and graduated from St. Katharine's School. Among the assets in her $170,063.96 estate was a pearl necklace valued at $2,600, a mesh bag and vanity box worth an estimated $2,600, and $53,000 in real estate.

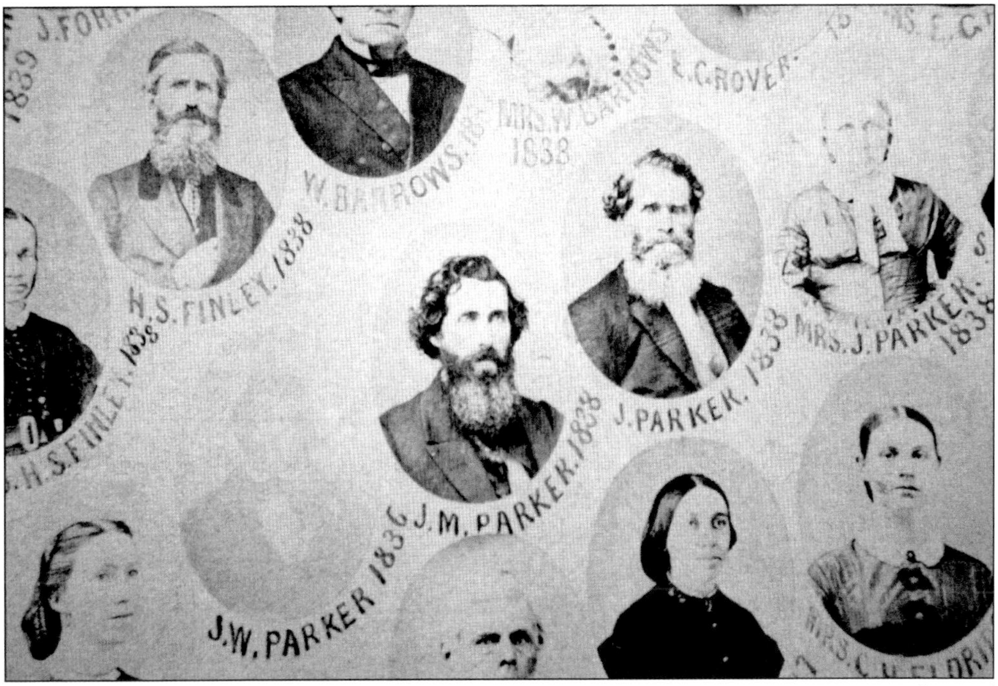

James Monroe Parker was born in Meshoppen, Pennsylvania, on May 20, 1824. He was educated there and worked in a woolen mill with his father until 1836. When he was 14 years old, he came to Davenport with his family. Parker worked as a clerk in general merchandising and dry goods stores for several years, after which he started work as a cashier at the bank of Cook and Sargent.

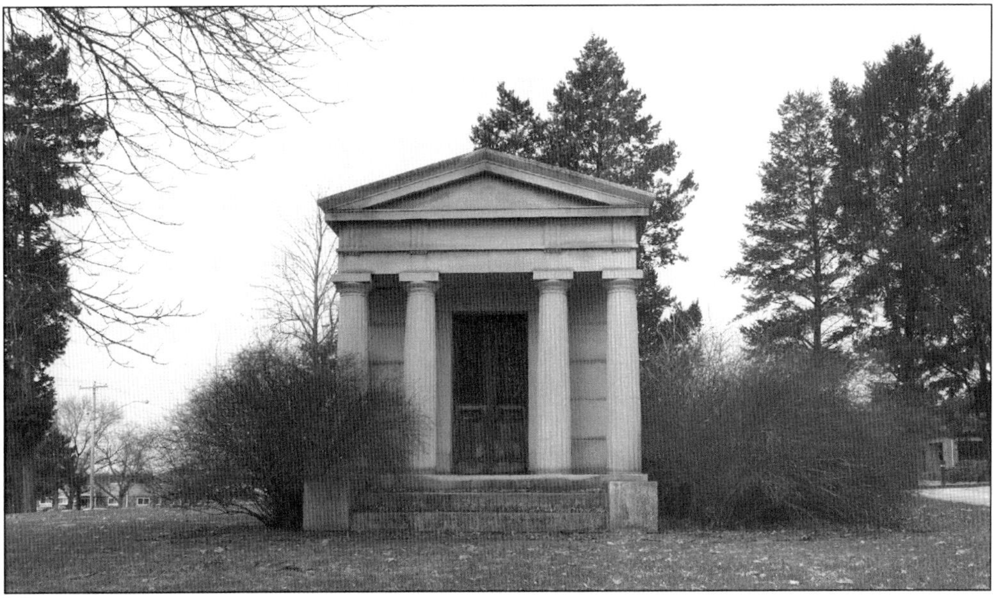

In 1853, James Monroe Parker became partners with Cook and Sargent and married Zerlina Wing. Three years later, he moved to Florence, Nebraska, and became the general manager of a Cook and Sargent bank branch there. It closed in 1860, and Parker took up farming. In 1869, his wife died, and he returned to Davenport, eventually remarrying. He invested and owned thousands of acres of farmland in Iowa and Nebraska.

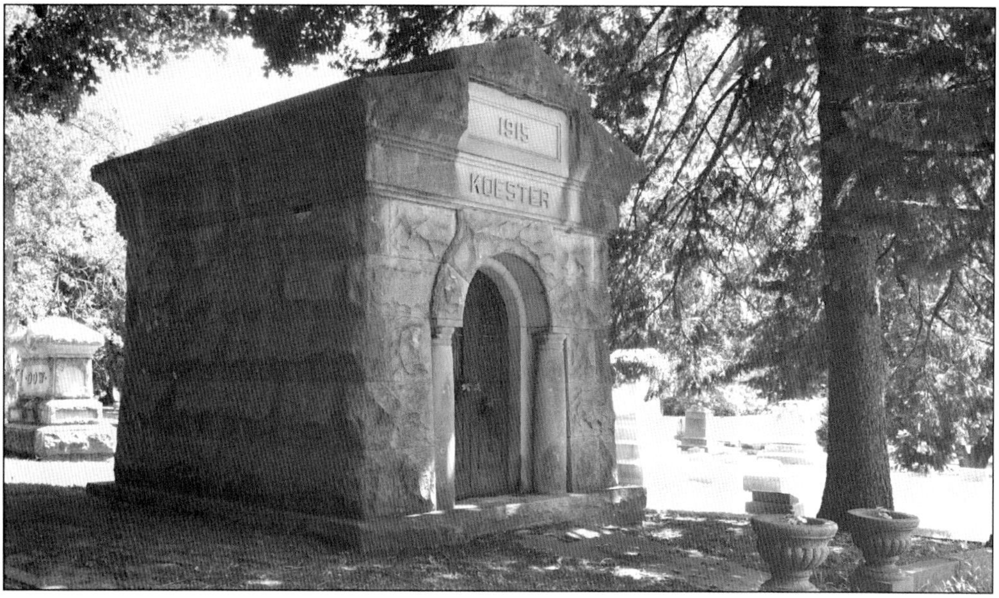

Gustav Koester was born in Germany and became an orphan at age five after his parents died of cholera in St Louis. His uncle, who was a minister in Muscatine, Iowa, took him in. Koester remained there until 1857 when he went to work in a St. Louis billiard parlor for his cousin. During the Civil War, he served as a cook in the 12th and 13th Missouri Regiments.

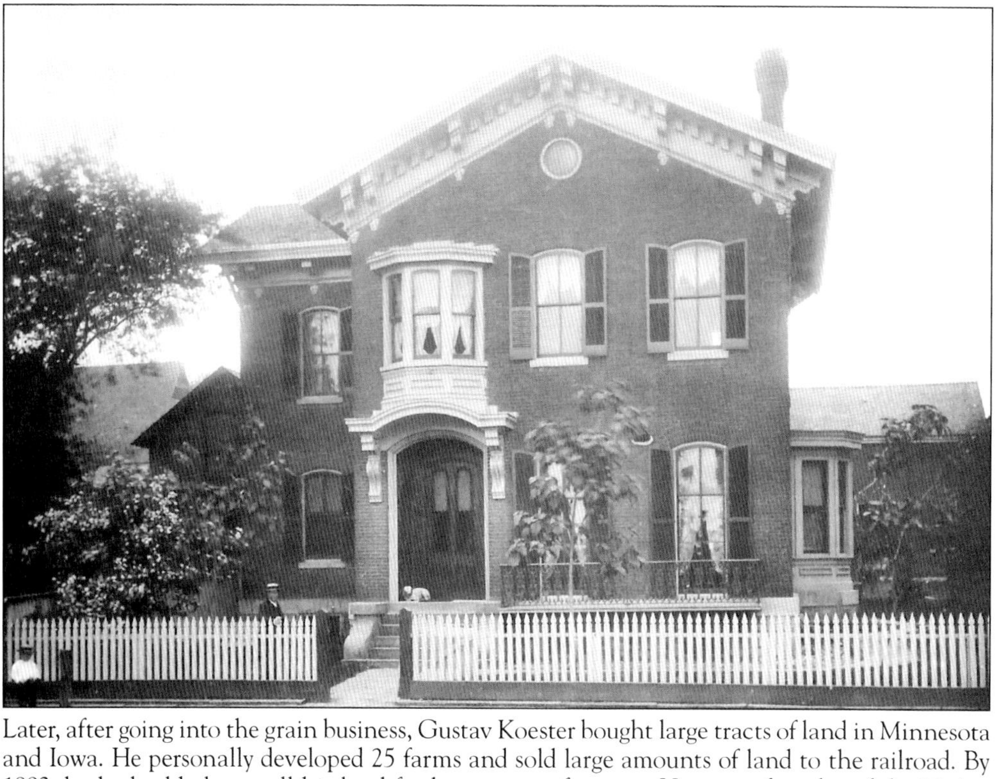

Later, after going into the grain business, Gustav Koester bought large tracts of land in Minnesota and Iowa. He personally developed 25 farms and sold large amounts of land to the railroad. By 1893, he had sold almost all his land for large sums of money. He was a founder of the Union Savings Bank and laid out the Norwood Park addition of Davenport.

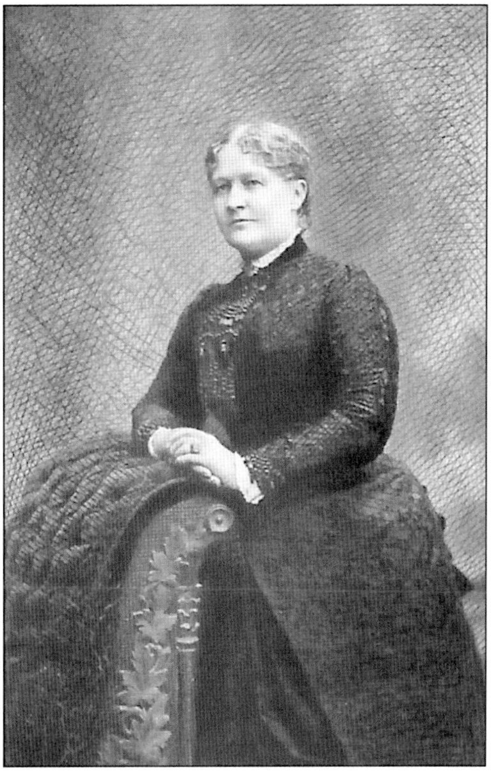

The ship *La Burgoyne* left New York on July 2, 1886, loaded with 511 passengers and 222 crew members. Two days later, on July 4, the ship collided with a sailing vessel named the *Cromartyshire*, tearing away its bow during a thick fog. The *La Burgoyne* sank, resulting in 553 passengers and crew members missing. When the fog lifted, the damaged *Cromartyshire* picked up the survivors. Anna Price Dillon, right, and her daughter Annie Dillon Oliver, below, were not among them. Witnesses reported fights taking place for seats on the lifeboats, including women and children being held at knifepoint. Only one woman from first class survived, having been saved by her husband. A board of inquiry exonerated the crew, though they were still widely accused of inappropriate behavior.

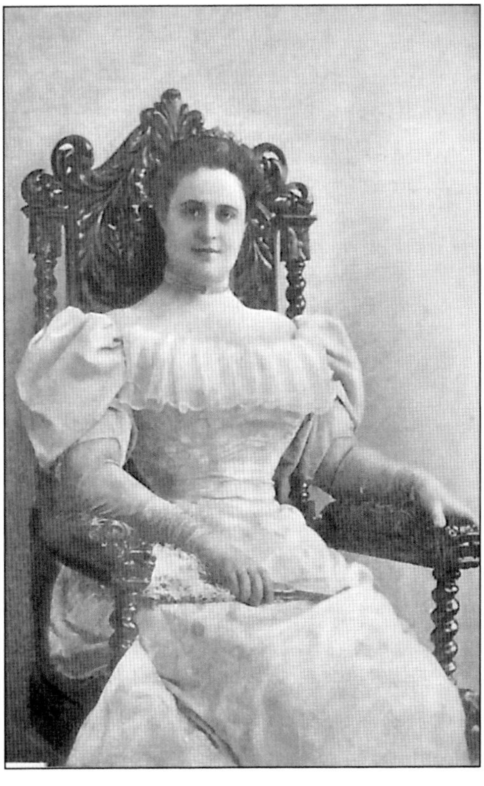

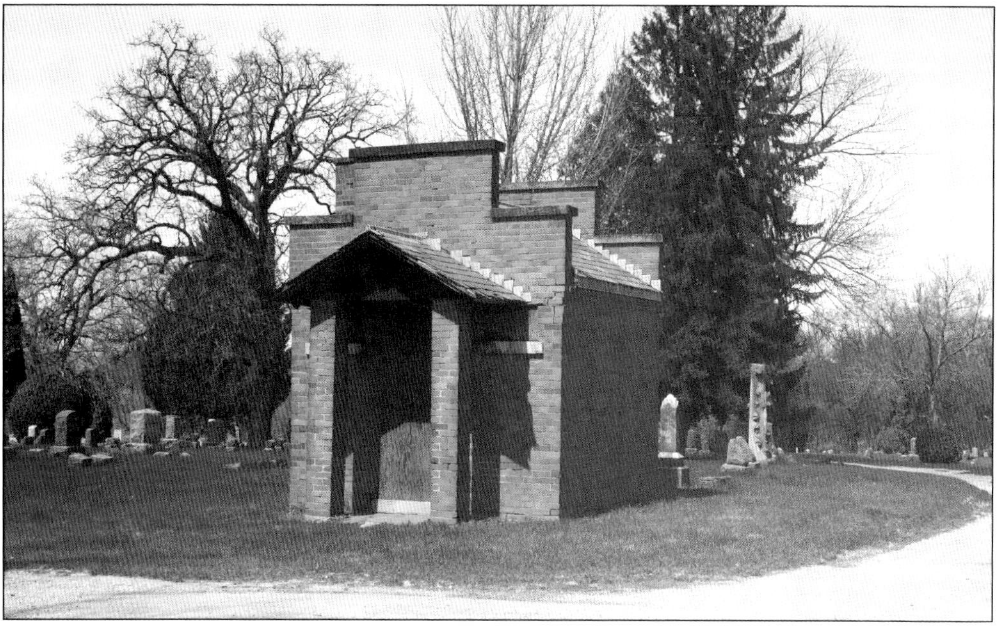

Anna Belle Nott died at her home at 120 Kirkwood Boulevard in 1912 from pernicious anemia, which at the time was incurable. She had been a lifelong resident of Davenport and was a cousin to James Elaine, a famous statesman. She had marked musical talent and was not only a member of the Daughters of the American Revolution, but also, for a time, was the regent of the Hannah Caldwell chapter.

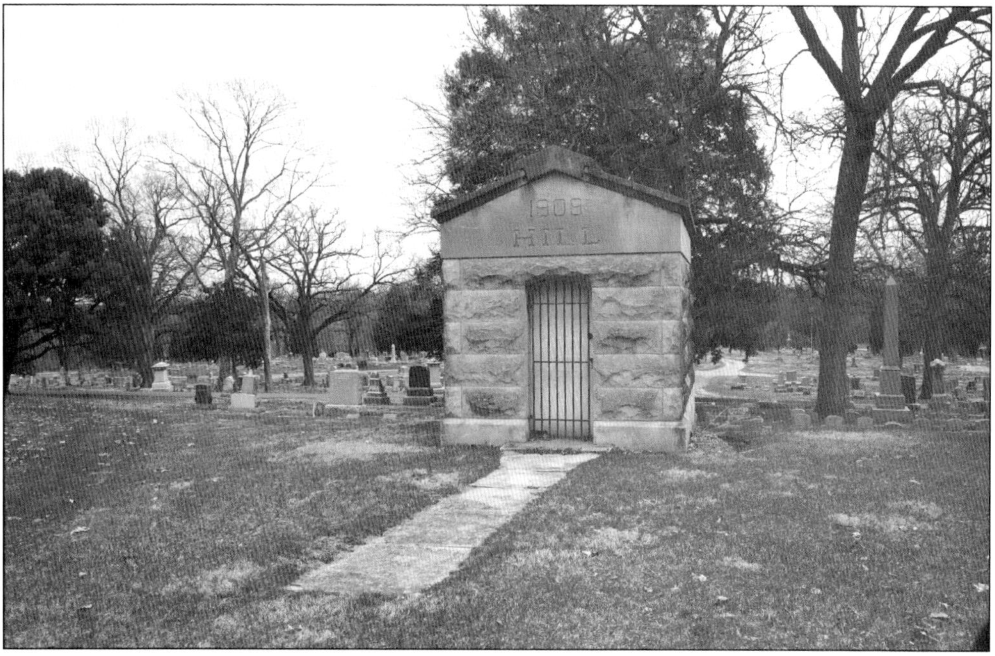

Genevieve and James Hill were children of W.H. Hill. Genevieve died from tonsillitis when she was 10 years old. James ran a business in Davenport called the Sunshine Outfitters for several years before moving to Madison, Wisconsin. He died there when he was only 30 years old. Both were buried in Oakdale Cemetery.

Henry F. Petersen was one of the sons of J.H.C Petersen, the founder of the well-known local department store. A diabetic, he developed jaundice while at the Panama Canal during a trip from New York to California. His health kept deteriorating after he returned to Davenport. His family originally settled in Maysville, and after various dry good merchants around downtown Davenport employed him, he went into business for himself.

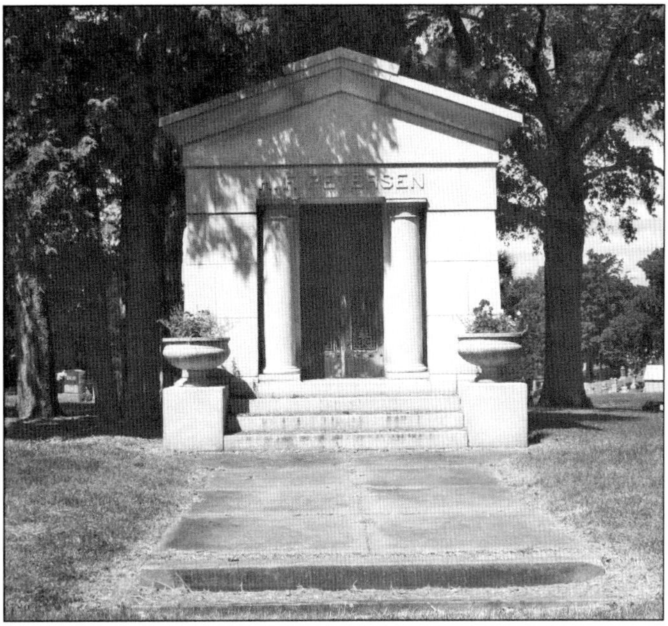

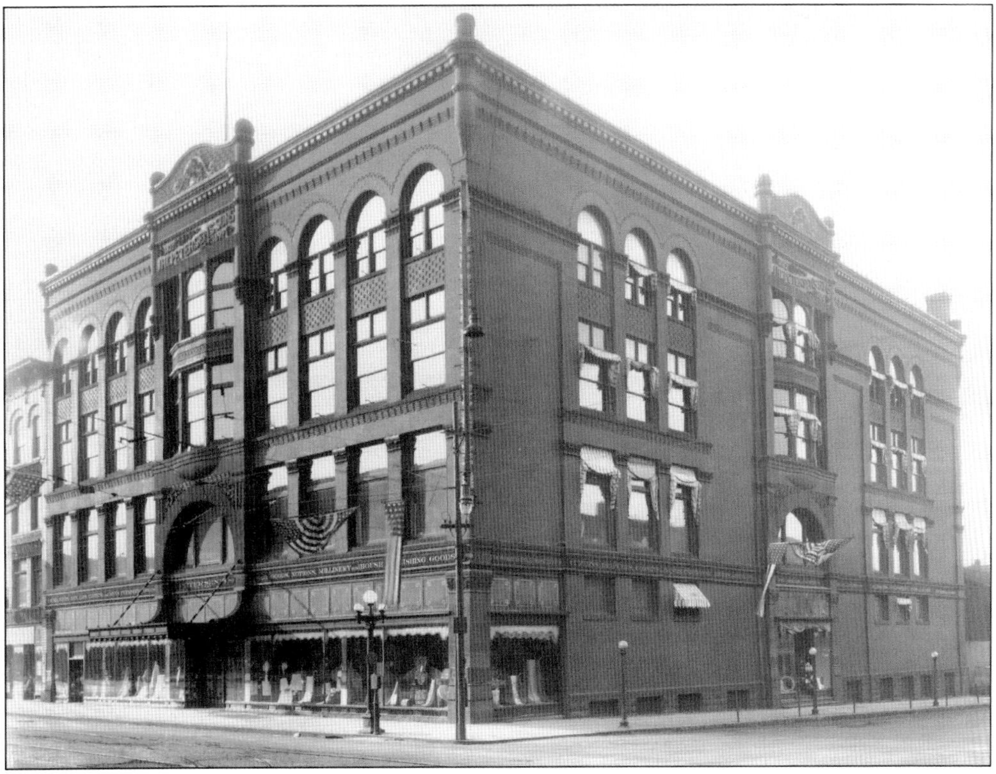

Henry F. Petersen, his father, and his brothers opened their own one-room store for a combined investment of $1,400. The large store at Second and Main Streets was built in 1892. Henry and his family worked well together, and eventually, Henry's son Arno joined the business. Henry, who was married to Clara Klug, was also director and vice president on the board of the Scott County Savings Bank.

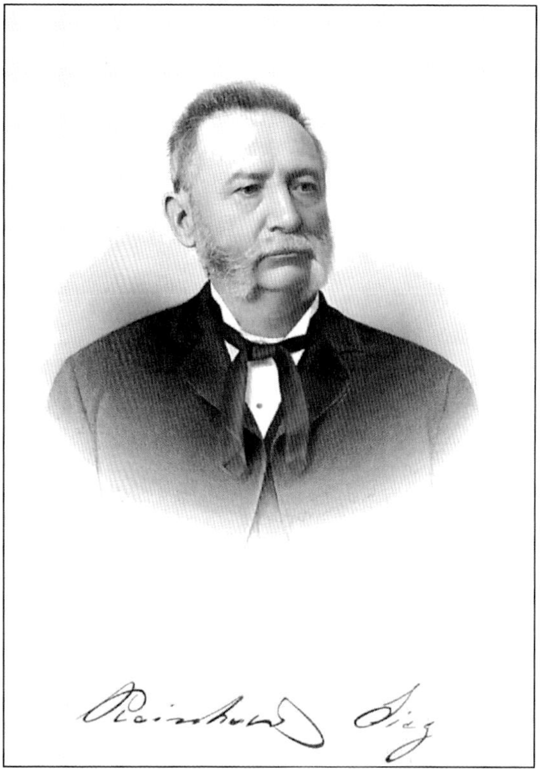

Born and educated during 1828 in Magdesberg, Germany, Reinholdt Sieg began his working life in a wholesale grocery store. He and his first wife eventually came to America, settling in Davenport and entering into the tobacco business. After the Civil War, Sieg quit that business and joined with Alexander F. Williams, selling heavy machinery for the iron industry. This new endeavor would eventually morph into the Sieg Iron Company.

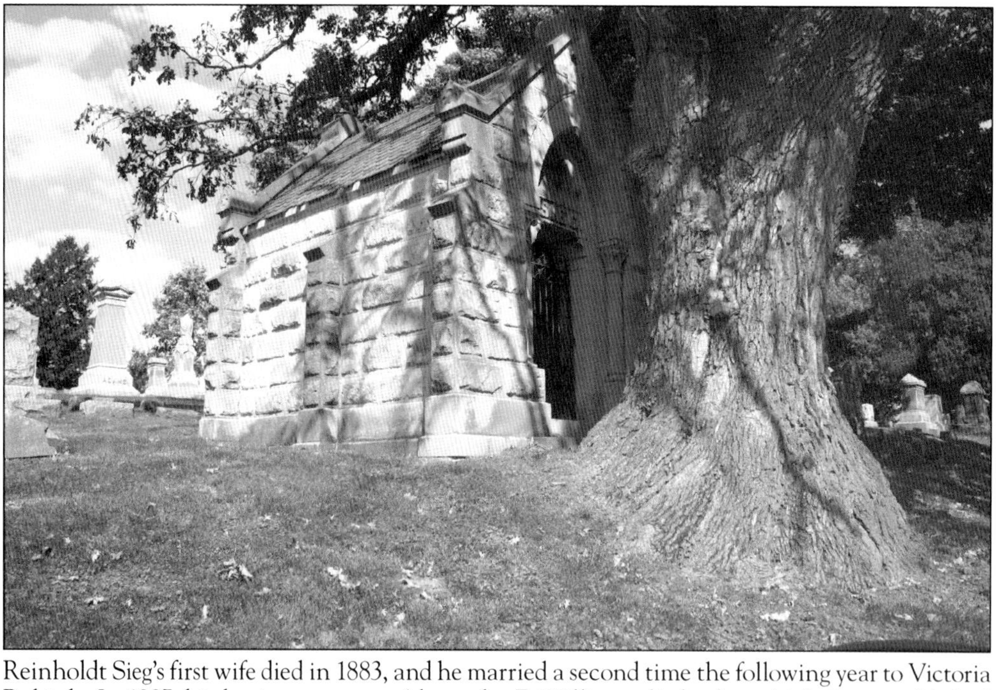

Reinholdt Sieg's first wife died in 1883, and he married a second time the following year to Victoria Robirds. In 1887, his business partner Alexander F. Williams died, after which Sieg established a stock company so that the employees, who had always held a responsibility for his business's success, could own a part. In 1890, Sieg passed away due to heart failure.

Two

MAYORS

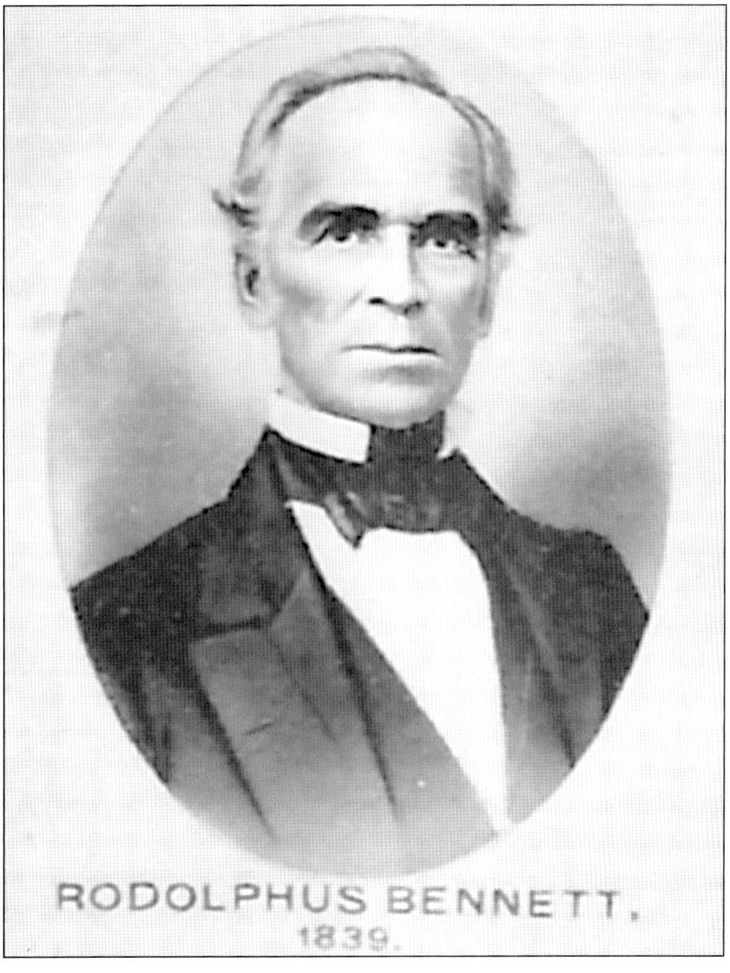

On January 25, 1839, the city of Davenport was created by territorial statute. A few months later, town officials were elected. Rudolfus Bennett was elected as the first mayor, with John Forrest and John Owens on the city council. James M. Bowling became treasurer. Apparently, not everyone liked his official position, and attendance at early sessions was poor, forcing meetings to postpone for lack of a quorum.

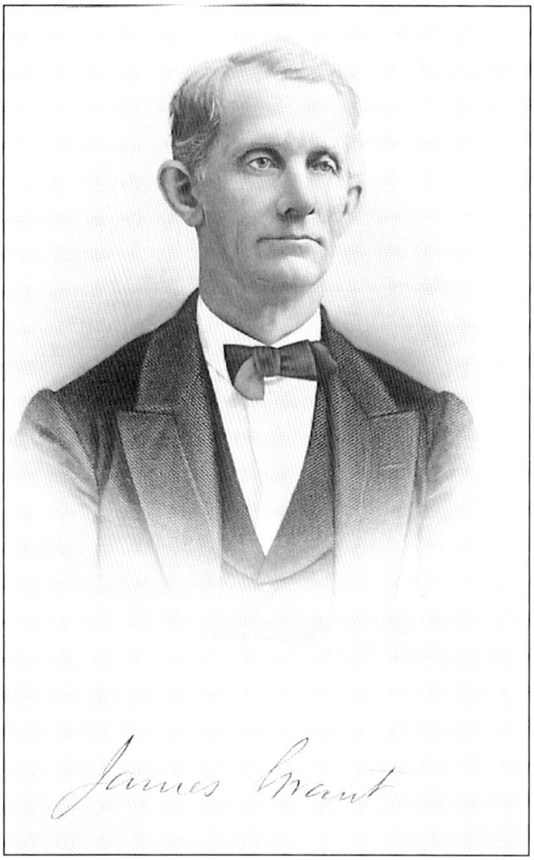

James Grant, born in North Carolina on December 12, 1812, came to Davenport in 1838. In 1841, he was elected a member of the House of Representatives of the Fourth Iowa Territorial Legislative Assembly. In April 1847, Grant was elected as district judge. He had supported Rockingham as the county seat. In 1851, Grant became the first president of the Chicago Rock Island Railroad.

James Grant was again elected a member of the Iowa House of Representatives in 1852 and was elected speaker. His private law library was said to have been the largest in the United States at 6,000 volumes. He was elected mayor of Davenport in 1854. Grant died in 1891 in Oakland, California. He had been married three times; his first two wives died.

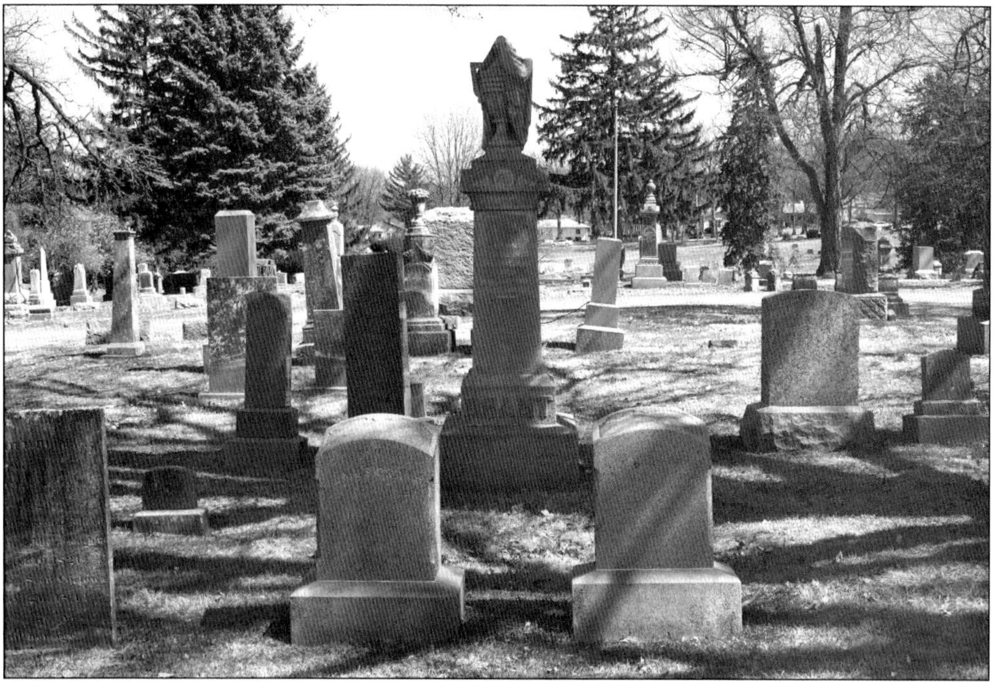

Hiram Price was born on January 10, 1814, in Pennsylvania. In 1844, he came to Davenport with $100 and opened a store. In 1847, Price was chosen to be the school fund commissioner, an office that he held for nine years. A year later, he was elected recorder and treasurer of Scott County, retaining that position for eight years. Price was a founder of the Sons of Temperance.

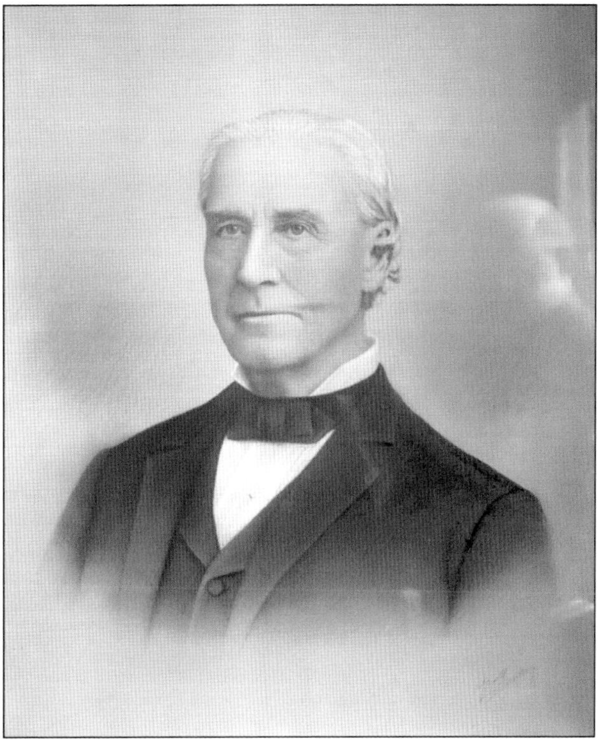

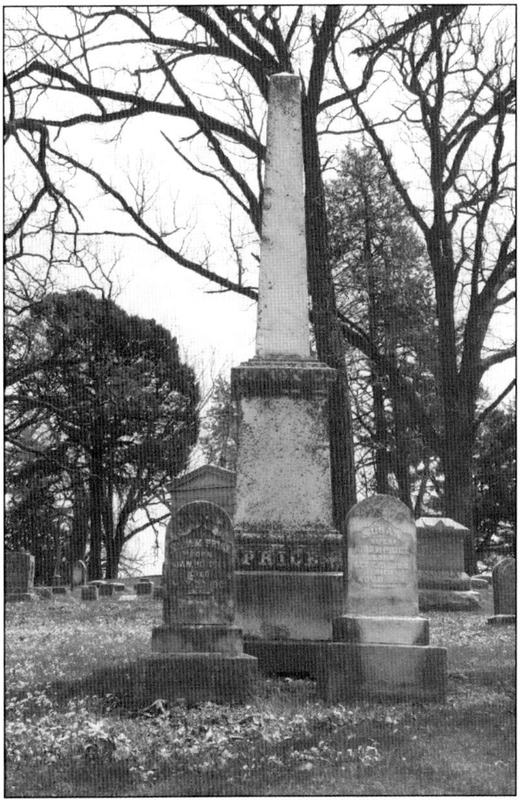

Called a "radical" and "King Hiram" by August Richter, the editor of *Der Democrat*, Hiram Price was a leader in the Whiskey Riot of 1855 in Davenport. He served as an alderman from 1852 until 1856. In 1860, Price was elected mayor of Davenport. In 1862, he was the successful candidate for representative to Congress. Price died in his Washington home from heart disease in 1901.

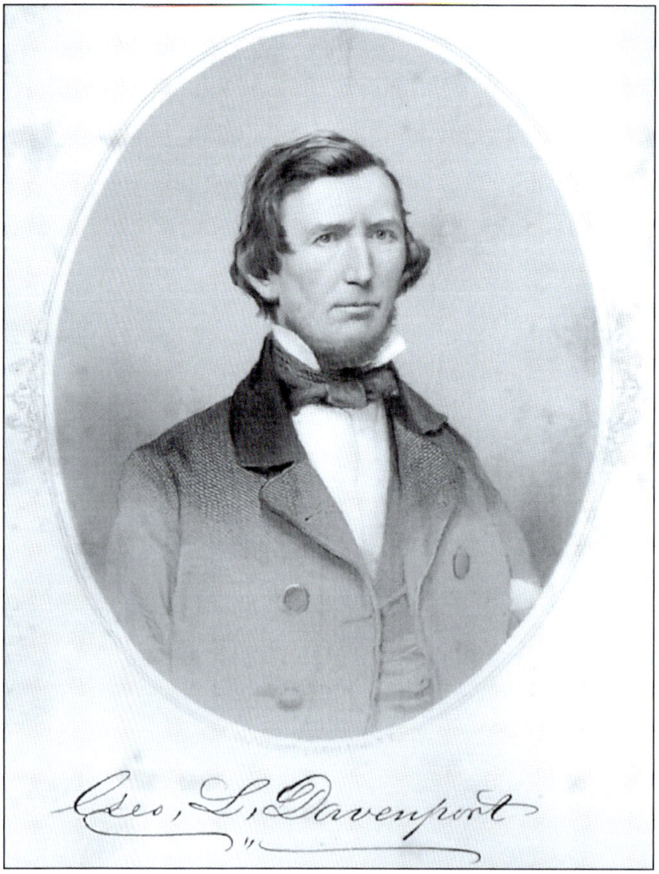

George L. Davenport was the oldest son of Col. George Davenport, a leading citizen in the early history of the area. He was born on Rock Island, now Arsenal Island, in 1817, the first white person to be born in this region. In 1832, Davenport was present at the Black Hawk Treaty with his father. He made the first claim in Iowa. The claim house on College Avenue still stands.

In 1850, George L. Davenport erected the first foundry and machine shop in the city of Davenport. He organized the first gas company in Iowa and served as its president for 22 years. Davenport later served as chairman of the board for the Chicago, Rock Island and Pacific Railroad for 10 years. On February 28, 1885, he died from heart disease in St Augustine, Florida.

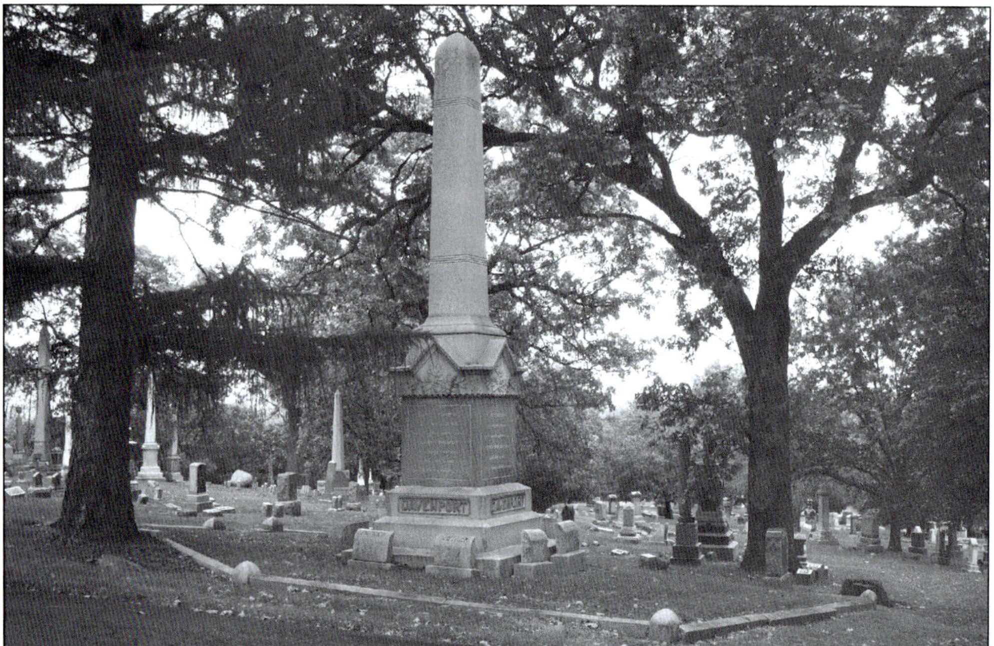

Ernst Claussen, the son of H.R. Claussen, was born in the town of Heide, Germany, on March 2, 1833. He was educated at the University of Kiel and enlisted as a volunteer in the Schleswig-Holstien Army against the Danes. Claussen came to America after the army's dissolution and stayed in St. Louis for 2 years. He then moved to Lyons, Iowa, in 1853 to work at his father's gristmill.

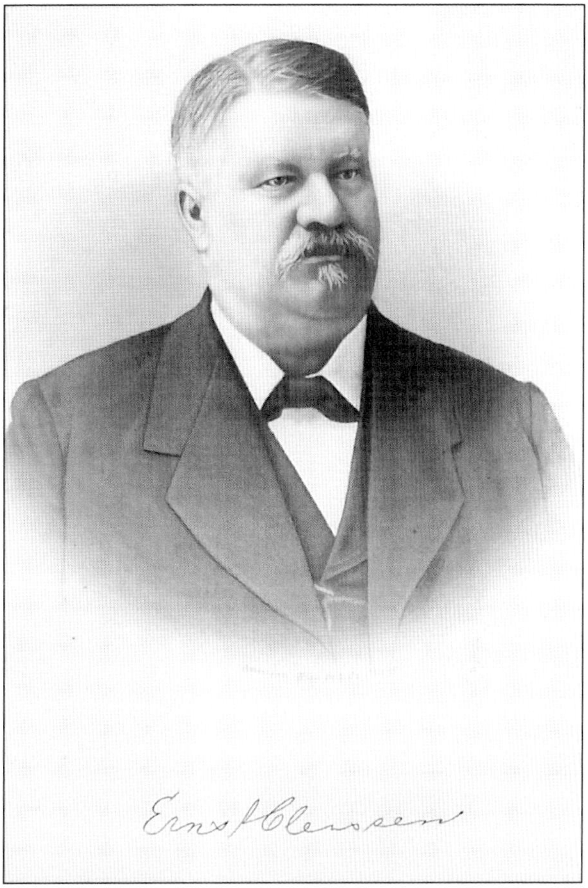

In 1861, Ernst Claussen joined the 1st Iowa Infantry as a sergeant and fought at Wilson's Creek. Afterwards, he returned to Davenport and continued as a lawyer. Claussen joined his father's firm in 1862 and continued to run it after his father left in 1869. Claussen was elected mayor of Davenport seven consecutive times and died in 1892. His funeral cortege consisted of 400 people on foot and more than 400 carriages.

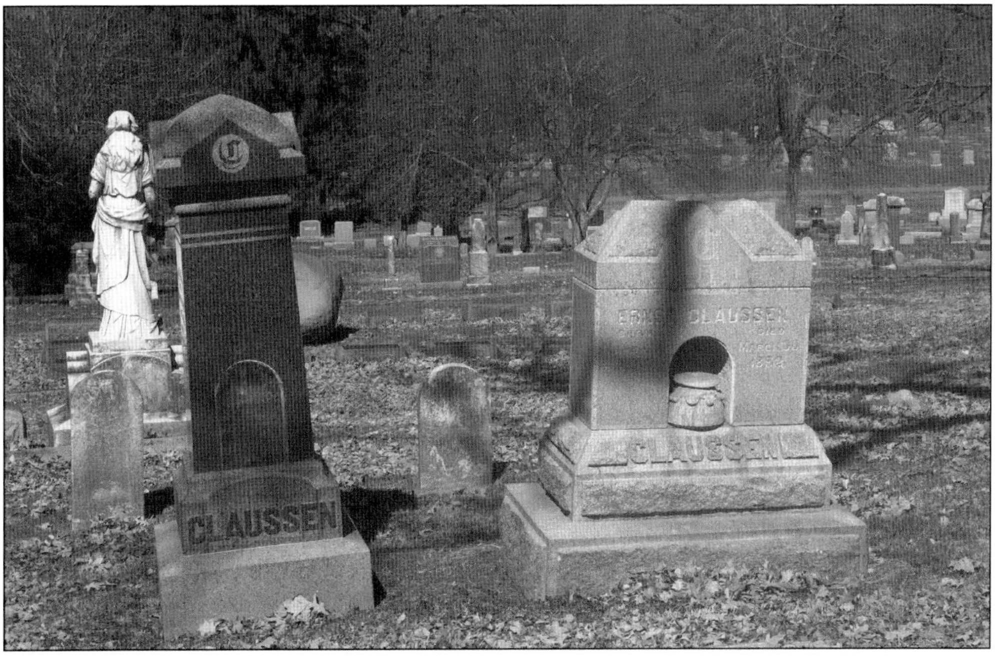

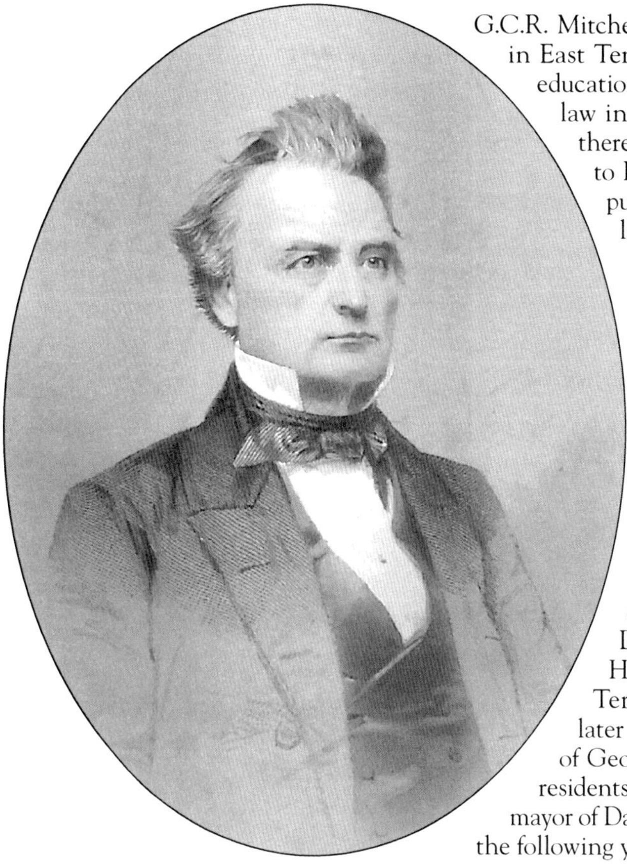

G.C.R. Mitchell was born on December 3, 1803, in East Tennessee. After receiving his basic education in Tennessee, he began to study law in Alabama. Mitchell practiced law there between 1822 and 1834, then came to Davenport, Iowa, in 1835 where he purchased land and began to practice law again.

In 1836, G.C.R. Mitchell opened one of the first law offices in Davenport. He was elected to the House of Representatives of the Iowa Territorial Legislature in 1843 and later married Rose Clarke, the daughter of George L. Davenport, one of the early residents of Scott County. Mitchell became mayor of Davenport in 1856 and a district judge the following year.

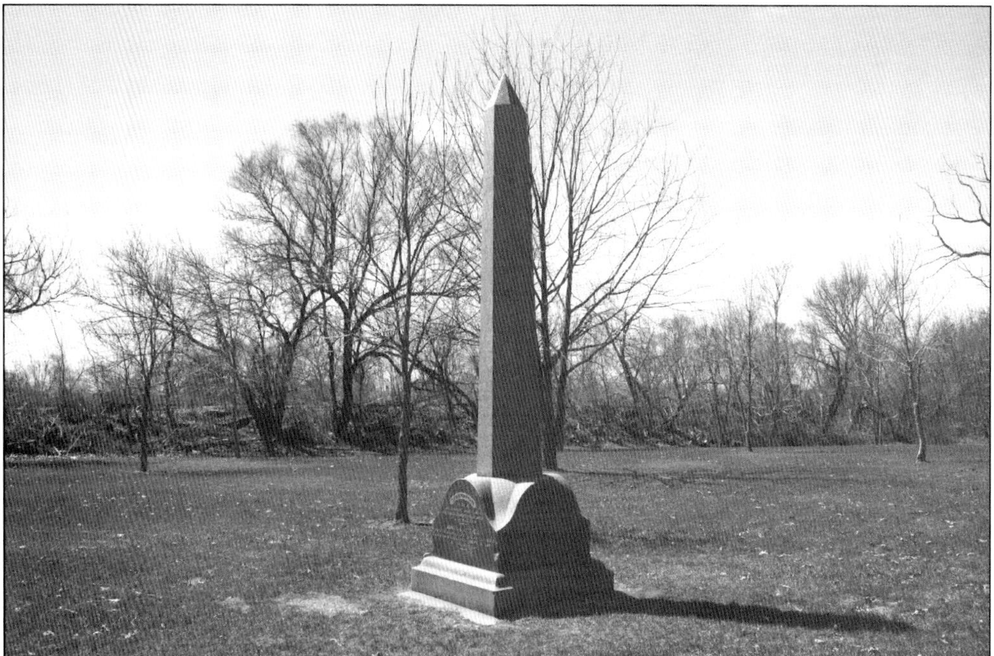

After arriving in Davenport in 1856, John C. Bills began practicing law. He, along with another lawyer, Hans Claussen, proved to the Iowa Supreme Court that a state amendment prohibiting alcohol had been adopted illegally. Bills also served as the president of the Davenport school board and served a four-year term to the Iowa State Senate. He was also a three-time mayor of Davenport.

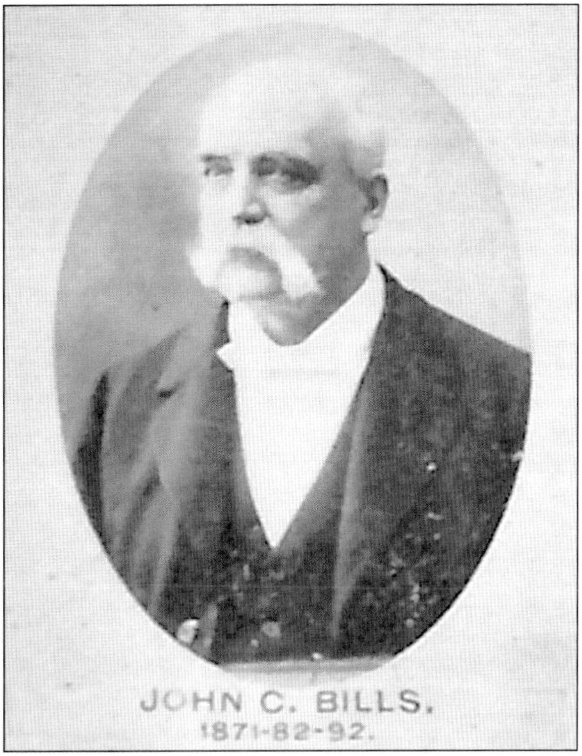

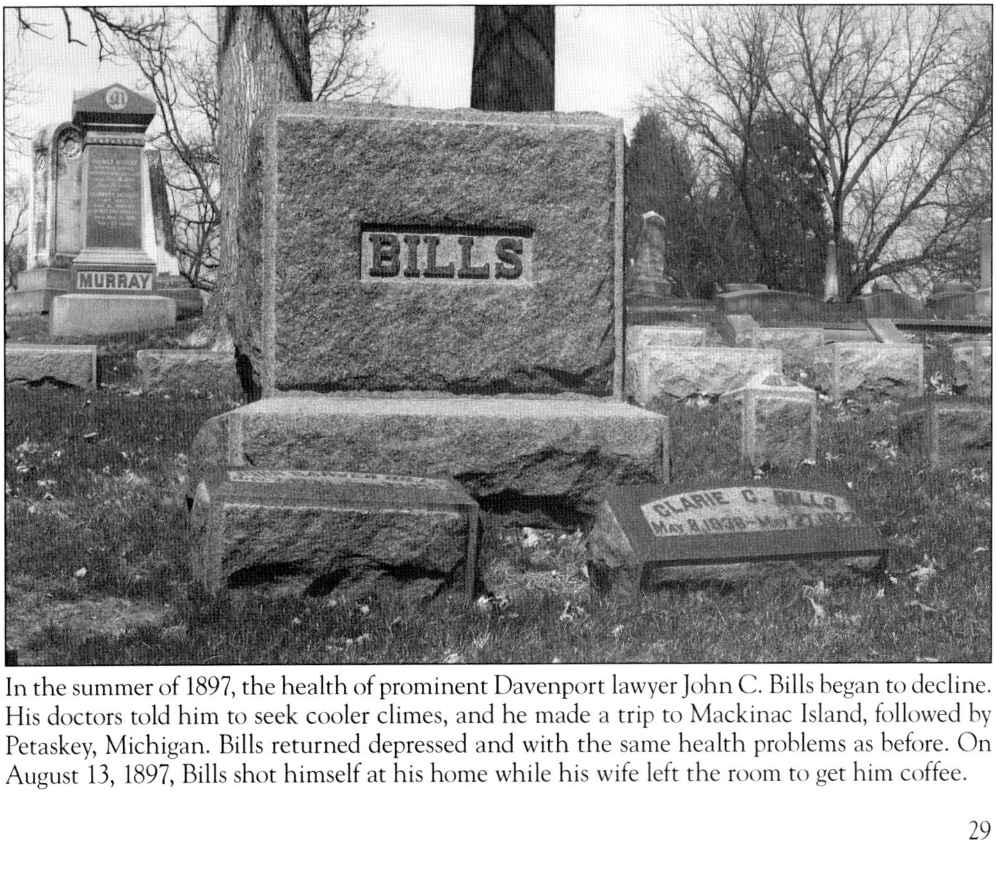

In the summer of 1897, the health of prominent Davenport lawyer John C. Bills began to decline. His doctors told him to seek cooler climes, and he made a trip to Mackinac Island, followed by Petaskey, Michigan. Bills returned depressed and with the same health problems as before. On August 13, 1897, Bills shot himself at his home while his wife left the room to get him coffee.

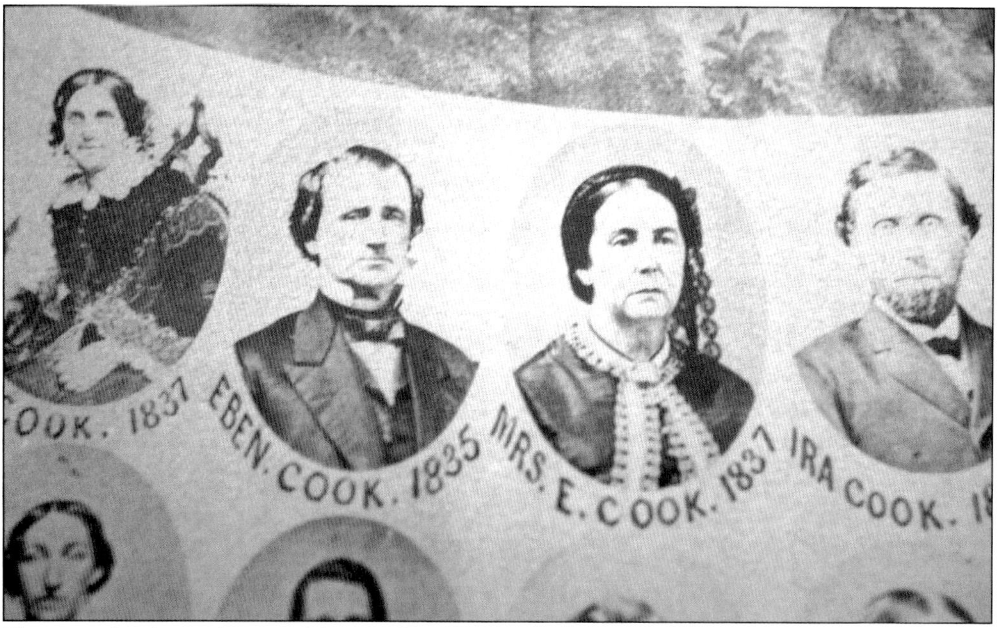

Ebenezer Cook was born in New York in 1810. He married Clarissa Bryant and entered the mercantile trade. Cook came to Iowa in 1837, and began reading the law. By 1840, he had become a lawyer. Cook began a successful practice, focusing primarily on collections. He was a member of the first Constitutional Congress of Iowa and was later elected mayor of Davenport. He died in 1871.

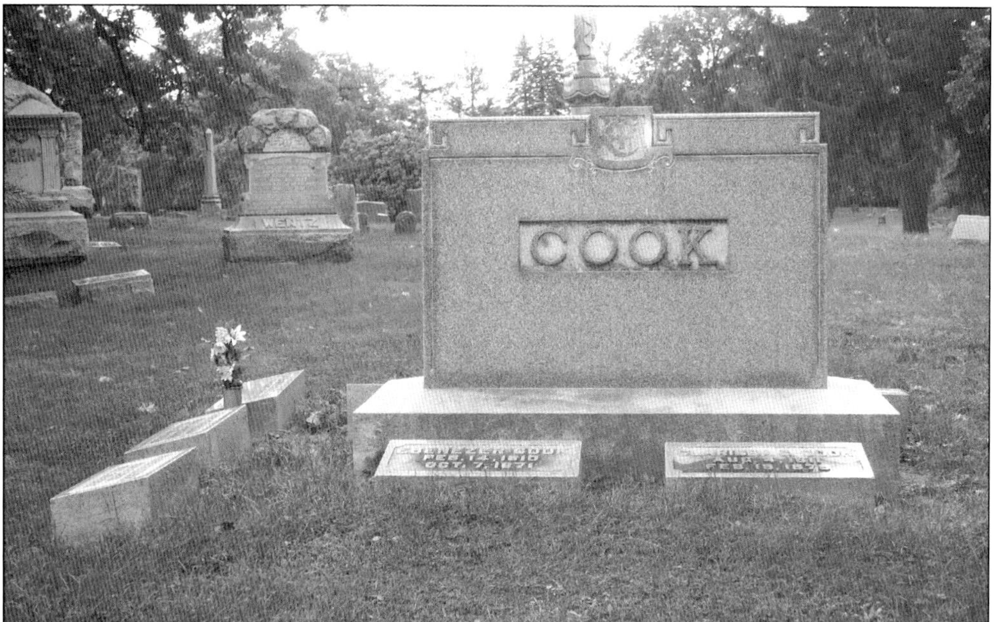

Clarissa Cook was born in 1811. After Ebenezer died in 1871, Clarissa paid for the building of the Trinity Episcopalian Church and its schoolhouse. She also paid for the building to house a permanent library for Davenport. After she died in 1879, she left funds from her sizable estate to build the Clarissa C. Cook Home for the Friendless, a home that cared for and housed old women.

George Sargent came to the town of Rockingham in 1837 and opened a general store. When the store failed, he moved to Blue Grass and lived there with his wife for several years. In 1846, he received several soldier's warrants, which were land grants awarded to soldiers as a reward for military service. He entered into business with local lawyer Ebenezer Cook, and they founded the firm of Cook and Sargent.

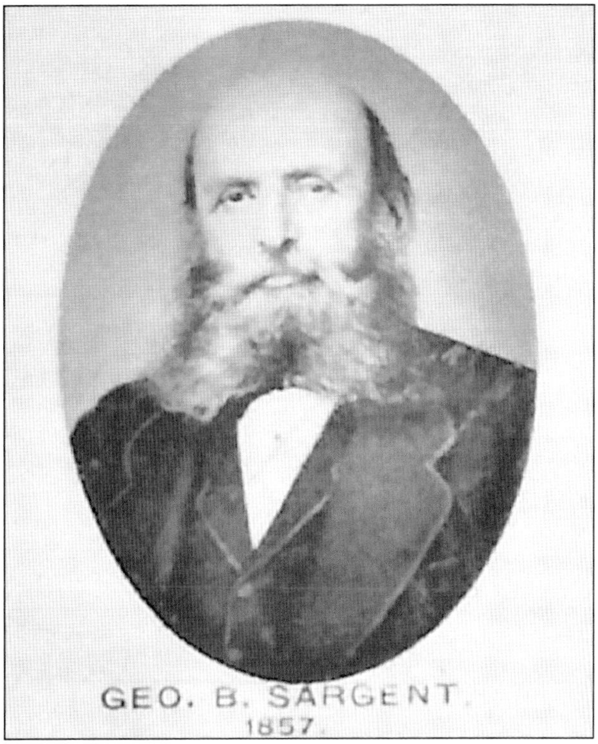

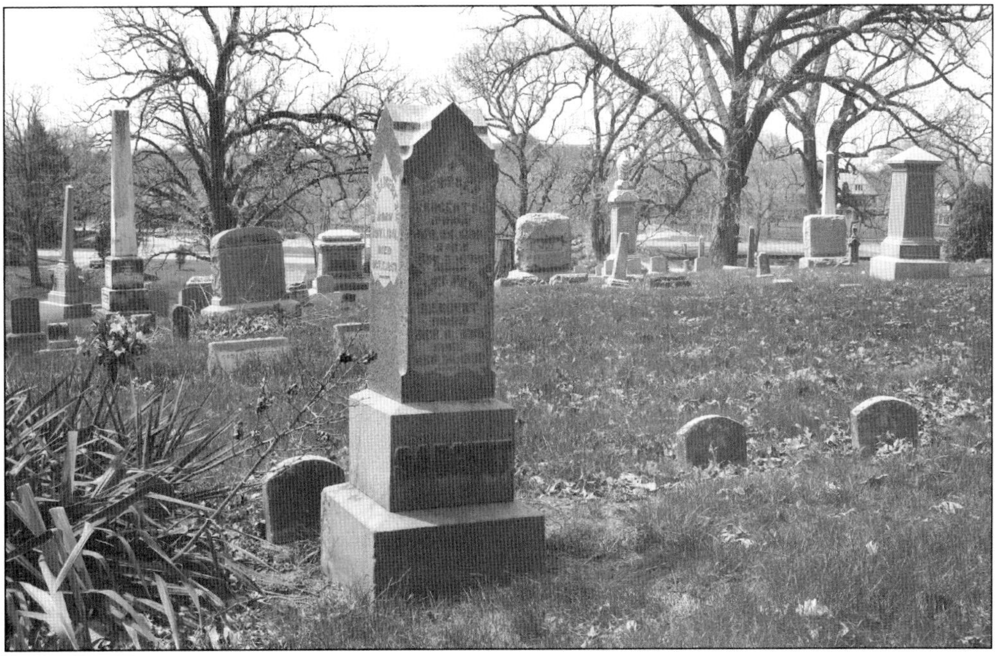

George Sargent and Ebenezer Cook opened the first bank in Davenport, but it closed after the Panic of 1857. Sargent was elected mayor of Davenport in 1858. Later, he moved around the country to pursue business interests in railroads and real estate. Sargent and his family eventually settled in Duluth, Minnesota. He went to Ems, Germany, in an attempt to recover his health at some of the area's medicinal springs. He died there in 1875.

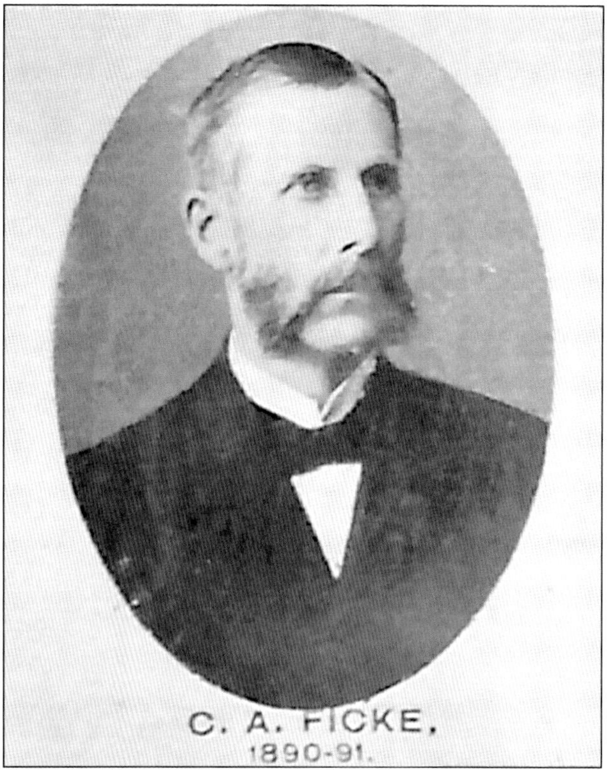

Charles Ficke was born April 21, 1850, in Boitzenburg, Germany. In 1852, at the age of two, he came to the United States with his family and settled on a farm near Long Grove, Iowa. He obtained his early education in the country schools of the area and worked for a year at a store in Lowden, Iowa, when he was 12 years old.

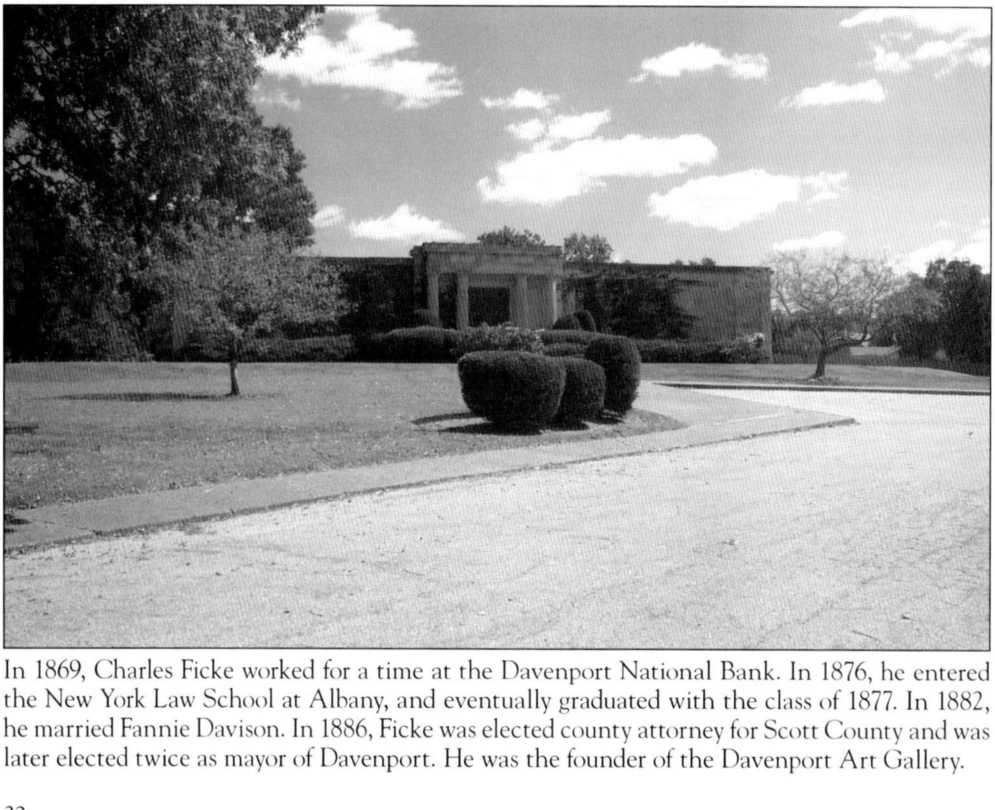

In 1869, Charles Ficke worked for a time at the Davenport National Bank. In 1876, he entered the New York Law School at Albany, and eventually graduated with the class of 1877. In 1882, he married Fannie Davison. In 1886, Ficke was elected county attorney for Scott County and was later elected twice as mayor of Davenport. He was the founder of the Davenport Art Gallery.

Enos Tichenor had bought property in Davenport in the 1840s. He was an antique dealer. In 1855, the temperance movement was in swing across the country. Tichenor was elected mayor of Davenport on the temperance ticket in the same year, winning over James M. Bowling, who ran as the Anti-Know-Nothing candidate.

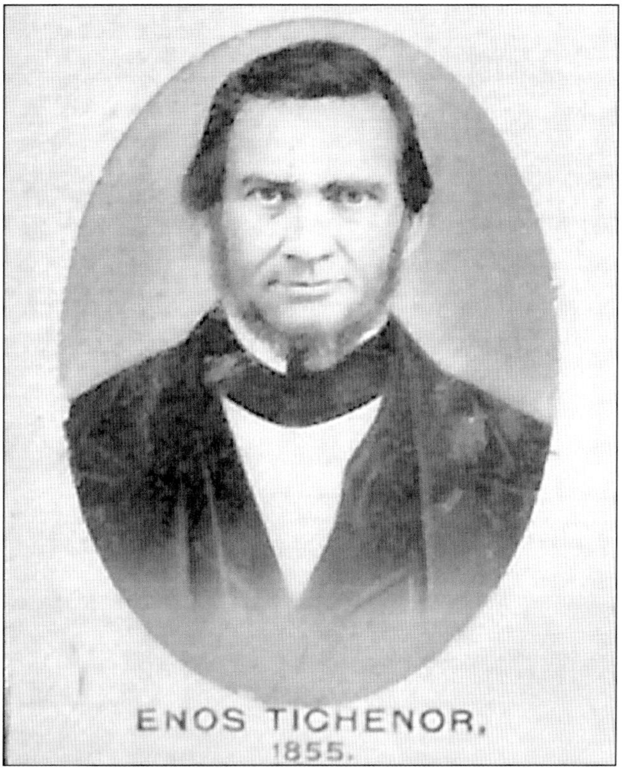

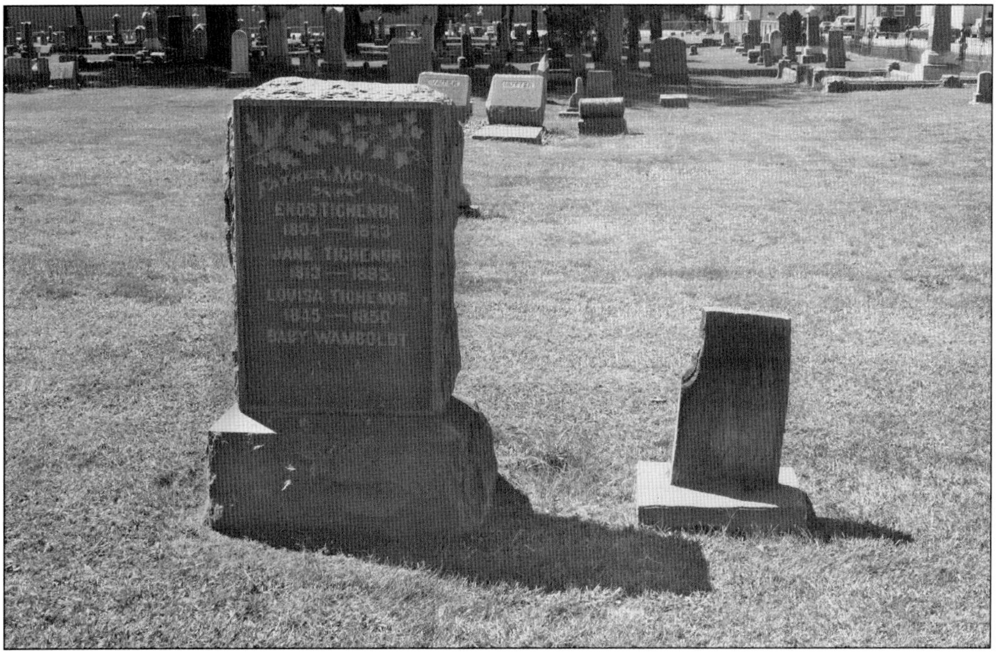

In the 1850s, prohibitionists held the majority on the city council and the mayor. The following summer, citizens in Scott County voted in the Maine Liquor Law. This law prohibited the making or sale of any alcoholic beverage in the state. The Whiskey Riot occurred in Davenport when Enos Tichenor was mayor. He died in 1873.

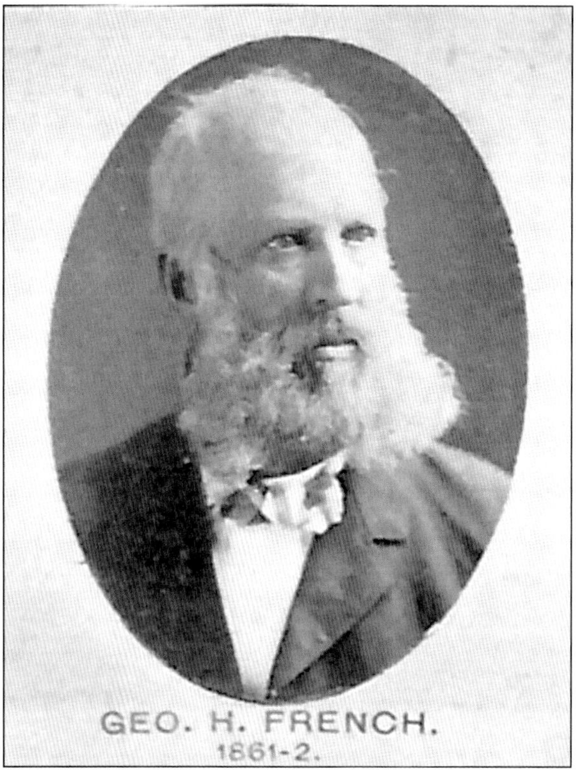

George French was born in Massachusetts in 1825. When his parents died, he had to raise two younger sisters by himself. In 1856, he and his family moved to Davenport because of his failing health and the fact that his brother-in-law, Episcopalian Bishop Lee, lived in the area. French soon entered into the lumber business. His company, French and Davies, supplied lumber to several Union camps during the Civil War.

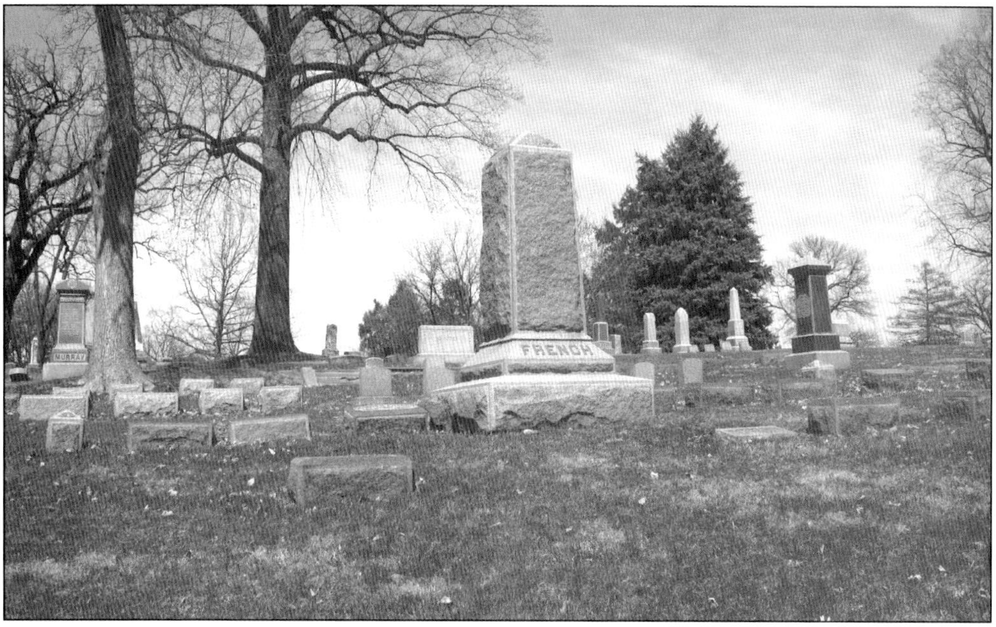

In 1858, George French was elected treasurer of the Davenport school board. He was later chosen as mayor of Davenport for two terms, and in 1864 and 1865, he served as an aide to the governor of Iowa. After the Civil War, he became president of the Davenport & St. Paul Railroad Company. French then began producing agricultural equipment with the Eagle Manufacturing Company. He died of cancer in 1888.

James Madison Bowling was born in Winchester, Virginia, on August 7, 1807, where he was raised and educated. His father, Jeremiah Bowling, was a mattress maker, and young James learned that trade from an early age and followed it until he came to Davenport in 1835. He settled in Buffalo Township at the mouth of Bowling's Creek on the Fourth of July. His aunt was married to Col. George Davenport.

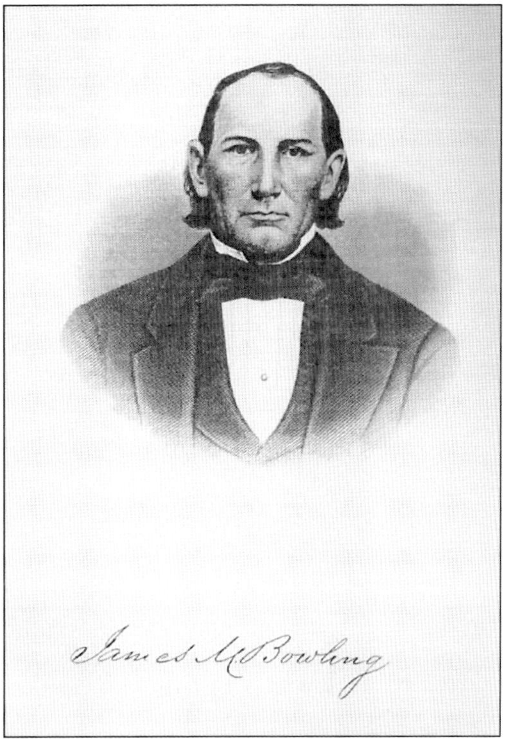

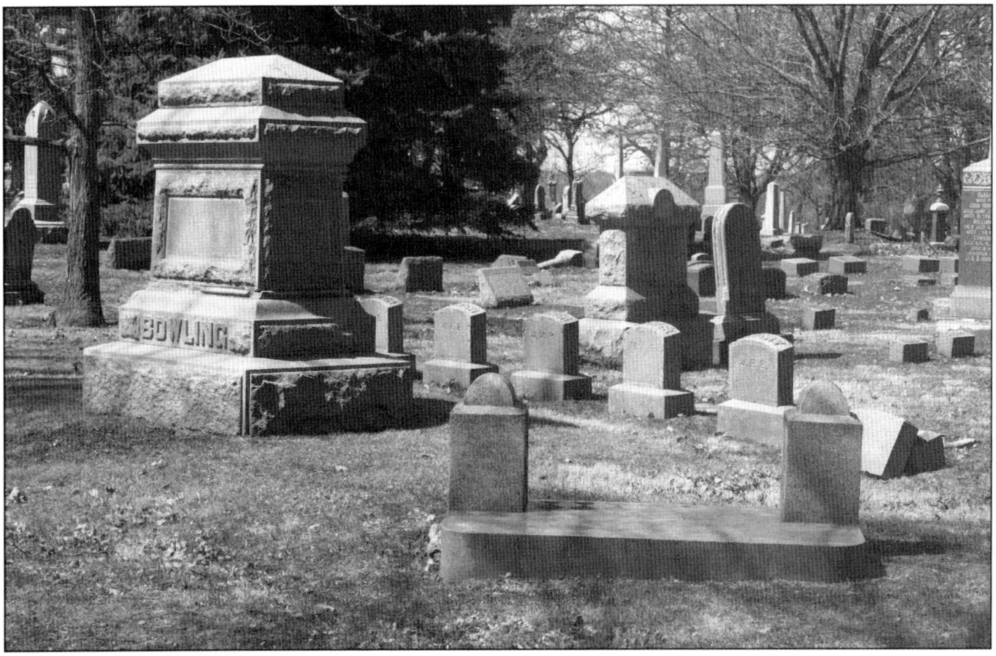

James Madison Bowling was elected mayor of Davenport in 1847 and 1848. In 1855, he ran and lost the mayoral contest as the Anti-Know-Nothing candidate. He worked in merchandising here with George L. Davenport until 1862. His son, William H.H. Bowling, was killed at Milieu, Georgia, on December 3, 1864. Another son, John C. Bowling, was confined for three months in Andersonville Prison.

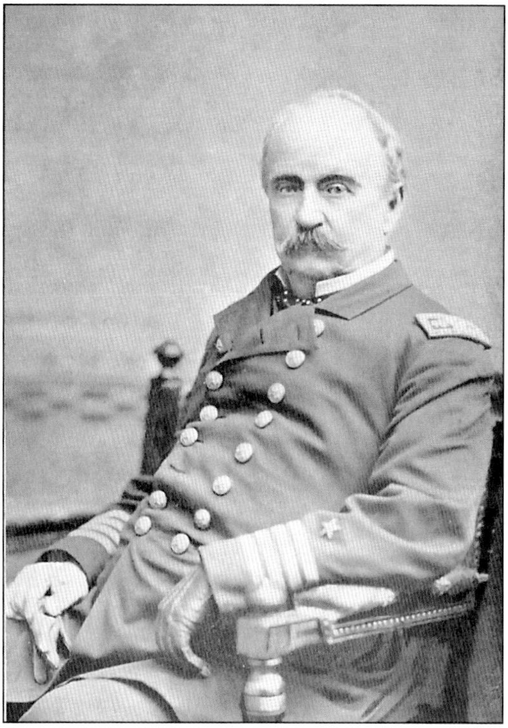

James Thorington was born in 1816 in Wilmington, North Carolina, and moved to Montgomery, Alabama, in 1827. He went to the University of Alabama at Tuscaloosa before studying law with John Thorington in Montgomery. He worked as a trader and trapper on the Upper Missouri and Columbia Rivers for two years before moving to Davenport, Iowa, in 1839.

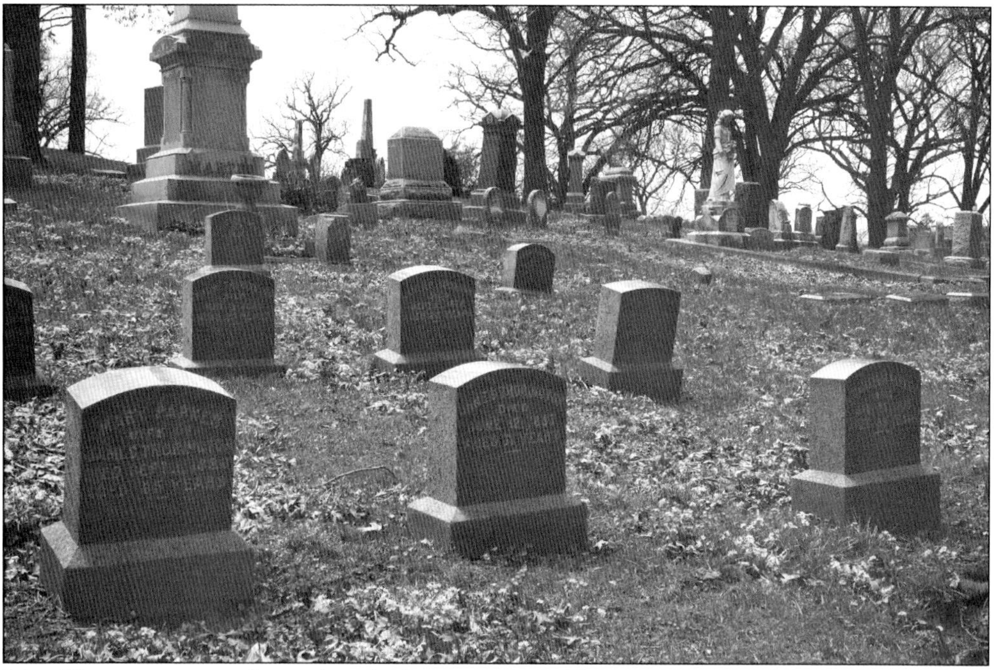

John Thorington was admitted to the bar in 1844 and began practicing law in Davenport. He was elected mayor of Davenport from 1843 to 1847, and later served in several public offices, including probate judge, clerk of the district court, and sheriff of Scott County. Thorington was elected to the 34th Congress in 1855 and served until 1857. He died while visiting his daughter in Santa Fe, New Mexico, on June 13, 1887.

John L. Davies was born in South Wales in 1813 and immigrated to America when he was 18, settling in Cincinnati. He moved to Davenport in 1841 and began working as a carpenter, eventually becoming a leading builder during the early days of Davenport. From 1837 through 1839, he served as a city alderman. After a time, he bought a sawmill and entered the lumber business.

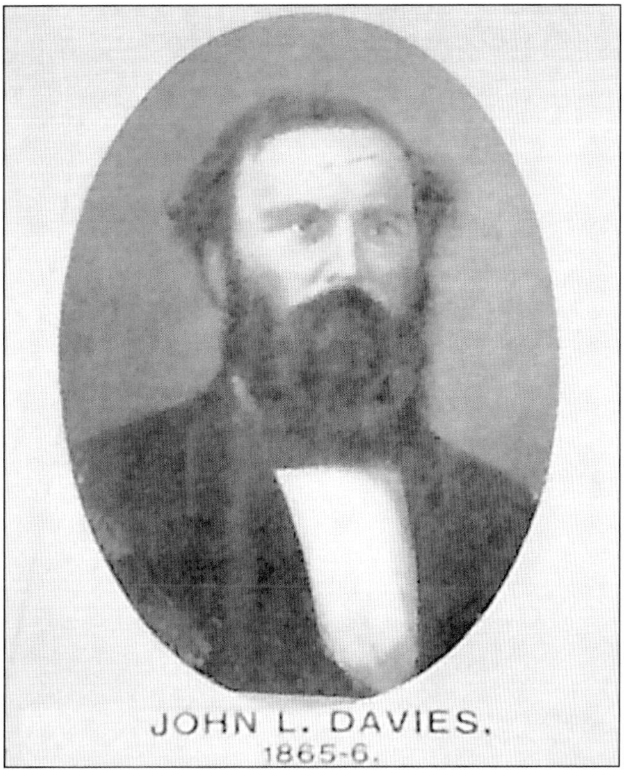

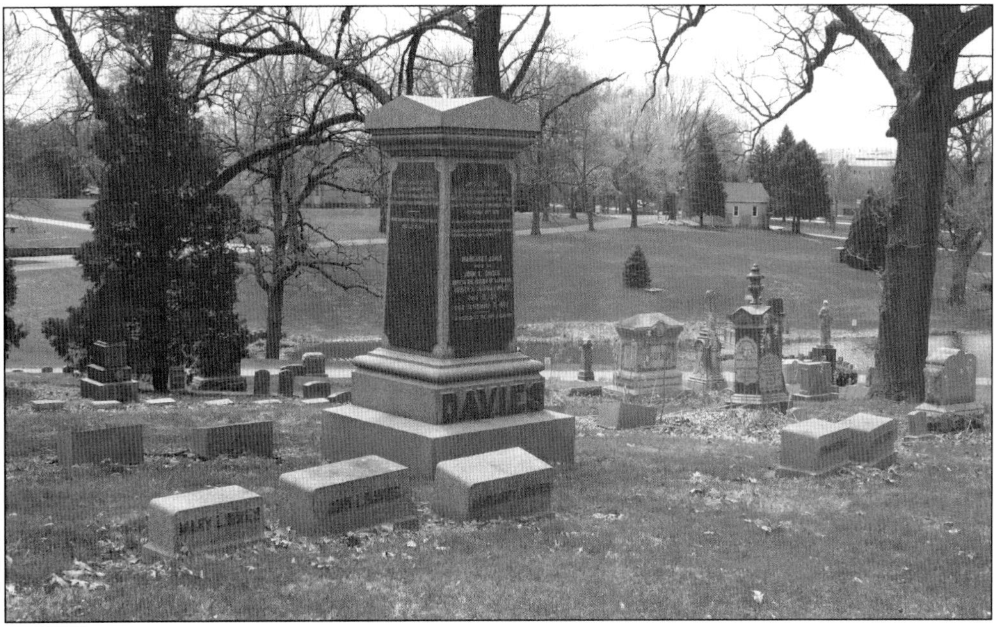

John L. Davies was a school board director, as well as a director of the First National Bank and the Davenport & St. Paul Railroad Company. He was a strong advocate of temperance in the 1850s and a cosponsor of the Maine Liquor Law in the Iowa Legislature. In 1865 and 1867, he was elected mayor of Davenport. He died in Davenport in 1872 from Bright's disease, which affects the kidneys.

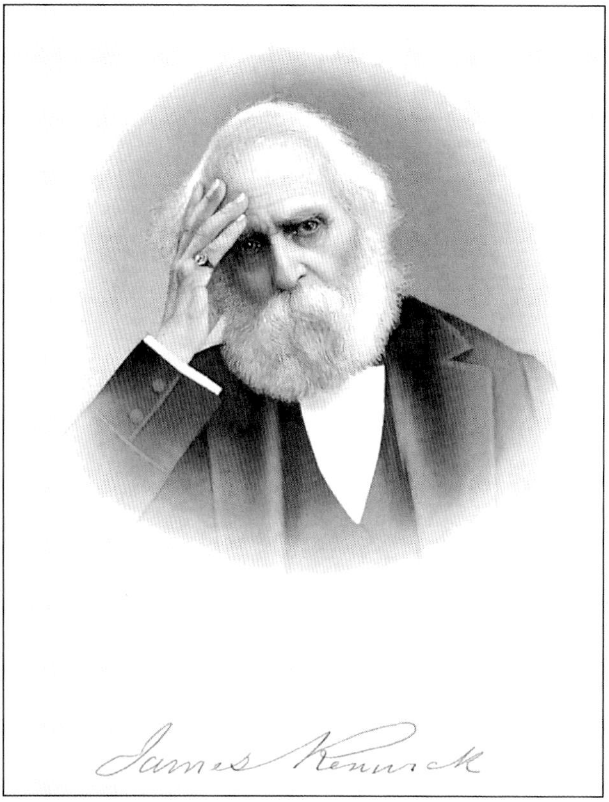

James Renwick was born in 1805 in Blentyre, Scotland. He began learning the business profession from his father, who was a woolen manufacturer, and continued working as a businessman in London. Renwick later moved to Liverpool with his family and worked as a ship-owning merchant, staying there for several years. In 1846, they moved to America and entered the lumber business, lasting in that industry for 27 years.

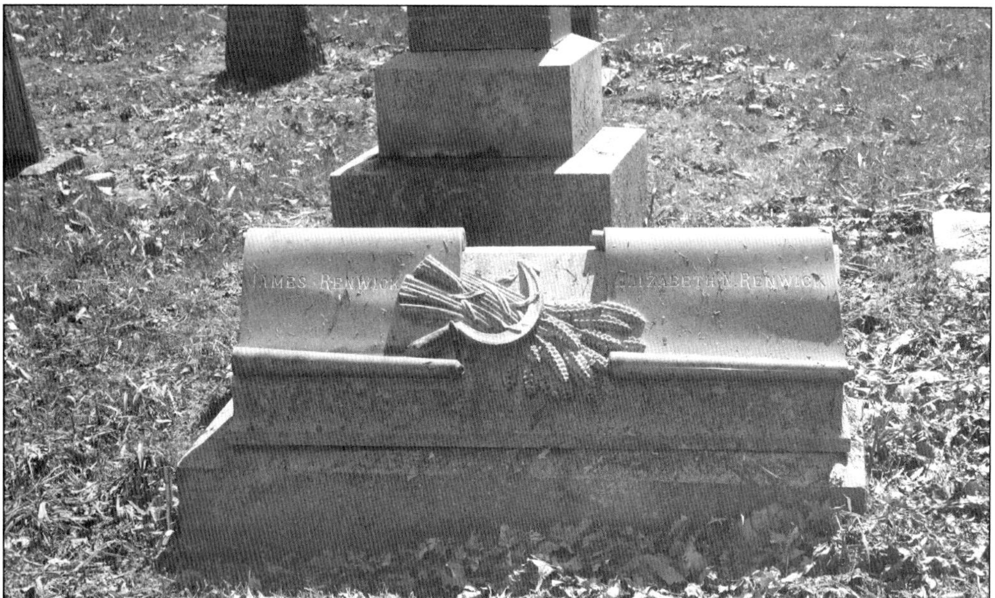

In 1849, James Renwick, and his son opened the first express business in Davenport and built a sawmill at Brady Street and Tremont Avenue. Renwick retired in 1870 and left the business to his son. He was elected mayor of Davenport in 1868. He lived with his two daughters and died in 1894 of old age at his home at the corner of Fifteenth and Brady Streets.

Jeremiah Henry Murphy was born February 19, 1835, in Lowell, Massachusetts. Murphy moved with his parents to Fond du Lac County, Wisconsin, in 1849 and later Iowa County, Iowa, in 1852. He graduated from the University of Iowa in 1857. After studying law, he was admitted to the bar in 1858 and commenced practice in Marengo, Iowa. In 1867, he moved to Davenport.

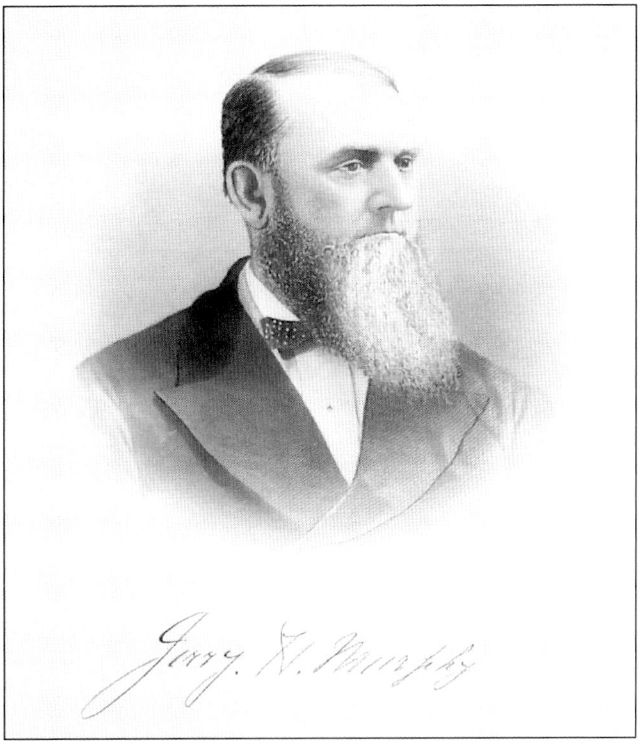

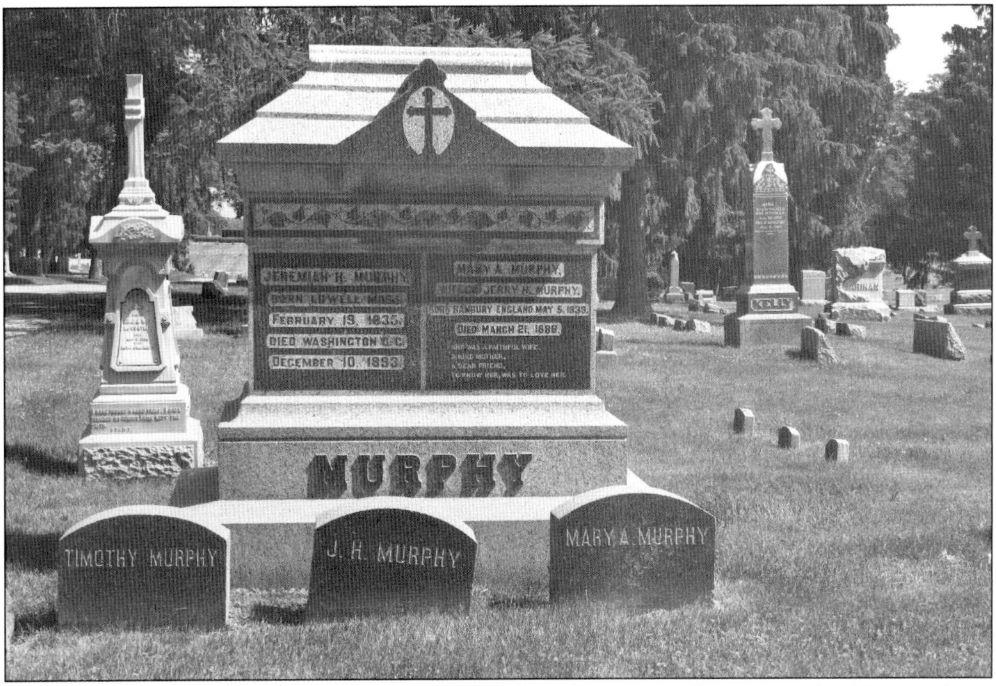

Jeremiah Henry Murphy was elected mayor of Davenport in 1873 and again in 1878. He served one term as a member of the Iowa Senate from 1874 to 1878. In 1882 and 1884, Murphy served as a US representative to Congress. Murphy was one of only two Democratic congressmen from Iowa to serve two or more full terms. He retired in Washington, DC, and lived there until his death in 1893.

Judge A.H. Bennett practiced law for more than 50 years in both New Hampshire and Davenport. While living in New Hampshire, he served as a state senator and as a representative to the state legislature. After he came to Davenport, he served as a district court judge after G.C.R. Mitchell resigned.

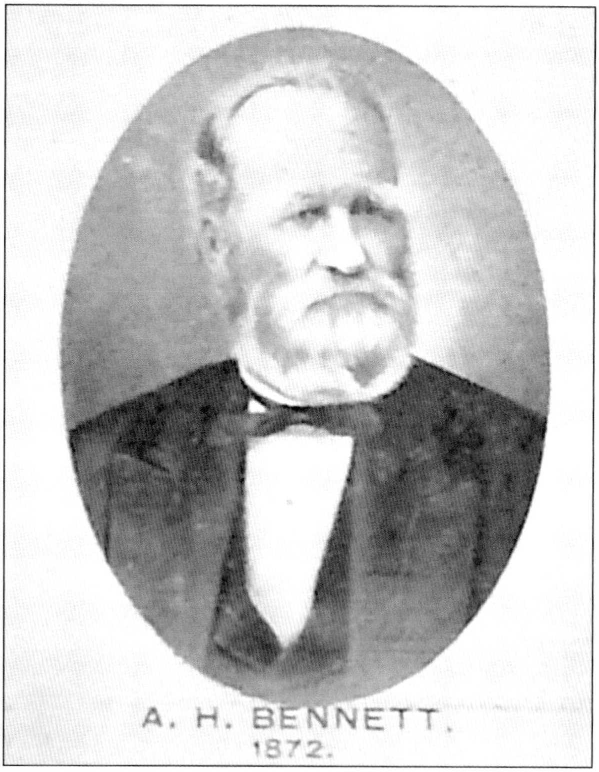

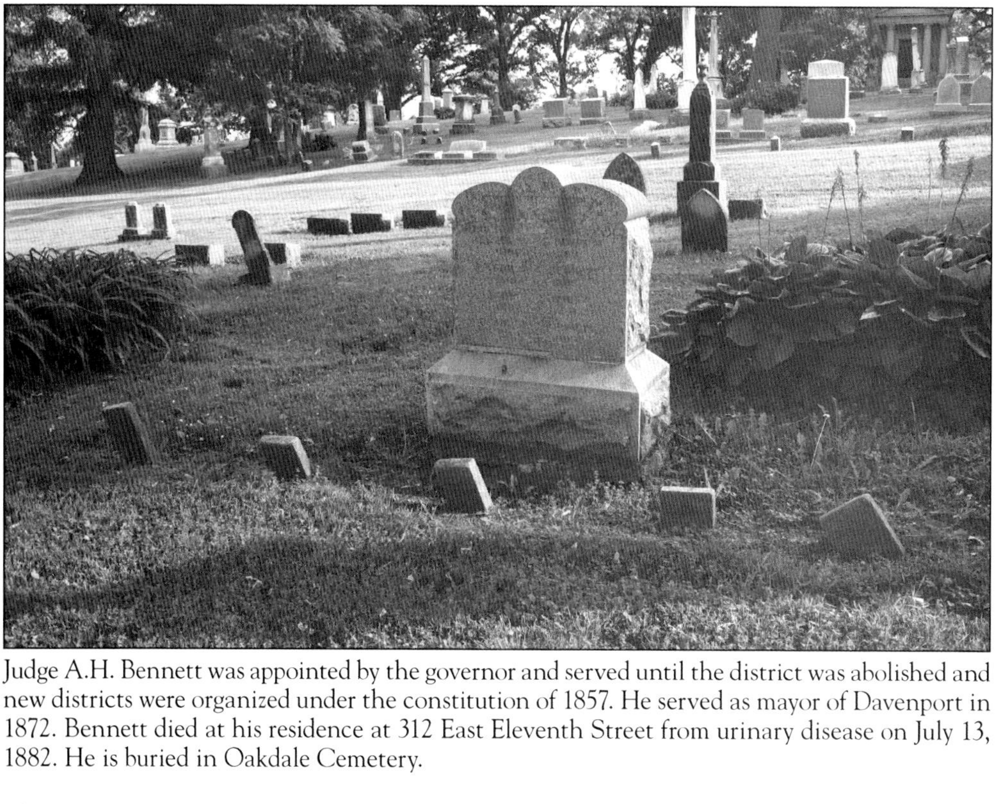

Judge A.H. Bennett was appointed by the governor and served until the district was abolished and new districts were organized under the constitution of 1857. He served as mayor of Davenport in 1872. Bennett died at his residence at 312 East Eleventh Street from urinary disease on July 13, 1882. He is buried in Oakdale Cemetery.

Three

Doctors

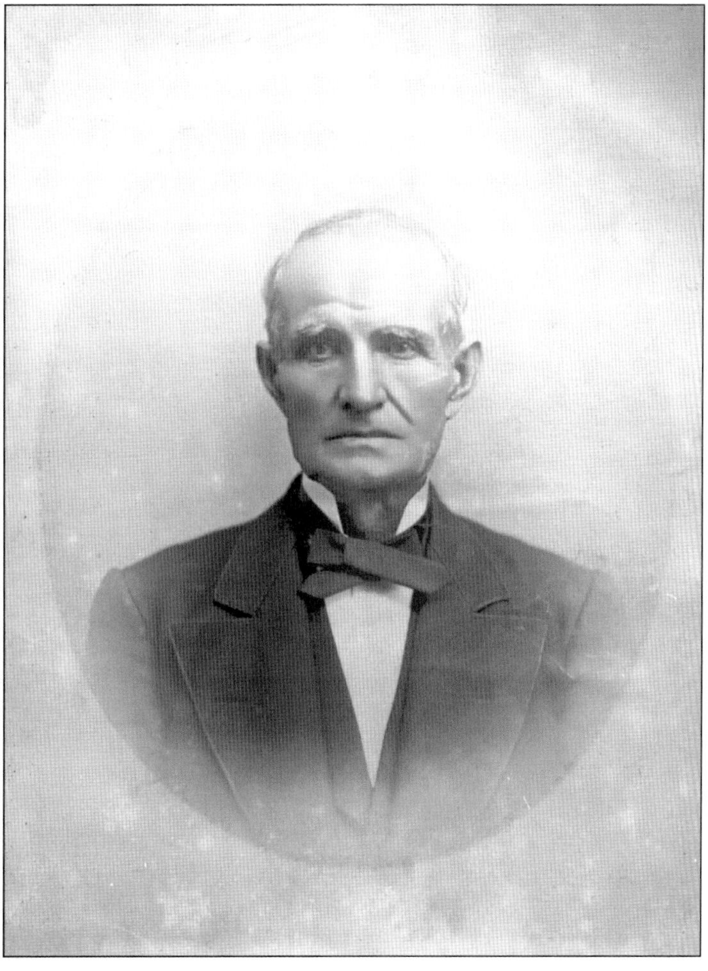

Jennings Price Crawford was born on August 27, 1855. He was educated as a doctor and finished his education in 1883. Crawford moved to Davenport the same year and established a medical practice. He was a surgeon at both St. Luke's and Mercy Hospitals, and he also served as the district surgeon for the Chicago, Milwaukee and St. Paul Railroad. Crawford died on March 24, 1907.

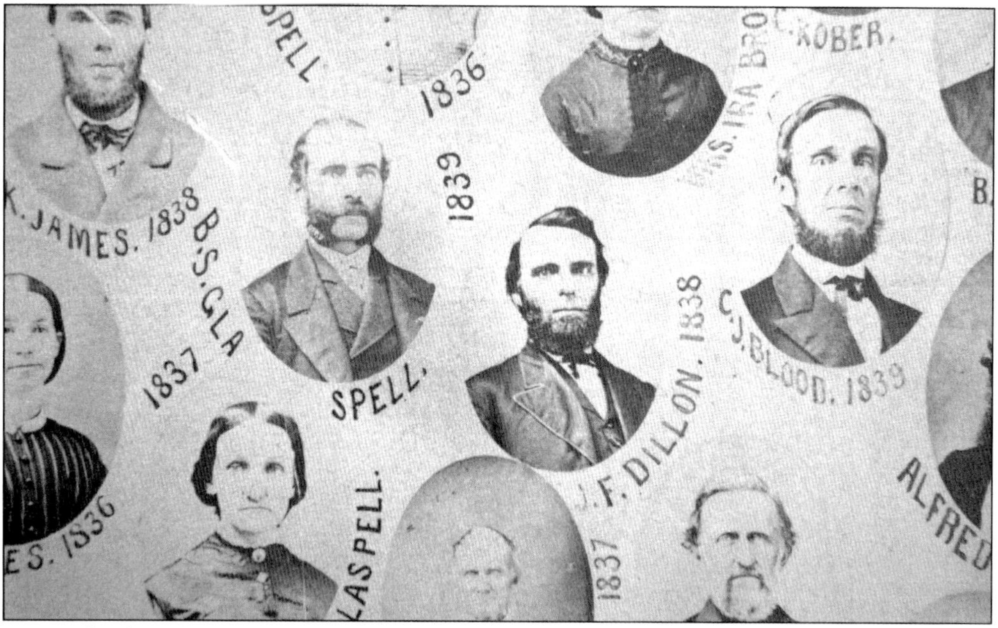

Cyrus Blood was born in New York in 1808. In 1839, he came to Davenport where he opened a select school between Third and Fourth Streets on the east side of Main Street. Starting in 1840, he farmed for six years before deciding to go into medicine. Blood graduated from Rusch Medical College in Chicago and practiced medicine with his brother-in-law.

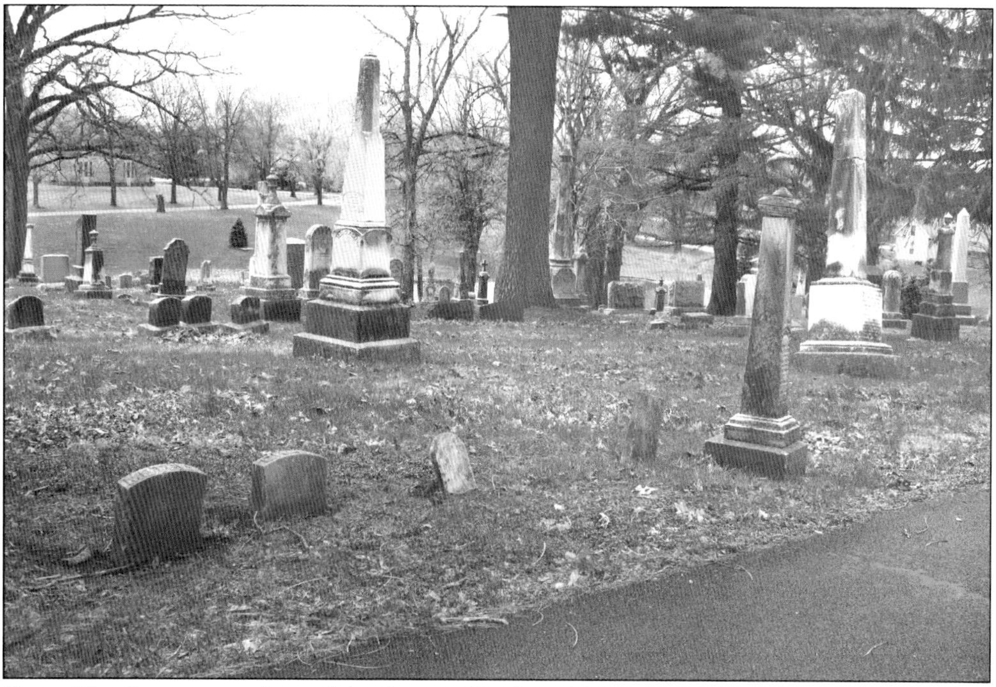

Cyrus Blood was a president of the Pioneer Settlers Association. In 1854, he became county commissioner, and in 1855, he became justice of the peace until 1860. Blood then retired, but in 1862, he worked as a clerk in the offices of Davison & True. Later, he again became justice of the peace. He died from heart disease complicated by pneumonia at his home at 1803 Summit Avenue.

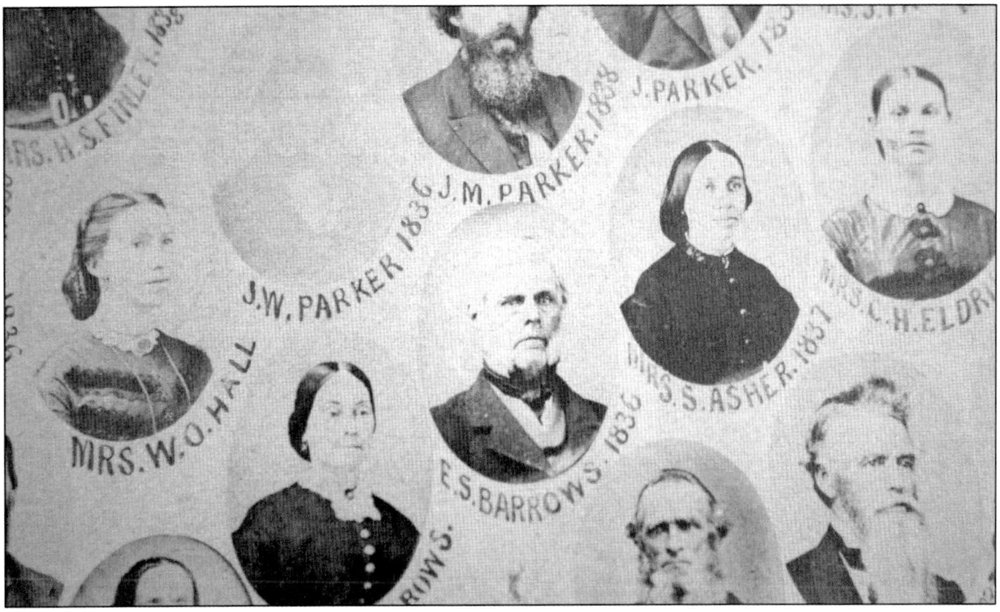

E.S. Barrows was born in Middlebury, Vermont, in 1799. For a time, Doctor Barrows was the only doctor in Iowa between Dubuque and Burlington. He was the first doctor in Scott County and the second in the territory. Doctor Barrows came to the area with his wife after serving in the US Army as a surgeon, which included service in the Seminole War in Florida.

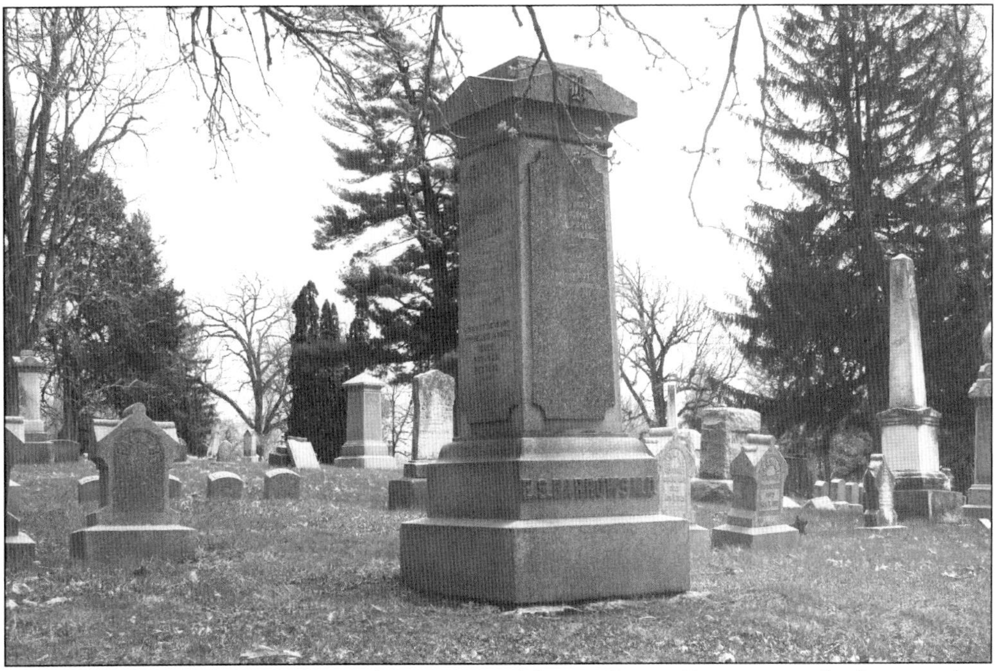

E.S. Barrows served as Antoine LeClaire's personal doctor. Doctor Barrows was the first president of the Scott County Medical Society and also helped found the Pioneers Settlers Association. He retired from the medical profession in 1860, and died from complications of a broken hip at his home on Sixth and Rock Island Streets in 1892. He was buried in an iron coffin, which was to help prevent body snatching.

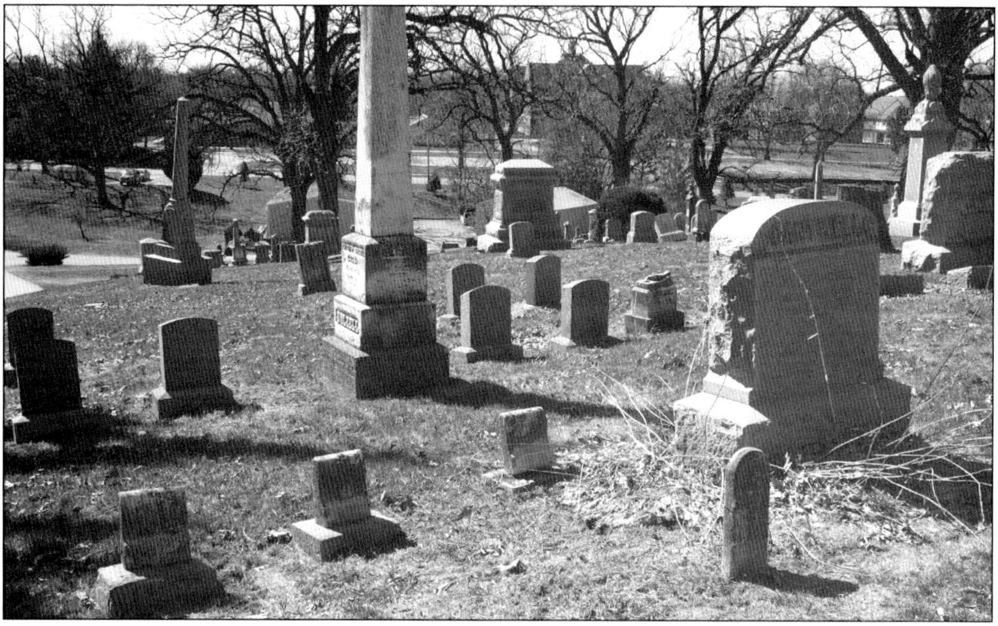

Alonzo William Cantwell began the study of medicine with a doctor in Hardin County, Ohio. He graduated from the University of Michigan in 1869 before arriving in Davenport. He eventually became a prominent doctor in the city, serving as physician to the board of health during a cholera outbreak in the city in 1873, as well as during a smallpox epidemic 10 years later. He died at Mercy Hospital in 1899.

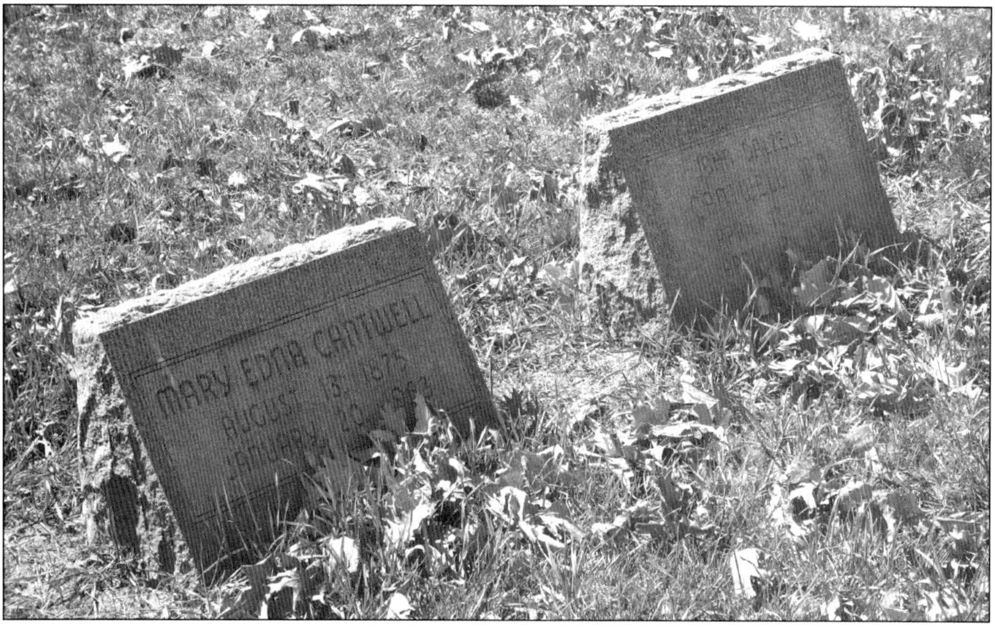

J.D. Cantwell, the son of Alonzo William Cantwell, was educated in Davenport and grew up to become a doctor himself. After attending Johns Hopkins University, he practiced medicine in Davenport. J.D. served as president of the Iowa State Coroners Association and was elected Scott County coroner in 1914. In 1918, he enlisted in the US Army. Afterwards, he came back to Davenport and again served as Scott County coroner.

Alfonse Hageboeck was born in 1867. He graduated from college in 1889 and started practicing surgery in 1891. Hageboeck had large real estate interests that included several residences. He was one of the founders of Davenport Locomotive Works and also served as the company's first treasurer and secretary.

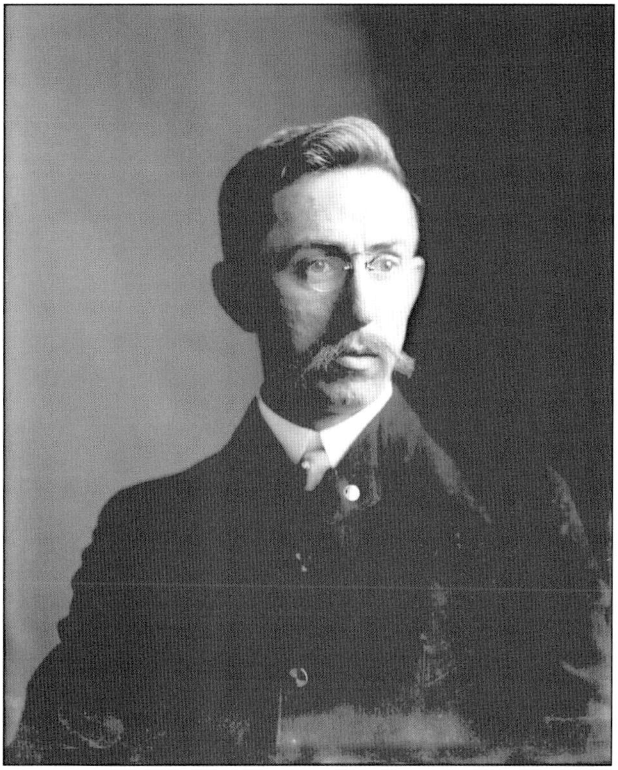

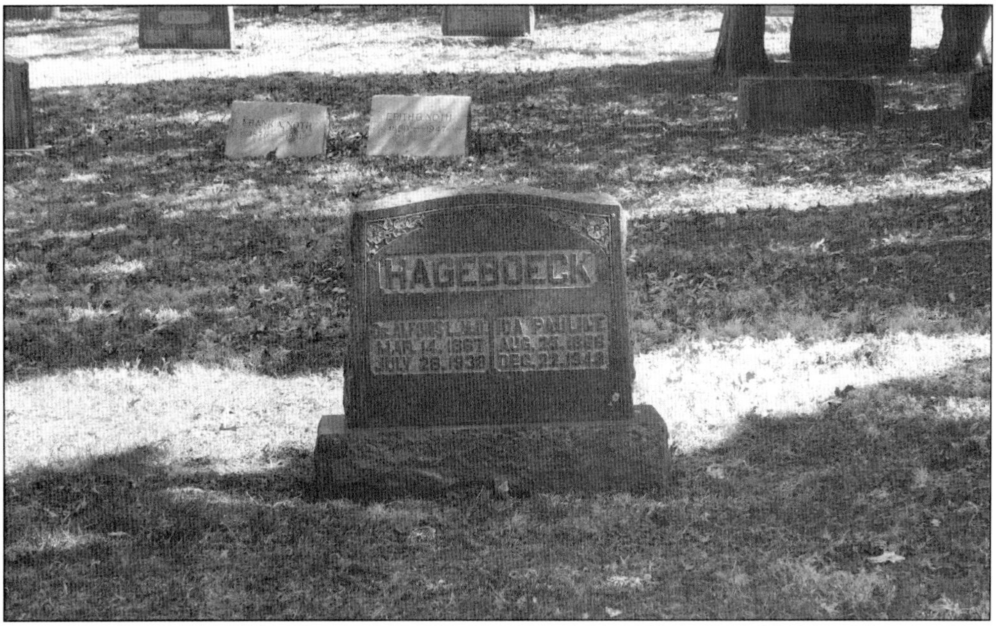

Alfonse Hageboeck held high positions at several companies. These included being the president of the Newcomb Loom Company and the American Pneumatic Action Company. He was also vice president of the Andrews Chemical Company. Hageboeck retired from his medical practice because of health problems in 1907. He died from a cerebral embolism at Mercy Hospital in Davenport on July 28, 1938.

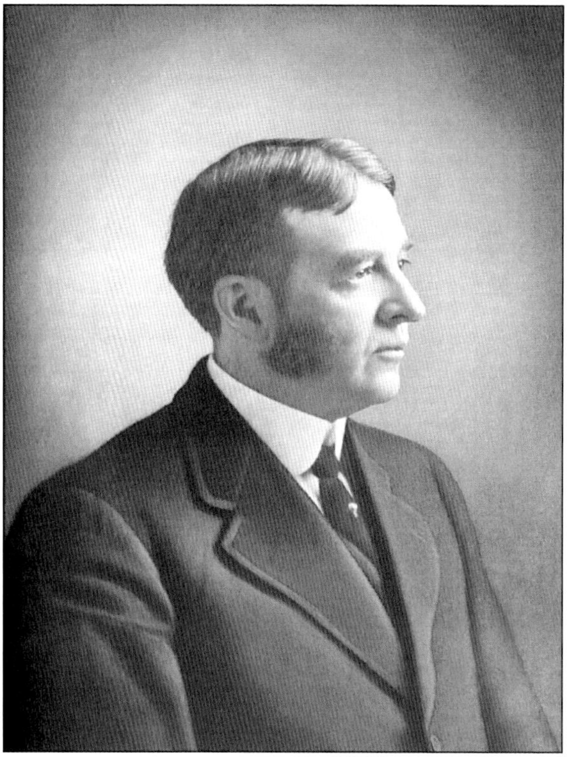

William Allen was born in Davenport in 1858. He began studying medicine in Iowa and later continued his studies for two years in Vienna, Austria. He inherited stock in the Davenport Central Railway and saw to it that the line was equipped with electric cars in 1888, making Davenport the second city in America to do this.

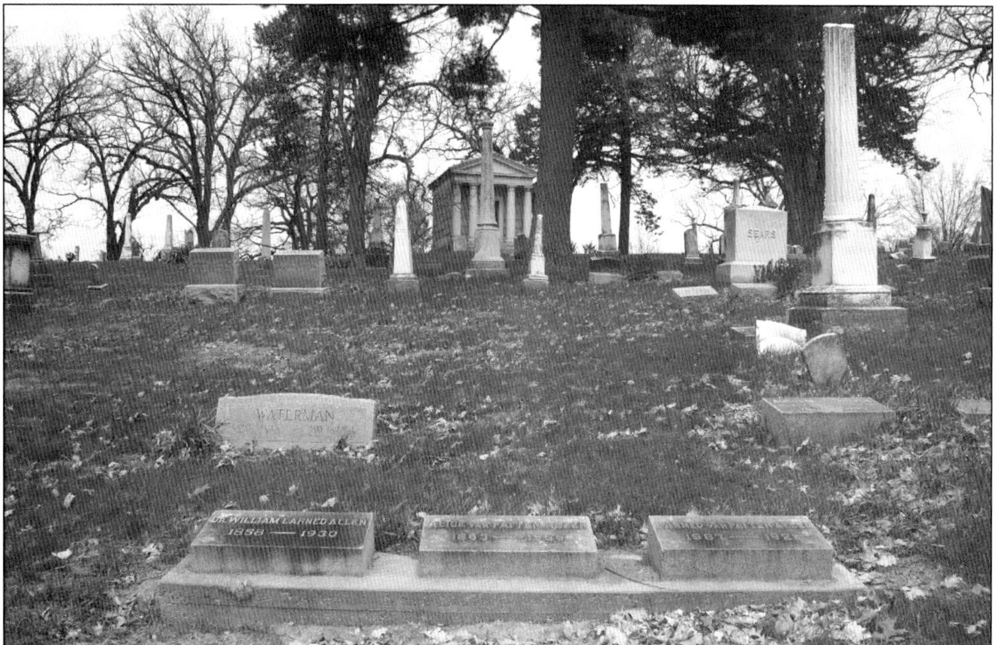

William Allen earned a successful reputation as a surgeon and founded St. Luke's Hospital in Davenport in 1891. He was president of the Davenport Academy of Sciences and the Scott County Medical Association. In 1900, he was elected to the presidency of the Iowa and Illinois District Medical Society. He died in 1930 from mitral insufficiency.

John Waterman Harris Baker was born in Chesterfield, New Hampshire, on August 21, 1821. In 1842, he graduated from Dartmouth Medical College, where he attended lectures by Dr. Oliver Wendell Holmes. Doctor Baker practiced in New Hampshire until 1853 and served as the regimental surgeon of the militia. He later went to California and opened an office in Calaveras County, where he served as a physician and dentist.

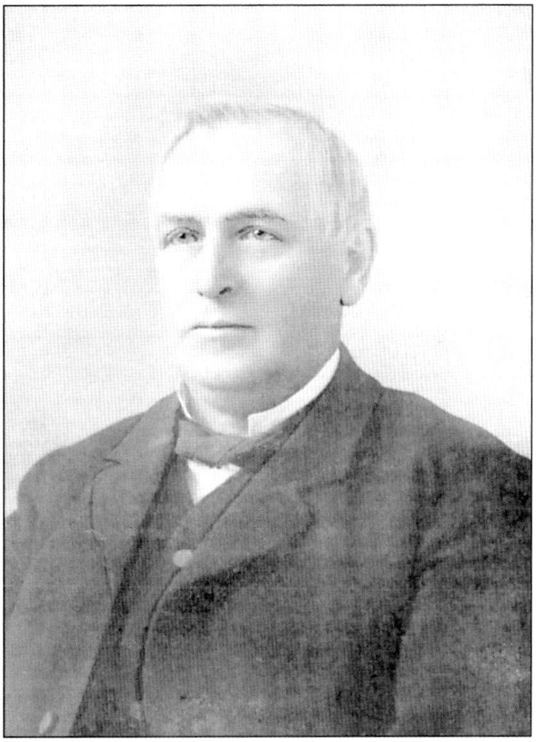

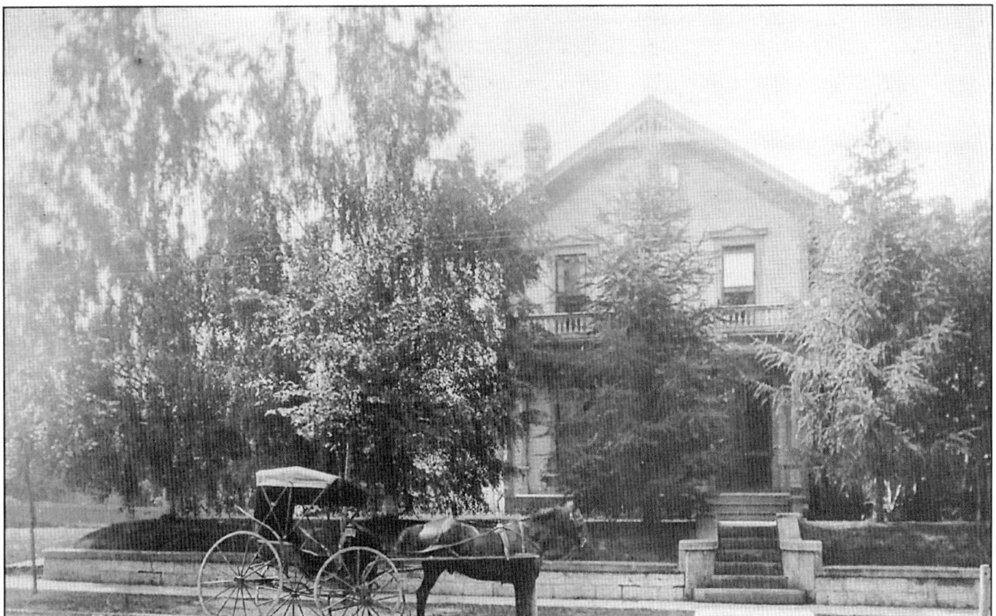

In 1855, John Waterman Harris Baker moved to Davenport and opened an office there. Doctor Baker was appointed surgeon of the 2nd Iowa Militia. During the Civil War, he was commissioned assistant surgeon and served for a time in the military hospital at Camp McClellan. Baker was a member of the Iowa and Scott County Medical Societies. He died on April 7, 1905.

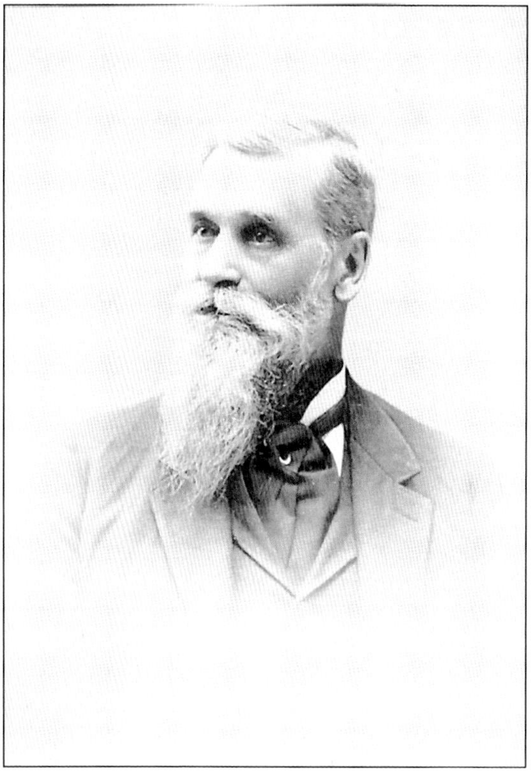

Lucius French was born February 2, 1832, in New York. At 16, he left home with $5 and attended Binghamton Academy in Binghamton, New York, for three years. Later, he went to his uncle, a physician, for instruction and then attended the Geneva Medical College and the Berkshire Medical College, graduating in 1853. In 1854, he practiced in Scranton, Pennsylvania.

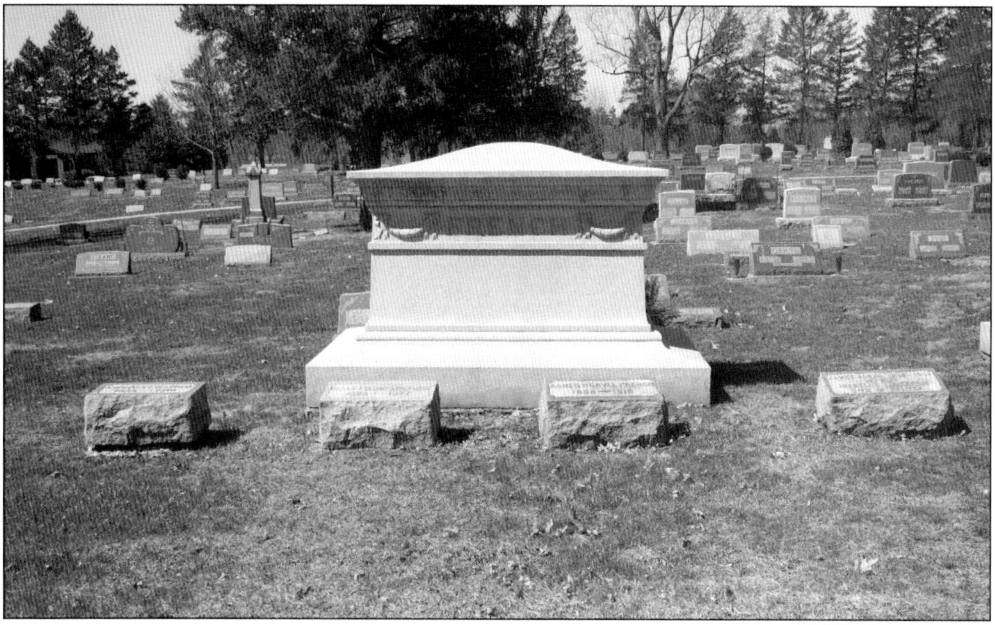

In 1861, Lucius French moved to Anamosa, Iowa. In 1862, he served as the assistant surgeon in the 31st Iowa Infantry. He resigned due to overwork in 1863. Also that year, he married Ellen Cook, daughter of Judge William L. Cook. She died in 1865 after moving to Davenport. He remarried Agnes Norval in 1867. French, a member of the Iowa and Scott County Medical Societies, died September 10, 1910.

William Kulp was born on September 19, 1836, in Wadsworth, Ohio. At 20, he started to study medicine, but trouble with his teeth lead him to specialize in dentistry. Kulp worked at various branches of business to support himself while completing his medical studies. In October 1859, he began practice in Muscatine, Iowa, and formed a partnership with H.G. Hall, a prominent dentist.

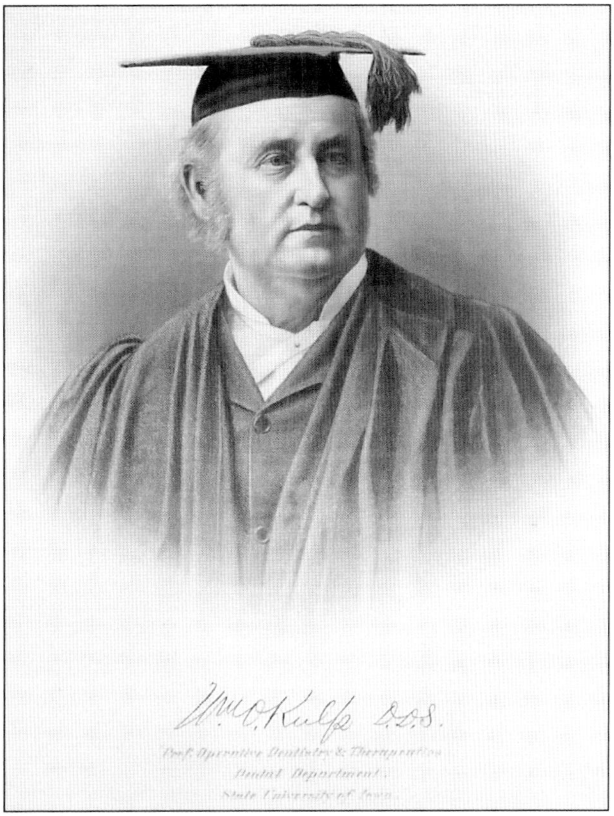

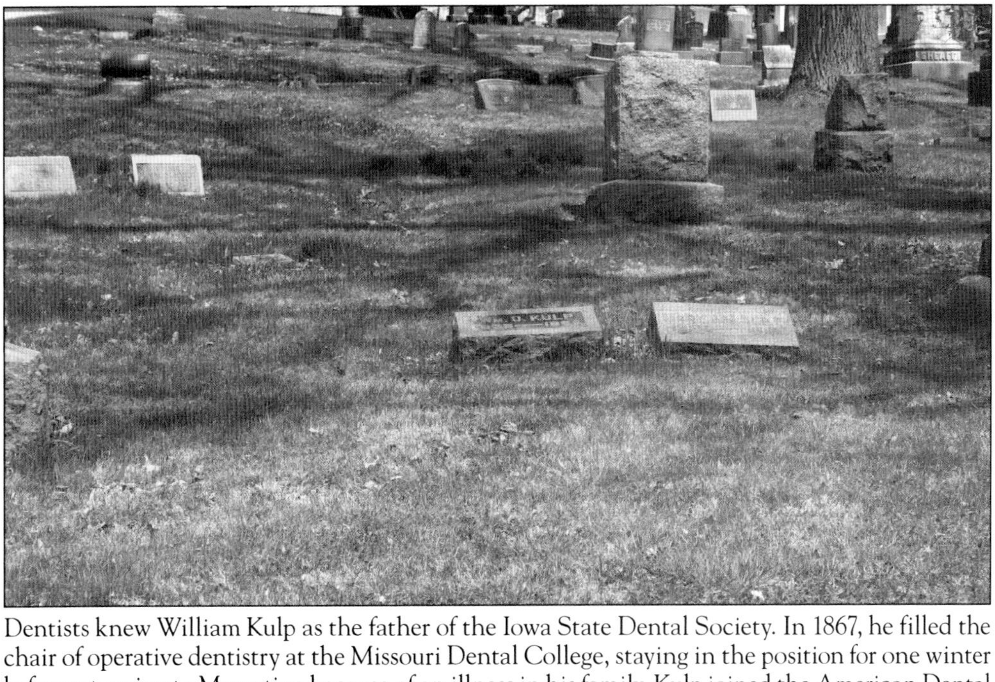

Dentists knew William Kulp as the father of the Iowa State Dental Society. In 1867, he filled the chair of operative dentistry at the Missouri Dental College, staying in the position for one winter before returning to Muscatine because of an illness in his family. Kulp joined the American Dental Association in 1864. He died from diabetes, and the funeral was held at the family home.

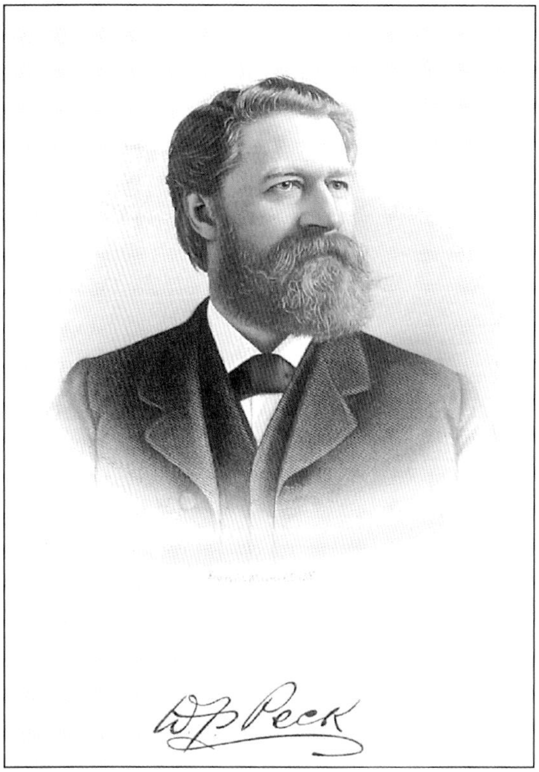

Washington Freeman Peck, born in Galen, New York, on January 22, 1841, graduated from Bellevue Hospital Medical College in 1863. At the close of his Bellevue service, Peck entered Lincoln General Hospital in Washington, DC, as a contract surgeon, but resigned after an attack of pneumonia. He moved to Davenport and opened an office on Third Street, close to Brady Street.

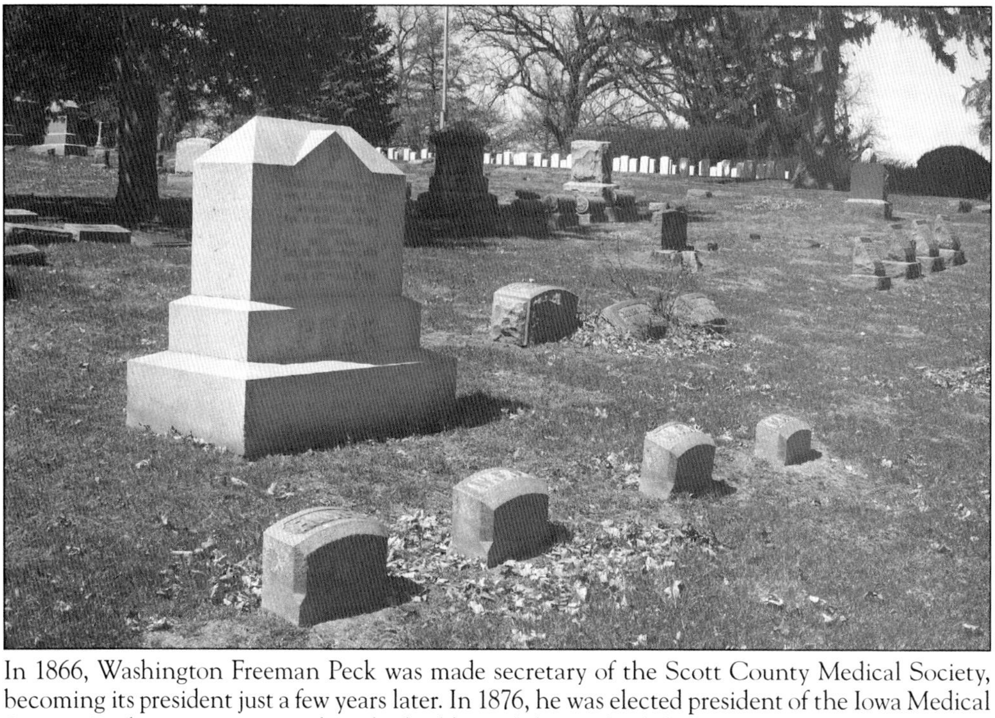

In 1866, Washington Freeman Peck was made secretary of the Scott County Medical Society, becoming its president just a few years later. In 1876, he was elected president of the Iowa Medical Society. Peck was instrumental in the building of the medical department at the University of Iowa, as well as in the founding of Mercy Hospital in Davenport. He died from heart disease.

Four

Lawyers and Politicians

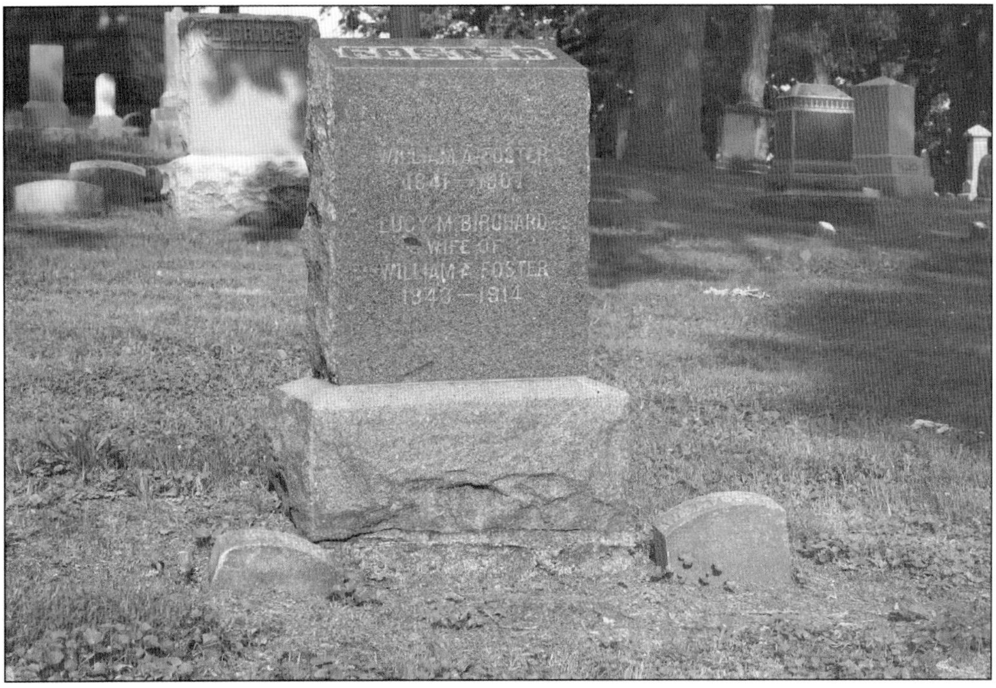

W.A. Foster was born in Scott County in 1842. He studied law with the firm Davison & True in Davenport, and was admitted to the bar in 1866. He opened a law office and in 1867, he married Lucy Birchard. In 1878, Foster was elected to the state senate. He achieved a reputation as a criminal lawyer, including serving as a lawyer in the Chicago Haymarket affair.

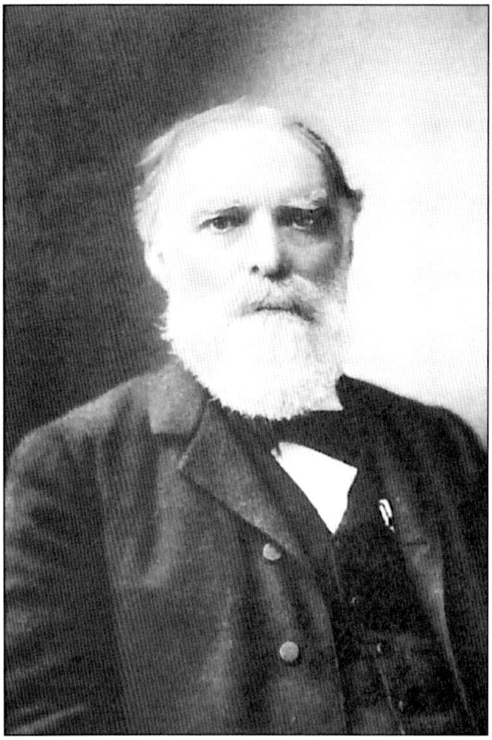

John F. Dillon, born in New York on December 25, 1831, moved to Davenport in 1838. At the age of 17, he began to study medicine with local physician Egbert S. Barrows. He attended two courses of medical lectures at the Keokuk Medical College and graduated when he was 21 years old. Soon after, Dillon gave up medicine and decided to study law.

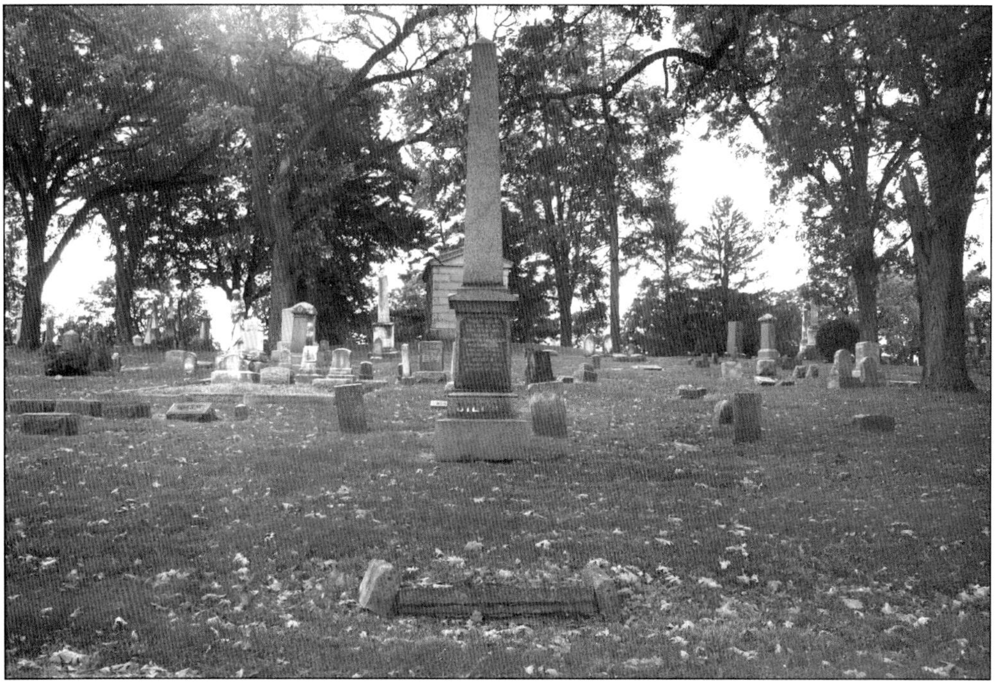

John F. Dillon was licensed as an attorney in Scott County, Iowa, in 1852. He was elected prosecuting attorney for Scott County. In 1858, he was elected judge of the seventh judicial district of Iowa. Dillon later served as a Chief Justice of the Supreme Court and was confirmed as circuit judge of the United States for the eighth judicial circuit. He died in 1914 at age 82.

Alexander W. McGregor was born in North Carolina on January 25, 1809. He came to Rock Island in November 1835 and was among the first attorneys admitted to the bar in the Territory of Wisconsin. McGregor bought a farm and, through some of his acquaintances, became a member of the real estate company that founded the city of Davenport.

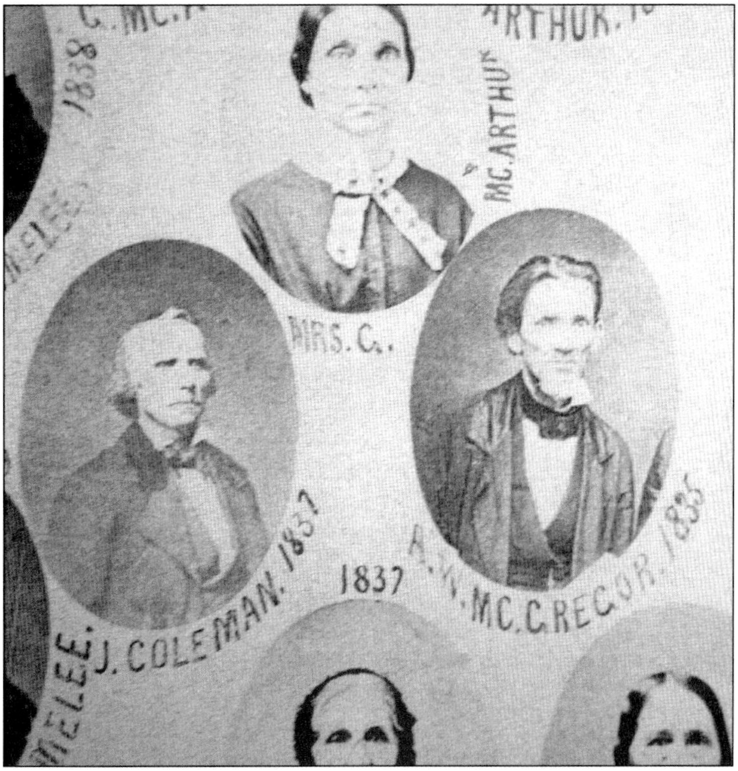

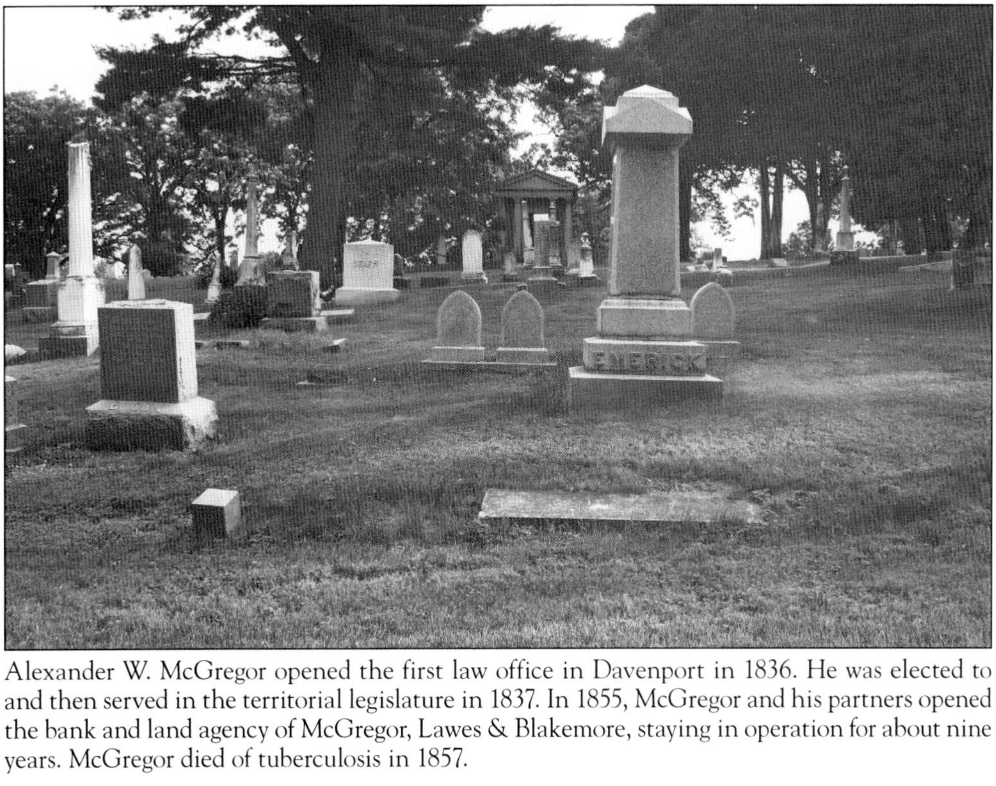

Alexander W. McGregor opened the first law office in Davenport in 1836. He was elected to and then served in the territorial legislature in 1837. In 1855, McGregor and his partners opened the bank and land agency of McGregor, Lawes & Blakemore, staying in operation for about nine years. McGregor died of tuberculosis in 1857.

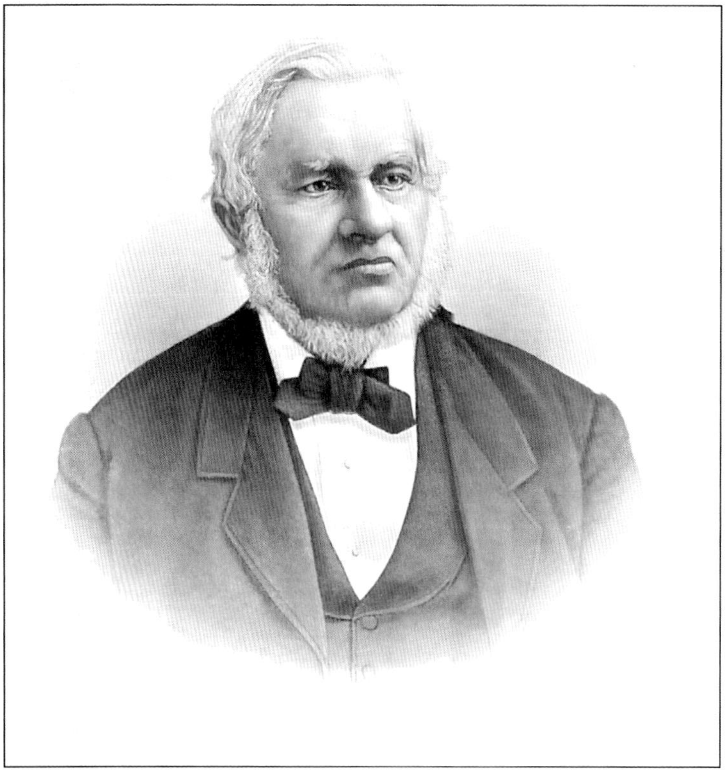

Hans Reimer Claussen was born in Schleswig-Holstein, Germany, on February 23, 1804. He practiced law until 1851, when he was exiled for his participation in the struggle of Schleswig-Holstein for independence from the Danish king. Claussen arrived in the United States in 1851 and settled in Davenport, where he began to study English and law.

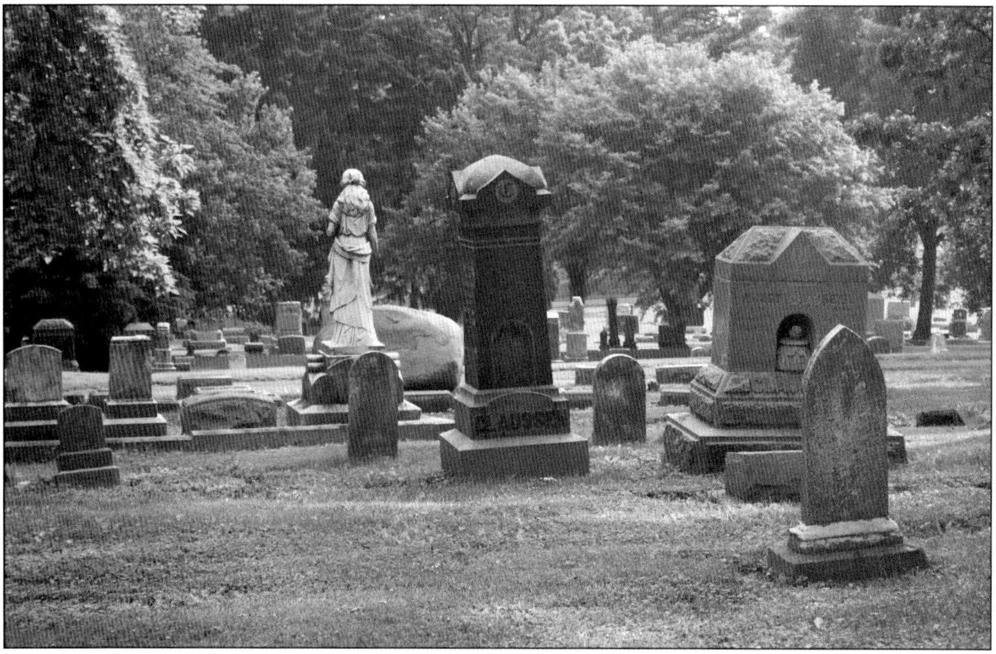

Hans Reimer Claussen was admitted to the bar in 1853. In the fall of 1858, he was elected justice of the peace, and reelected in 1860. He eventually took his son Ernst Claussen as a partner in his firm. In 1869, he was elected to the state senate, serving four years and then retiring. He died March 14, 1894, at 90 years old.

Albert Bollinger was born in Lancaster, Illinois, in 1839. At the beginning of the Civil War, he enlisted in the Union army and served as a secretary to Gen. William Tecumseh Sherman and as a recruiter. After the War, he learned to be a carriage maker and opened a carriage-making factory in Geneseo, Illinois. After many successful years, he moved to Davenport and became a salesman for the Sieg Iron Company.

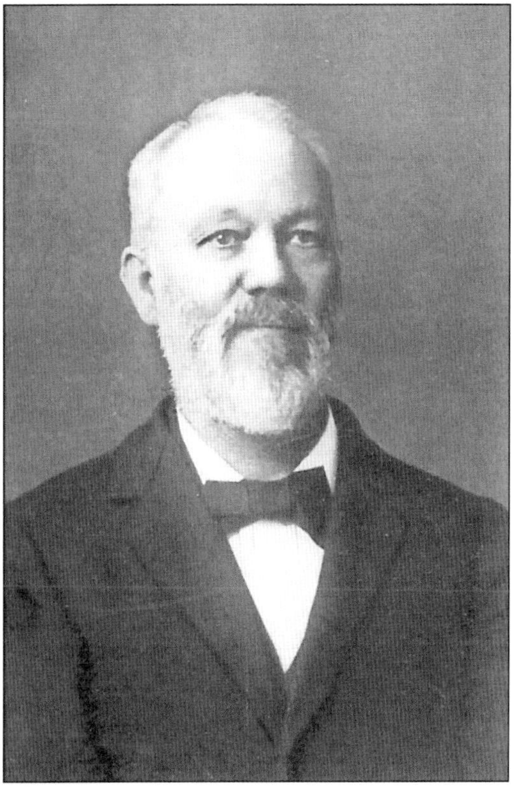

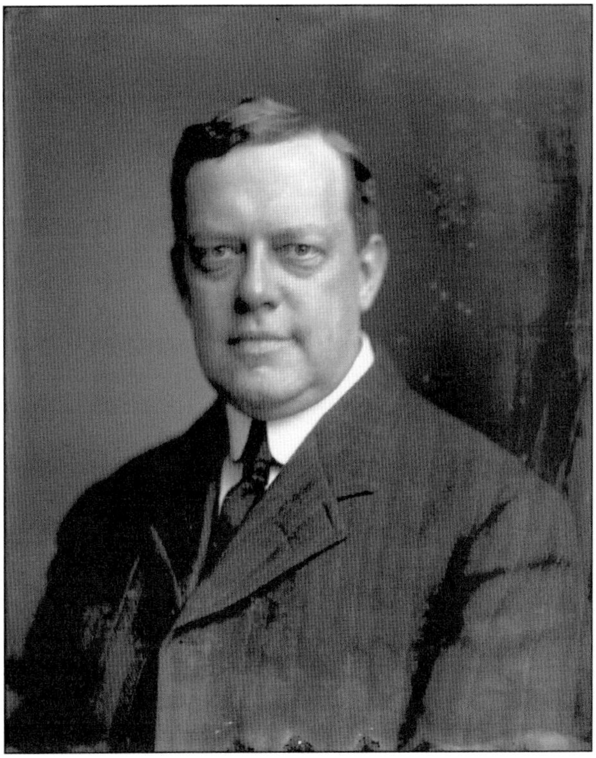

James Bollinger, the son of Albert Bollinger, was born and educated in Davenport as a lawyer and joined the bar in 1889. He practiced in Davenport for several years and was appointed a district court judge. After he left this position, he entered into a partnership with Louis Block. The partnership dissolved in 1932, and Bollinger went independent for a time, then he entered into another partnership with Judge Maurice Donegan. He died in 1951.

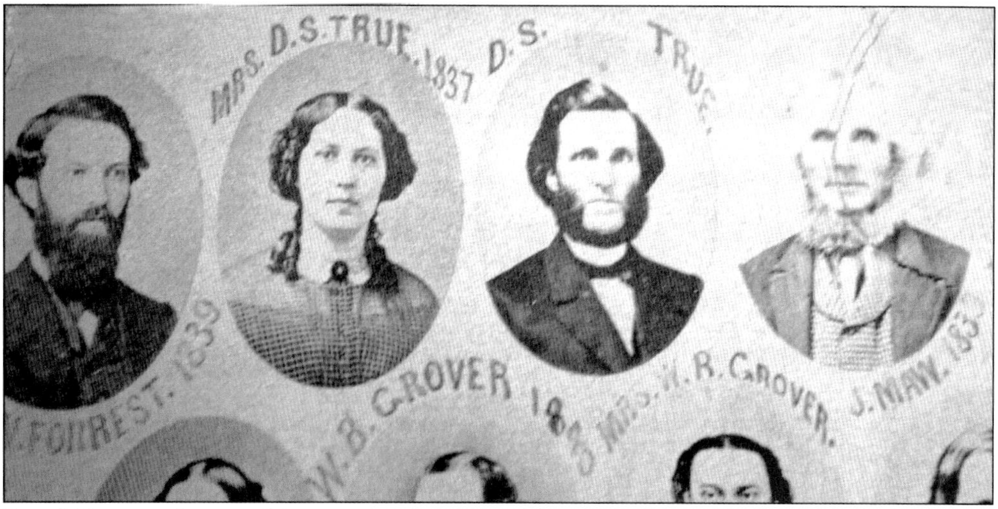

David True was born in Maine in 1823. Working his way up from the local school and then through college, True became a school principal for a time. He eventually left the position to travel Europe, after which he settled in Davenport and opened a law practice in 1852. Two years later, he and another young lawyer, Abner Davison, formed the firm Davison & True.

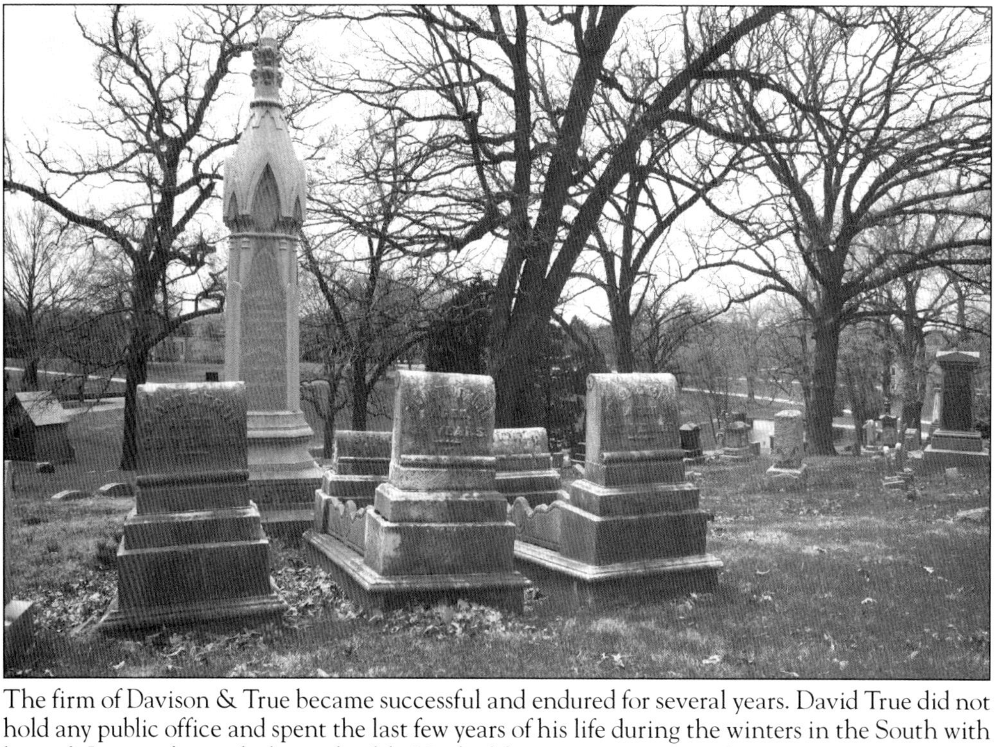
The firm of Davison & True became successful and endured for several years. David True did not hold any public office and spent the last few years of his life during the winters in the South with his wife Jennie, due to declining health. He died from consumption in his room at the Newcomb House on April 23, 1873, at the age of 50.

Joseph Reed Lane was born in Davenport, Iowa, on May 6, 1858. He graduated from the State University of Iowa at Iowa City in 1880. In the same year, he was admitted to the bar and started practice in Davenport. Lane was a member of the Davenport City Council and was elected to the 56th Congress in 1899, staying there until 1901. He died in 1931 from nephritis.

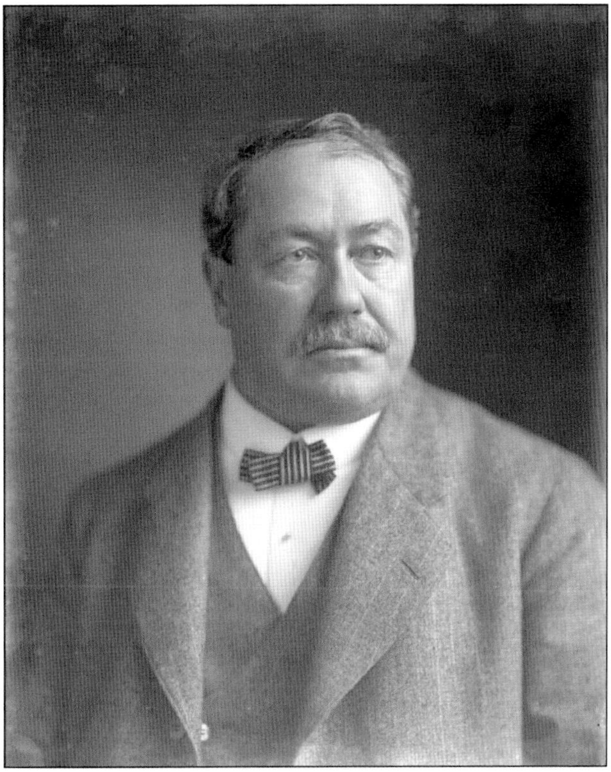

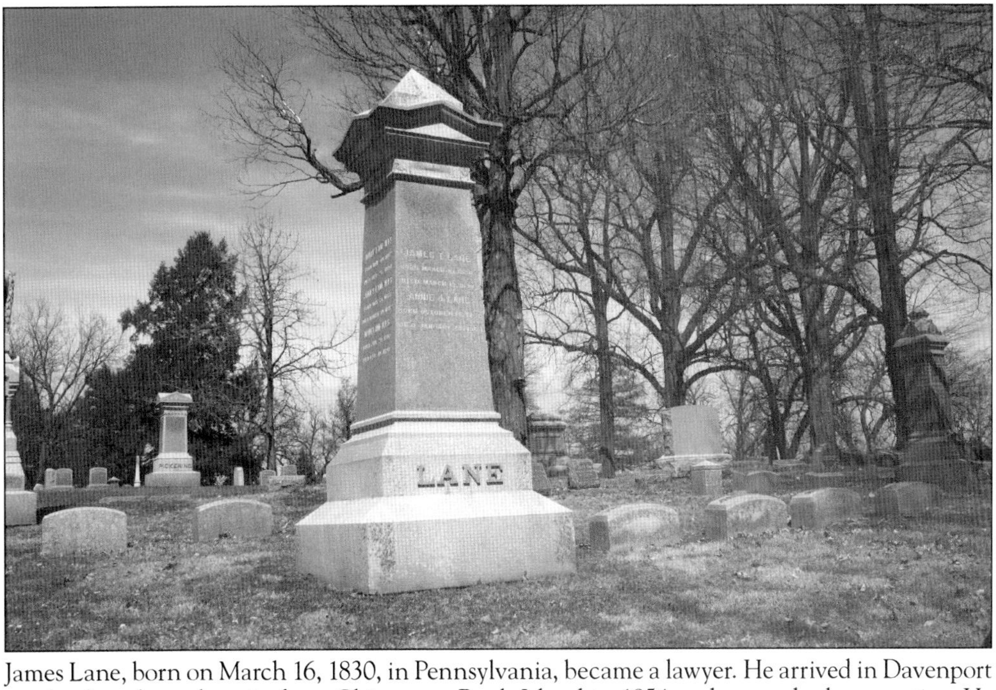

James Lane, born on March 16, 1830, in Pennsylvania, became a lawyer. He arrived in Davenport on the first through train from Chicago to Rock Island in 1854 and opened a law practice. He was elected three times as city attorney of Davenport and to the state legislature in 1861. In 1873, he became the US district attorney for the state of Iowa.

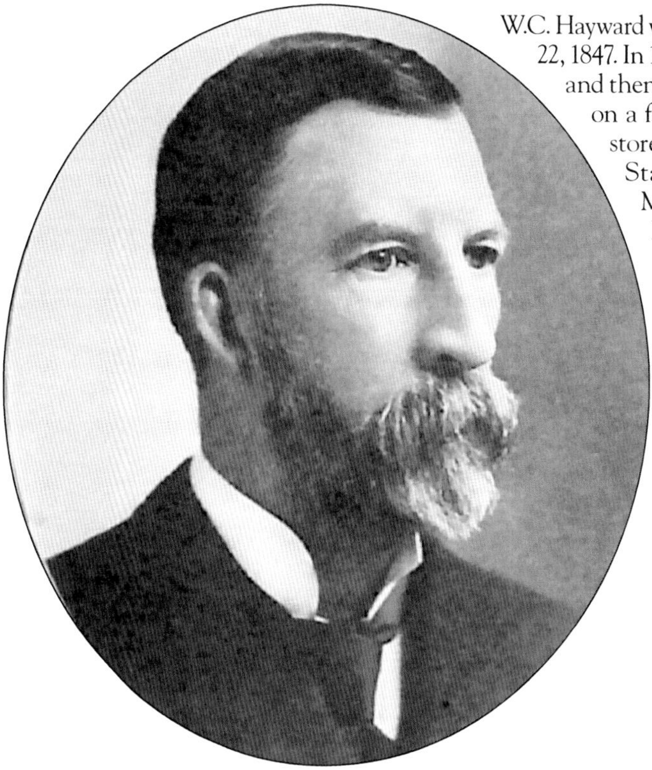

W.C. Hayward was born in New York on November 22, 1847. In 1861, his family moved to Minnesota and then to Iowa in 1867. Hayward worked on a farm before becoming a clerk in a store and teaching. He attended the State College of Agriculture and Mechanical Arts in Ames, Iowa. Hayward moved to Winnebago County and was elected county surveyor.

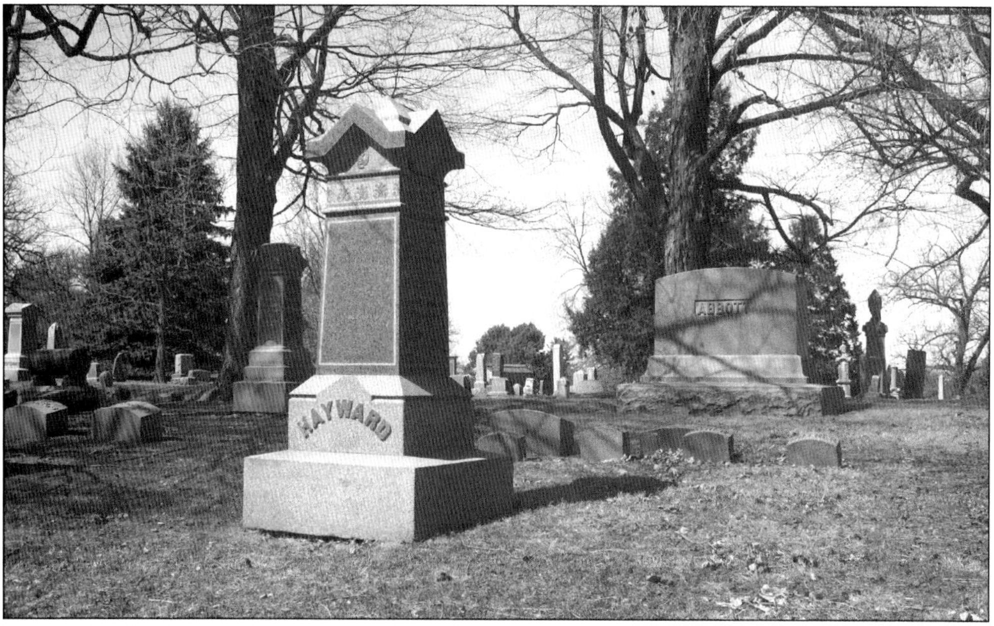

In 1886, W.C. Hayward became a resident of Davenport. He helped organize the Union Savings Bank of Davenport and was president of the Davenport National Bank. Hayward was a member of the school board for nine years, and in 1897, he was elected to the state senate and then again in 1901. He was elected Secretary of State in 1906 and was reelected twice. He died from a stroke of apoplexy.

Five

Businessmen and Farmers

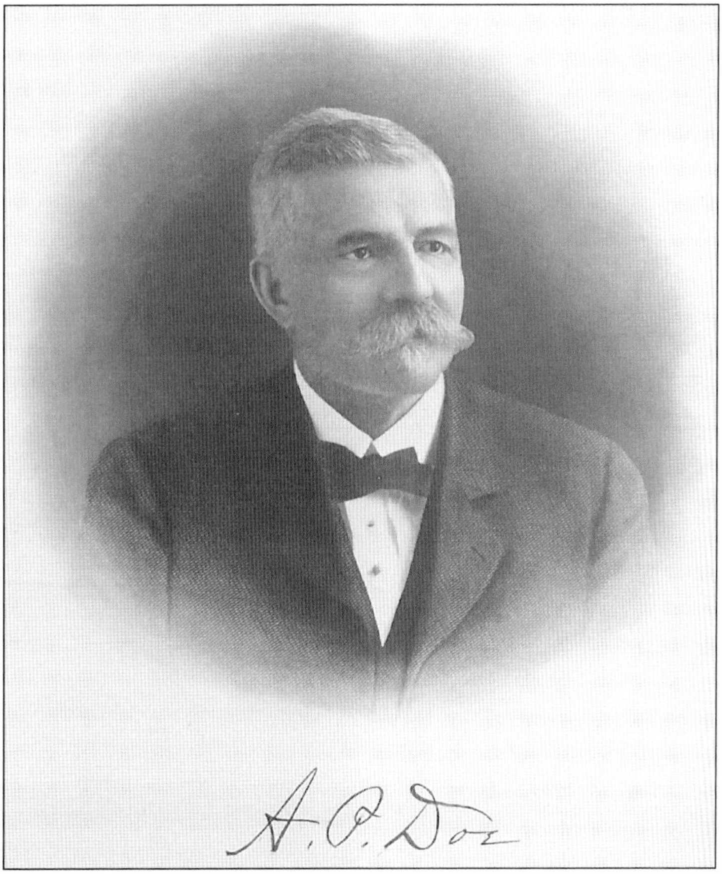

Alonzo P. Doe was born in March 1837 in Windham, Maine. He learned skills as a machinist, manufacturing rifles for the Civil War. He came to Davenport in 1866 and began business as a wholesale shoe merchant, lasting for 35 years. He was a vice president and president of the Iowa National Bank, retiring in 1901. Doe helped establish the orphans' home. He died from heart trouble in 1910.

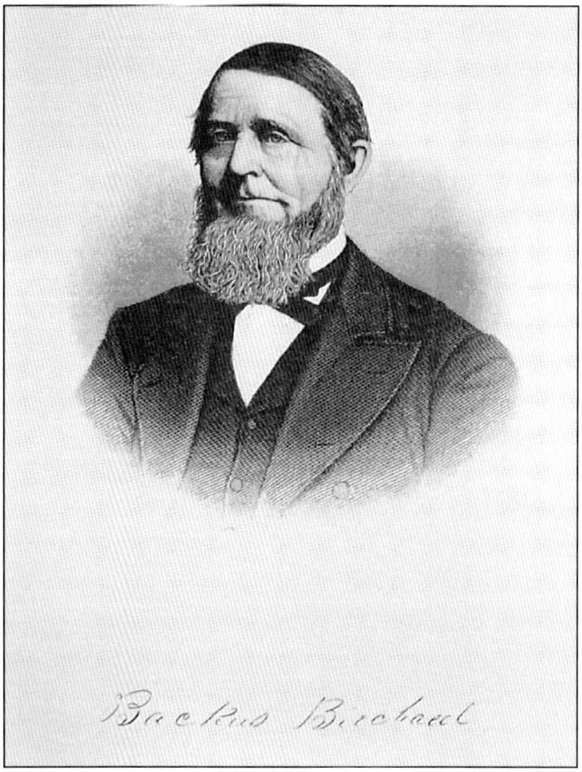

Bachus Birchard was born in Pennsylvania in 1812. He lived on his father's farm until he was 22, then left and found employment in New York as a mason. After three years, Birchard began work as a mason superintendent on the Erie Canal. In 1839 and 1840, he came west, spending time doing stonework in Milan, Illinois. While he was in the area, he purchased a home in Pleasant Valley, Iowa.

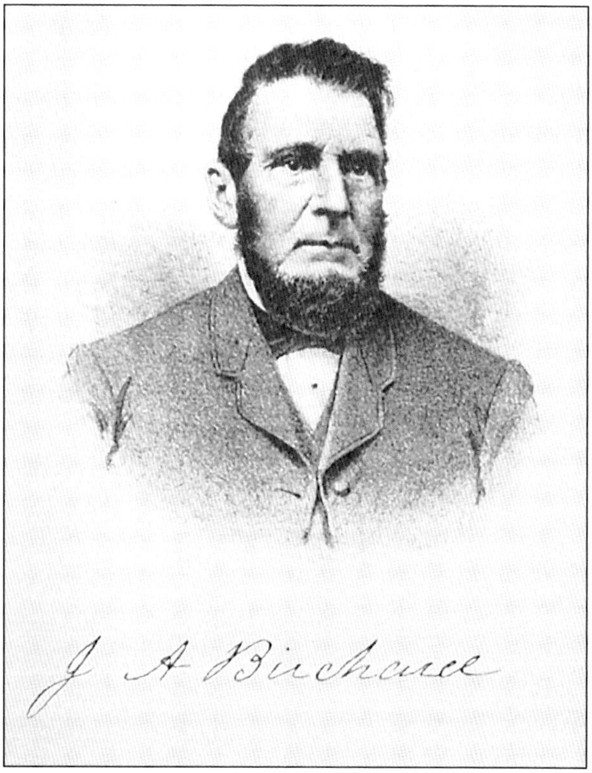

Jabez Birchard was born and raised a farmer in Pennsylvania. He and his wife moved to Davenport in 1838, where he once again took up his farming profession. They helped name the town of Pleasant Valley and lived there their entire lives. Jabez, a member of the first Iowa Legislature, was made lame in a 1860s buggy accident. He died in Pleasant Valley in 1871.

In 1832, the Black Hawk Treaty was signed. Translating between the US government and the Native Americans was Antoine LeClaire. An interpreter, LeClaire spoke English, French, and Spanish, as well as several native dialects. As a stipulation of the treaty, he received a large portion of land on the Iowa side of the river. Some of this land would become the city of Davenport.

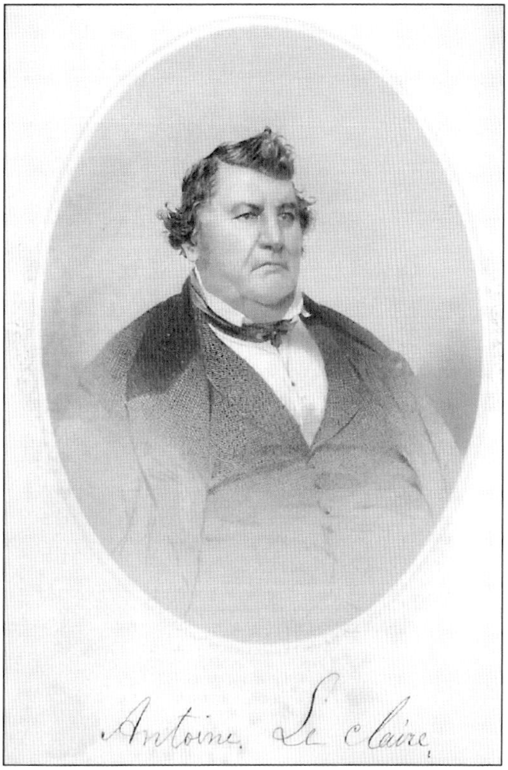

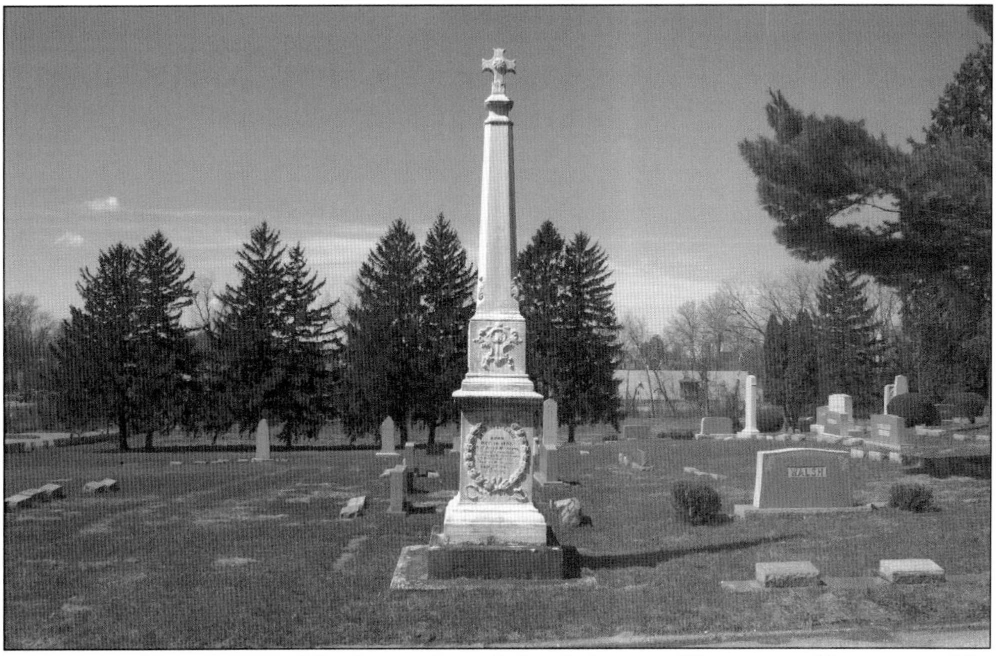

Antoine LeClaire was one of the driving forces behind the city of Davenport. He was a wealthy man who contributed greatly to the development of the city, donating his own money to religious groups who wanted to build churches there. LeClaire and others were responsible for bringing the first railroad into Iowa, and he donated his home to be used as the first railroad depot in Iowa.

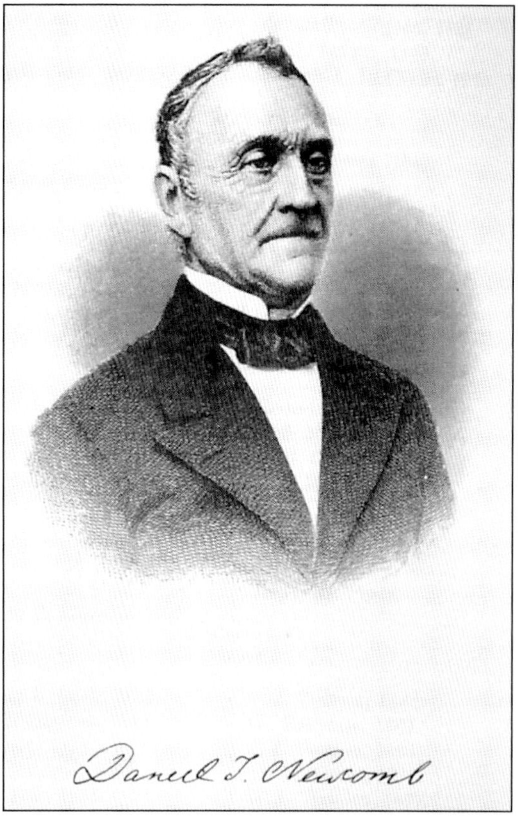

Daniel Tobias Newcomb was born in Pittstown, New York, in 1791. During the War of 1812, he participated in the Invasion of Plattsburg in 1814. In 1822, he moved to Essex County, New York, to develop a large tract of land situated in what is now the town of Newcomb. He moved to Davenport in 1842 and died of apoplexy on December 22, 1870.

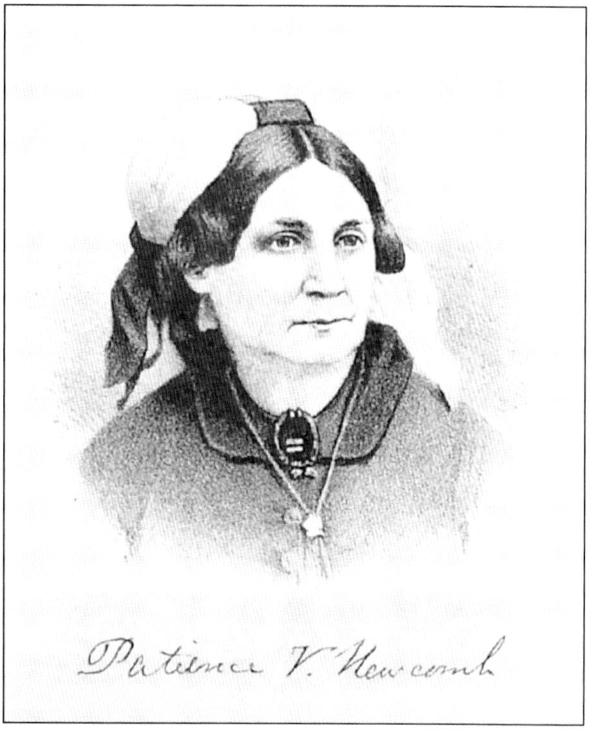

Patience Newcomb, born on February 4, 1793, in New York, served as president of the Soldiers' Aid Society of Davenport, and was a founder of the Soldiers' Orphans' Home. Newcomb also frequently donated to the Davenport Academy of Science. She died of old age on August 21, 1891, in Rochester, New York.

Daniel Moore was born in Leicester, England, on September 25, 1819. In May 1830, he immigrated to Philadelphia, Pennsylvania, and later moved to Cincinnati, Ohio. To achieve this, Moore crossed the Allegheny Mountains, floated down the Ohio River in a skiff, and later came to Cincinnati by flatboat. He worked in steam boating and as a baker in St. Louis, Missouri.

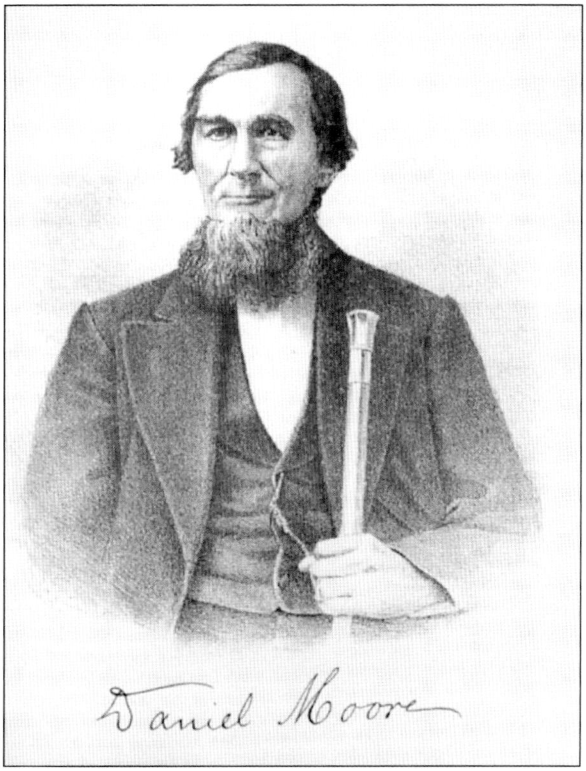

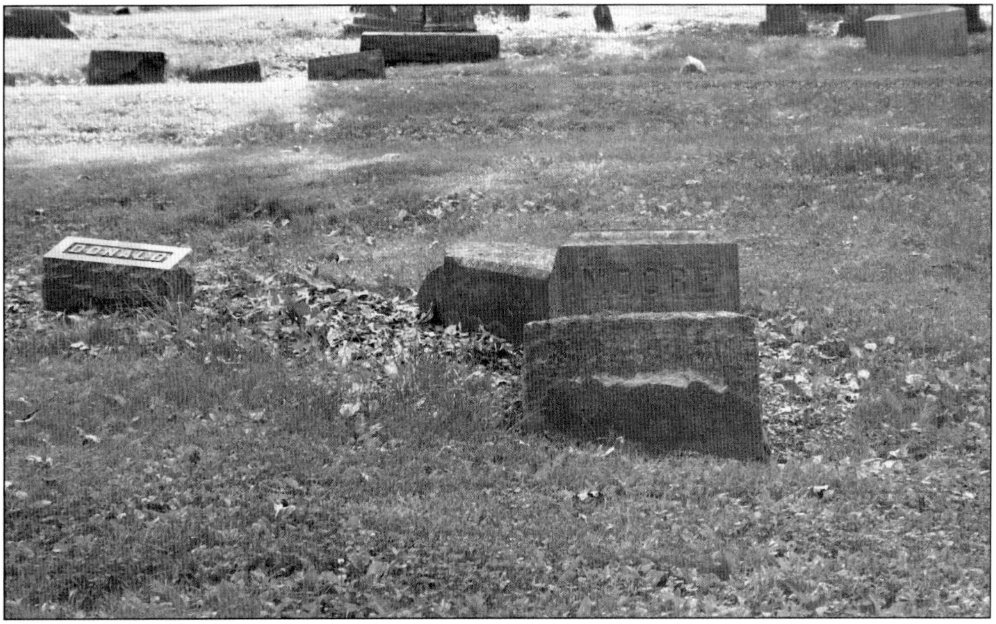

In 1841, Daniel Moore moved to Stephenson (now Rock Island) and founded his baking business there. In 1842, he had moved across the river to Davenport where, from that year to 1851, Moore was the only baker and butcher serving that city. He retired in 1873. In 1881, Moore was president of the pioneer association and was helped organize the Davenport Fire Department. He died from pneumonia in 1885.

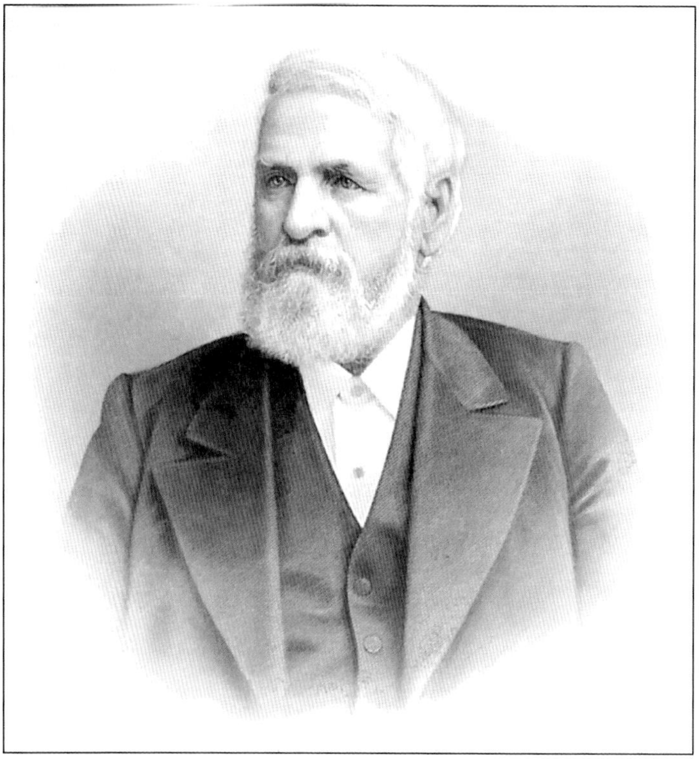

Israel Hall, born in 1813, was a native of Halifax, Vermont. He remained on his father's farm until he became a carpenter's apprentice in 1830. He continued working with different builders until 1835, when he went into business for himself. He moved to Davenport in 1838 and continued working in construction.

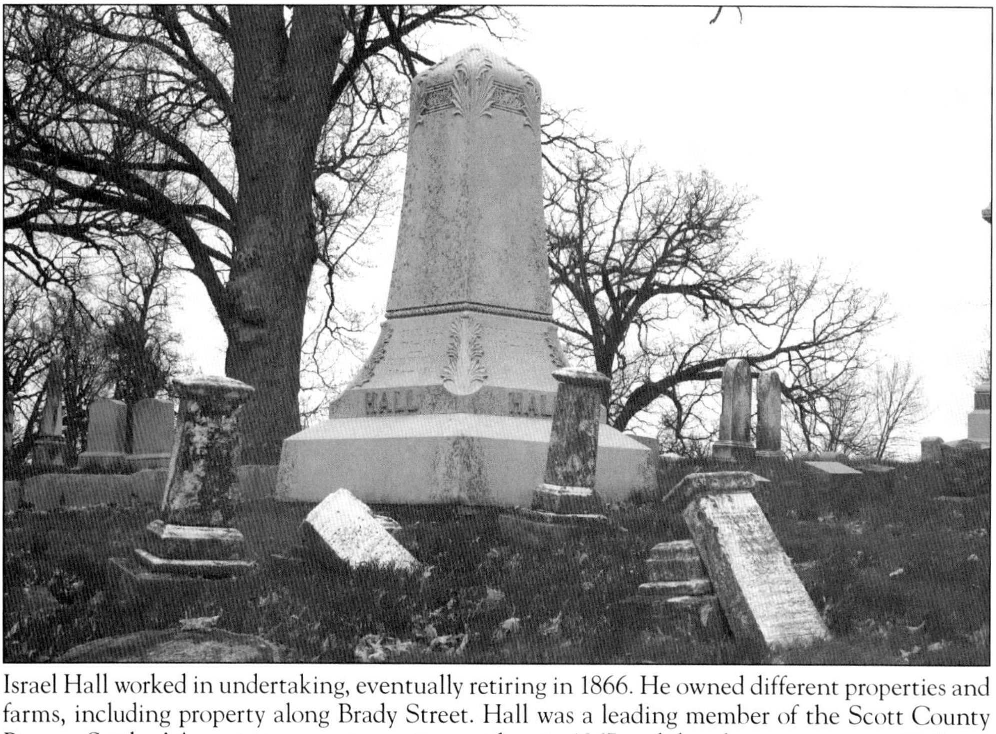

Israel Hall worked in undertaking, eventually retiring in 1866. He owned different properties and farms, including property along Brady Street. Hall was a leading member of the Scott County Pioneer Settlers' Association, serving as its president in 1867 and then later as treasurer. Hall was also the secretary of the Oakdale Cemetery Company. He died from a stroke in 1896.

Israel Barr was born in Pennsylvania in 1831. In 1846, he moved to Iowa with his parents. Barr received his education in local schools. He eventually worked as a teamster on a canal boat and as a carpenter in Davenport. Eventually, Barr purchased a farm close to Davenport.

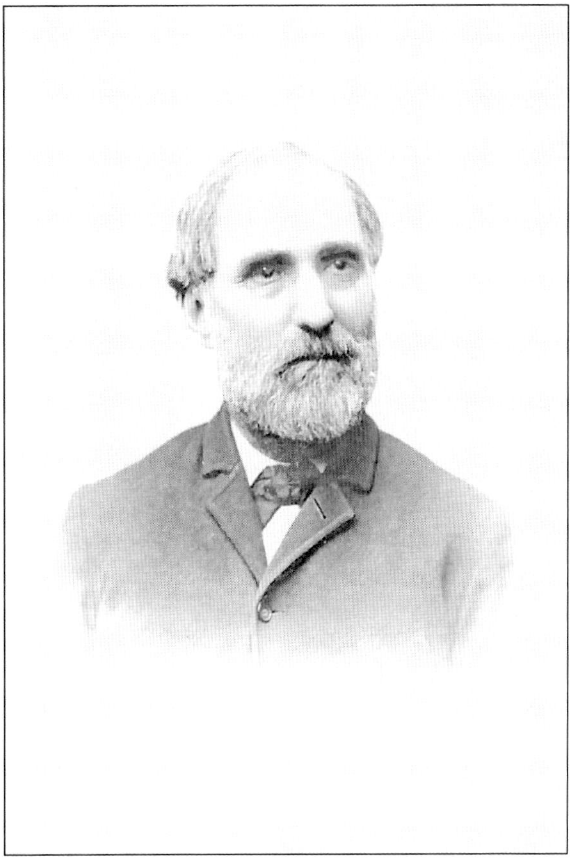

Israel Barr was a leading Scott County farmer known throughout the Midwest for raising shorthorn cattle. He was awarded numerous premiums at fairs and displayed an interest in thoroughbred horses. In 1856, Barr married Sarah West. He died in 1878, soon after having suffered a stroke at his farm along Jersey Ridge Road.

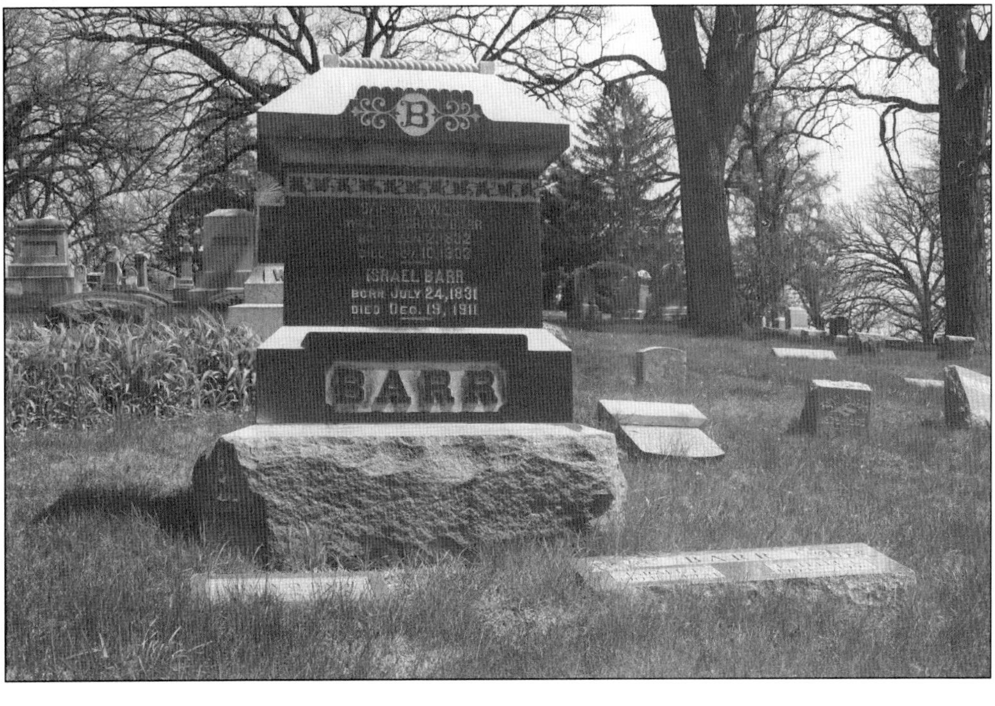

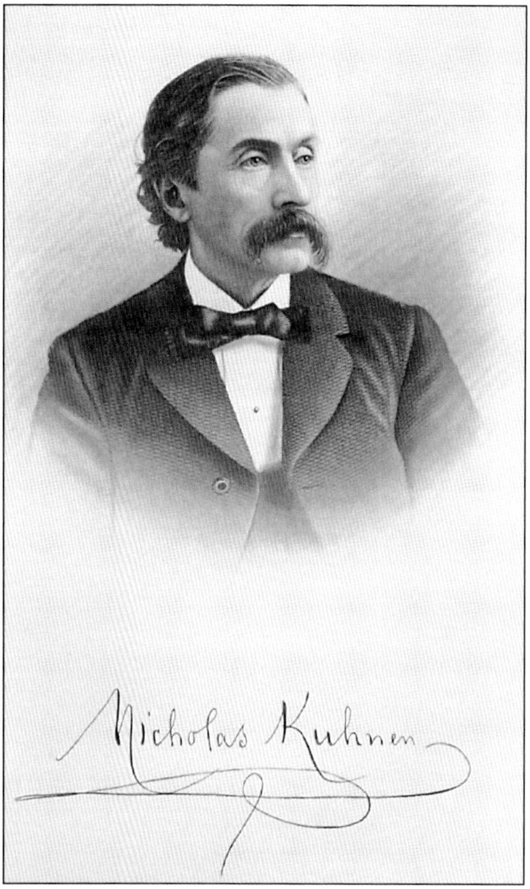

Nicholas Kuhnen was born in Prussia on May 19, 1828. A cigar maker by profession, he came to the United States in 1846 to ply his trade in various places over a period of several years. Kuhnen eventually came to Davenport in 1854. Initially, he made his own cigars, but soon he was one of the leading businessmen in Davenport and, later, the state of Iowa.

Nicholas Kuhnen was an organizer of both the German Savings Bank and the Davenport Glucose Manufacturing Company. In 1861, Kuhnen married Mary Alexander. The couple had one son and three daughters. Kuhnen died on April 22, 1892, and was first buried at Pine Hill Cemetery, but in 1918, he was moved and reburied at Oakdale.

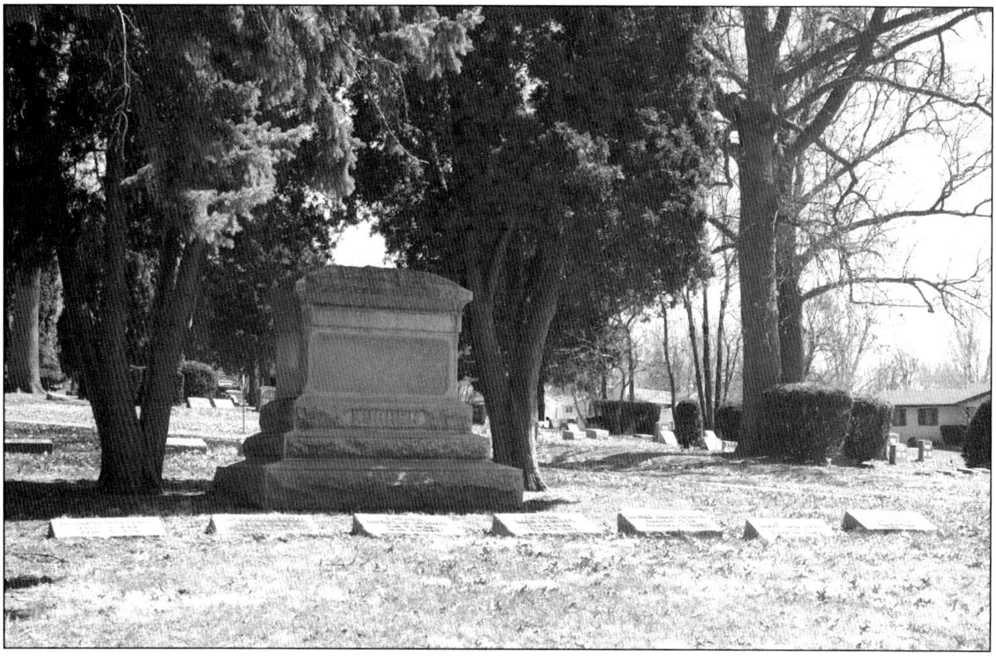

August Steffen, born in Germany in 1824, came to New York in 1848, and then moved to Cincinnati, Ohio. After a short time, he soon moved on and eventually settled in Natchez, Mississippi. Steffen set out for California in 1850, where he achieved some success as a gold prospector.

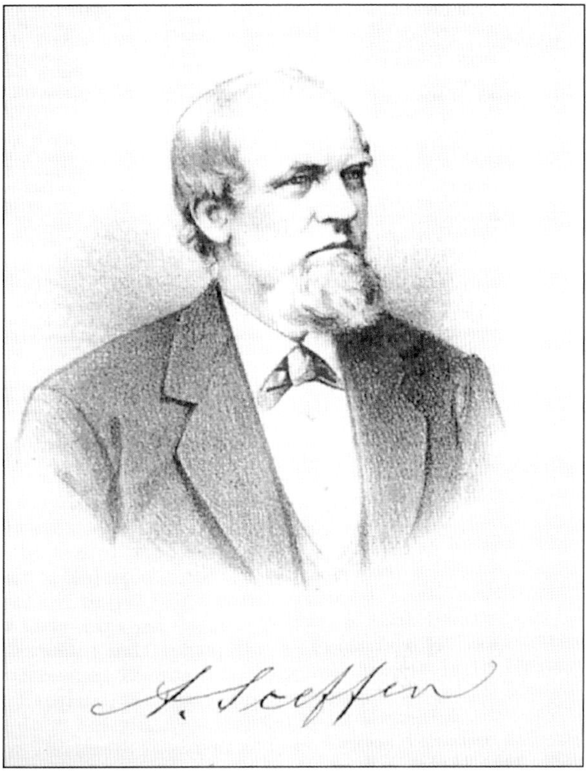

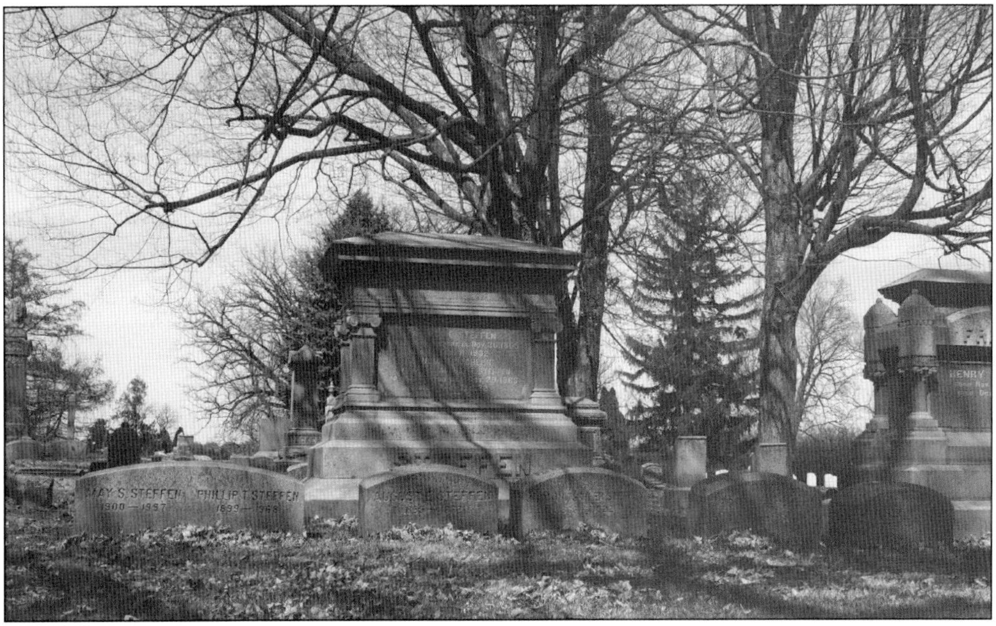

August Steffen used the money that he had gained from gold prospecting to open a grocery store in Davenport, Iowa. He also began selling dry goods and entered into the grain business. Steffen held leadership positions in different businesses, including president of the Davenport Plow Company. In 1856, he married Margarethe Gehrlicher. In 1876, he erected the August Steffen building. He died on October 8, 1899.

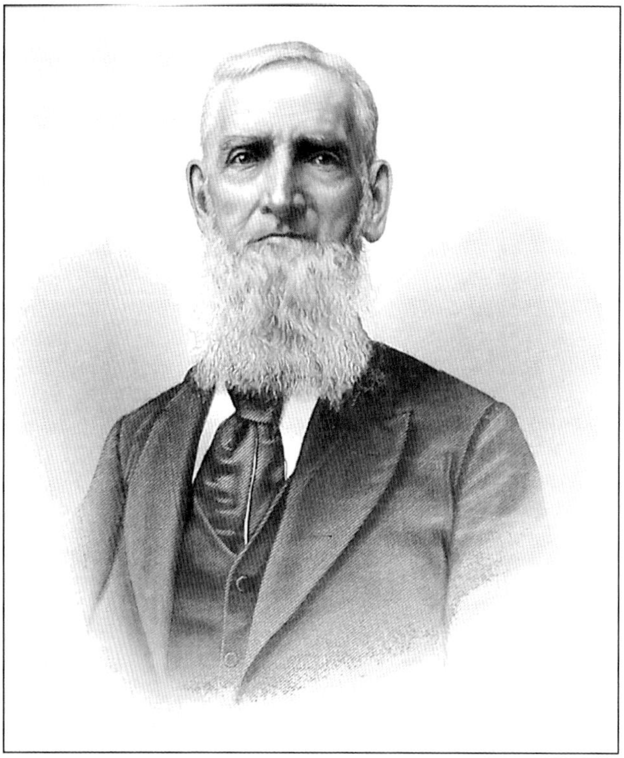

J.J. Humphrey was born in Albany, New York, in 1811. He operated a store from 1836 until 1841 in which he recalled listening to Daniel Webster give a speech. After running a business in Wisconsin and then in Albany, Humphrey set out for the gold fields of Australia in 1853. Although he did engage in mining for a while, Humphrey once again successfully engaged in the merchant trade while there.

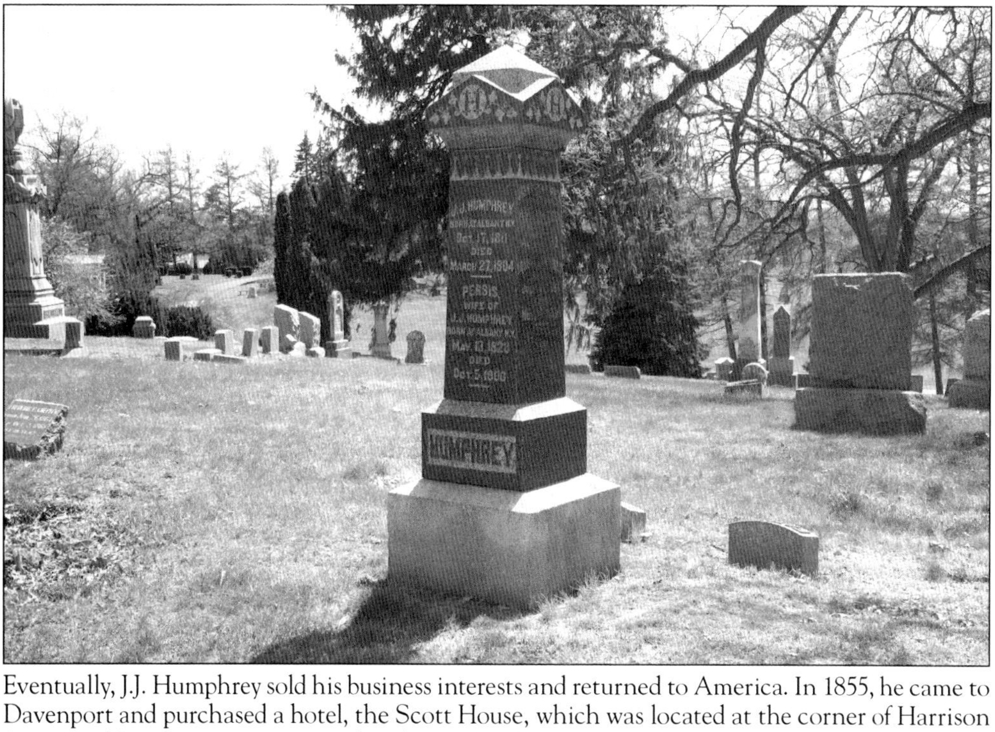

Eventually, J.J. Humphrey sold his business interests and returned to America. In 1855, he came to Davenport and purchased a hotel, the Scott House, which was located at the corner of Harrison Street and River Drive. He catered to farmers and ran the hotel for several years before retiring in 1878. He died from old age at the age of 93.

John Holst was born in Hamburg, Germany, on April 11, 1816. At age 11, he became a sailor and traveled all over the world. In 1836, Holst became ill in New Orleans, ending his sailing days. He joined the Louisiana volunteers under General Taylor and fought the Creek Indians in Florida for two years. Holst returned to New Orleans and worked in a store.

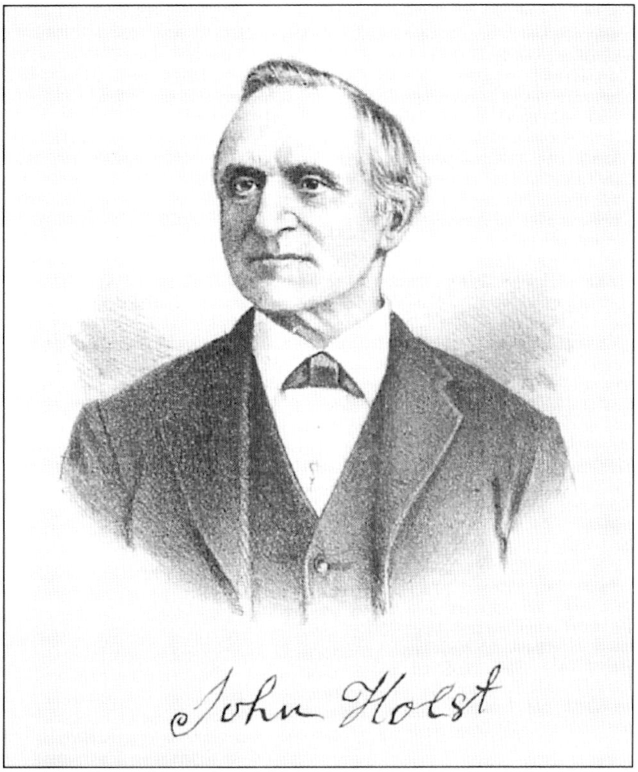

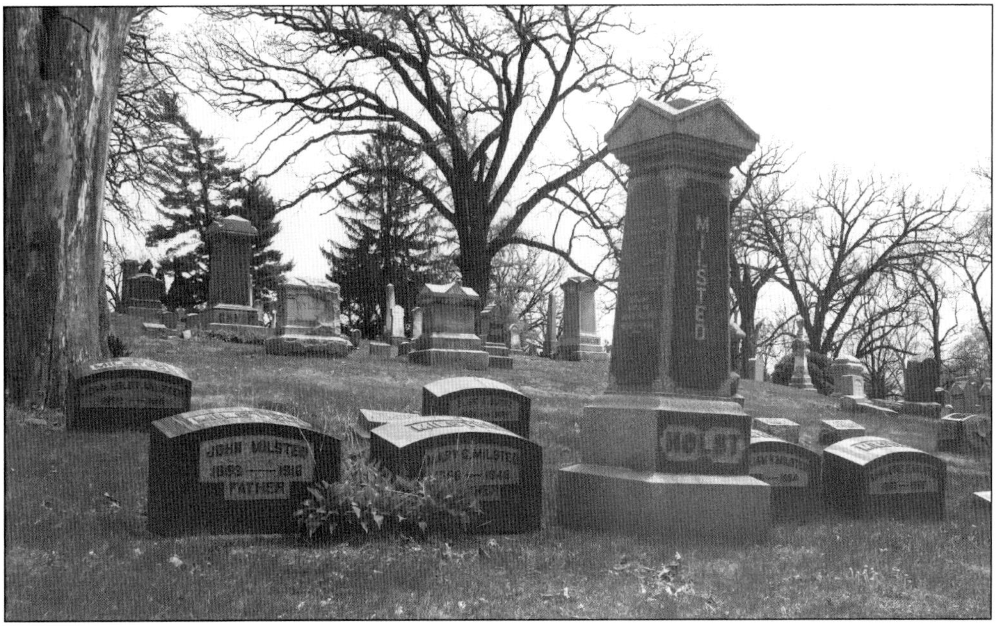

In 1845, John Holst bought a farm in Clinton County, Iowa. In 1846, he enlisted in the Civil War as a teamster and was involved in several engagements. When he returned home, he sold his farm and came to Davenport, where he worked as a clerk for a while. He ran a grocery and speculated in real estate. He retired in 1866 and died at his home in 1882 from dropsy, which is an accumulation of fluid beneath the skin that causes swelling.

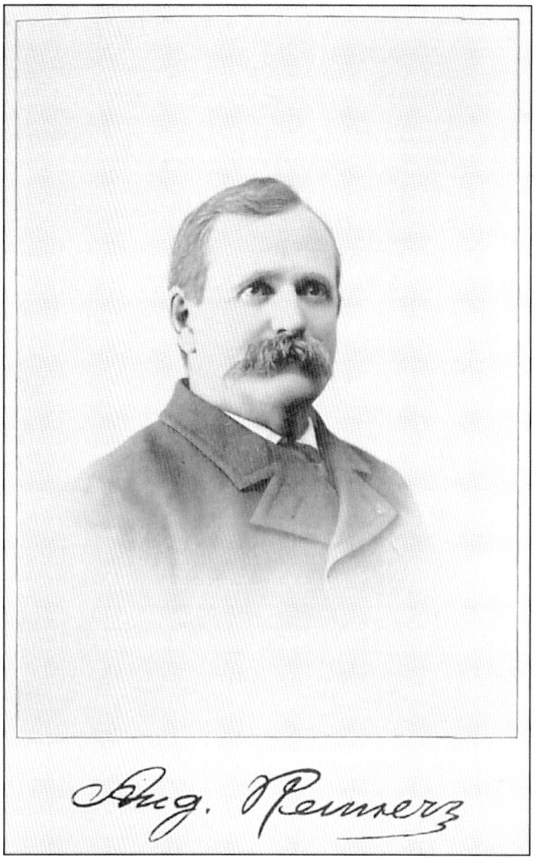

August Reimers was born in Schwein, Germany, on September 23, 1841. In 1849, he came to St. Louis with his mother and brothers. He eventually became a baker's apprentice and, later, a candy maker. During the Civil War, he fought in several battles with the 3rd and 15th Missouri Infantry and was wounded twice. After his service, he returned to St. Louis and began working in a candy factory.

In 1871, August Reimers moved to Davenport and opened a candy factory that eventually became Reimers and Fernald, which ended up doing good business in the West. He was elected alderman but lost the race for mayor in 1891. A Civil War veteran, Reimers was a member of the Grand Army of the Republic. He was married twice and died from pneumonia in 1908.

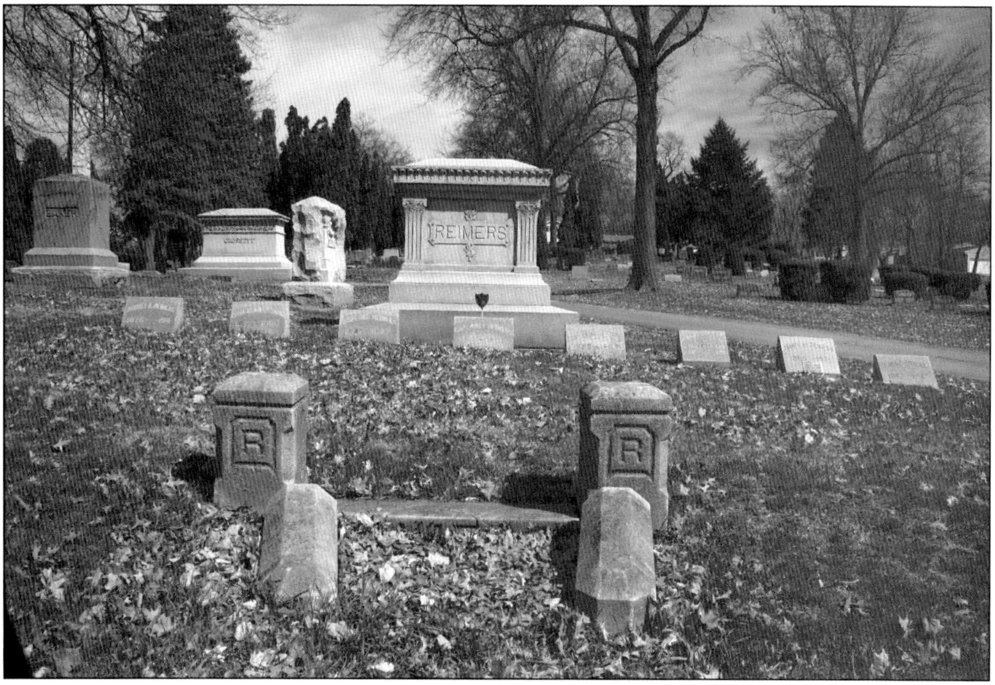

Born June 17, 1831, and educated in Ohio, George Cable came from a successful family. In 1866, he moved to Davenport and eventually entered into the lumber and coal business with his father, Hiram. After his father retired and his business partner, John Hornby, died, Cable reorganized the former firm of Hornby and Cable into the Cable Lumber Company, from which he retired as president.

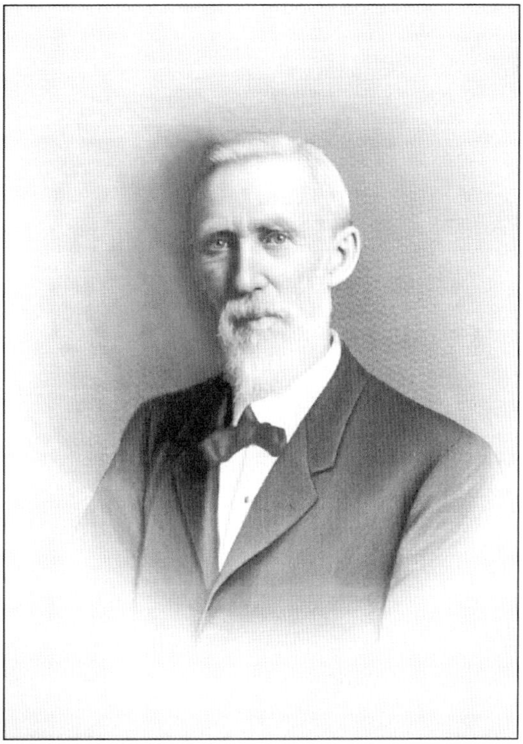

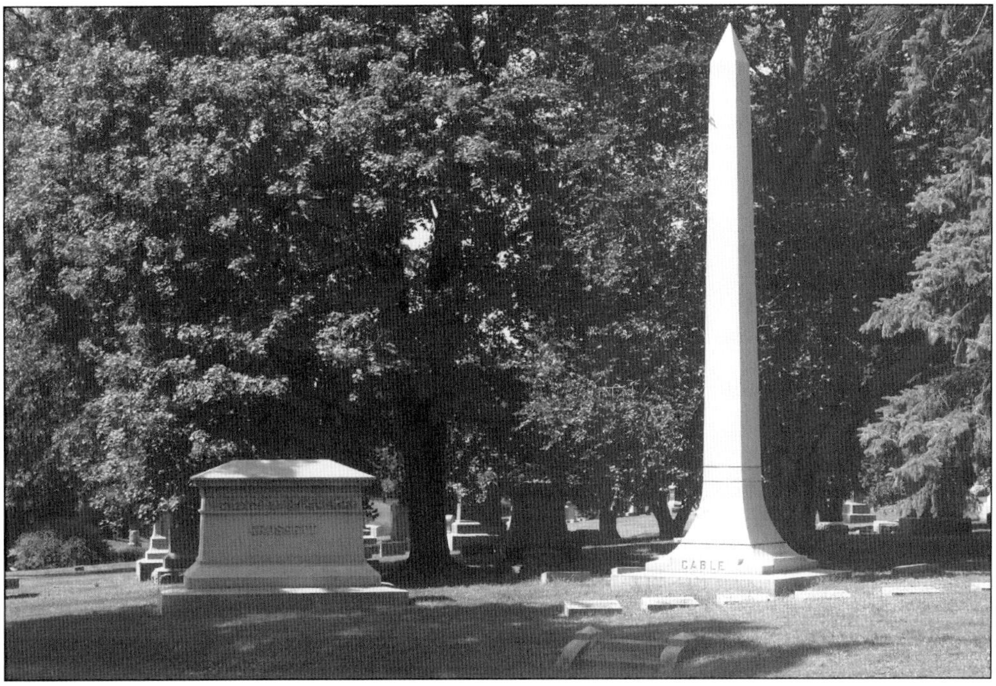

The Cable lumber mill closed with the decline of logging in the region but continued to hold interests elsewhere. George Cable also served as vice president of two other lumber companies—one in Texas, the other in Arkansas. Cable was an elder in the Presbyterian Church and a member of the Masonic Lodge. He died in 1911 at his family home when he was 80 years old.

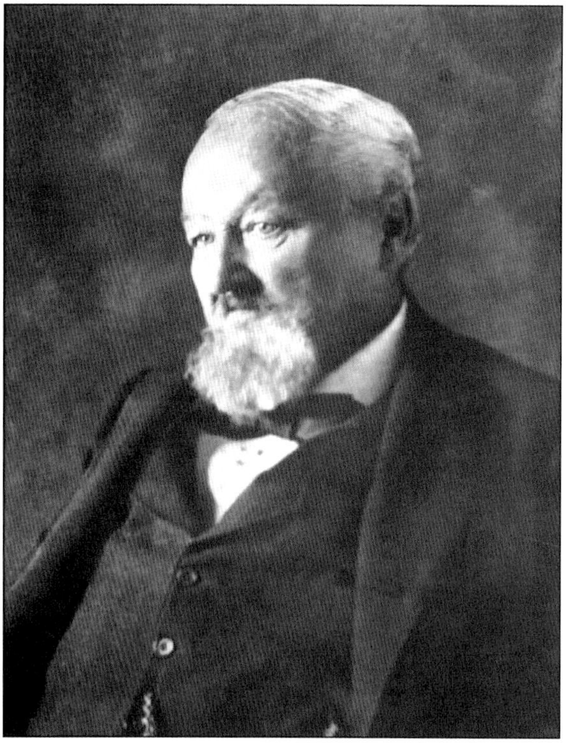

John H.C. Petersen was born in 1821. He apprenticed for five years in the dry goods trade, and then went on to work as a clerk for eight years. In 1860, Petersen came to Scott County, Iowa, and purchased a 160-acre farm in Hickory Grove Township to take up farming. A short time later, he opened a factory in Davenport that manufactured matches.

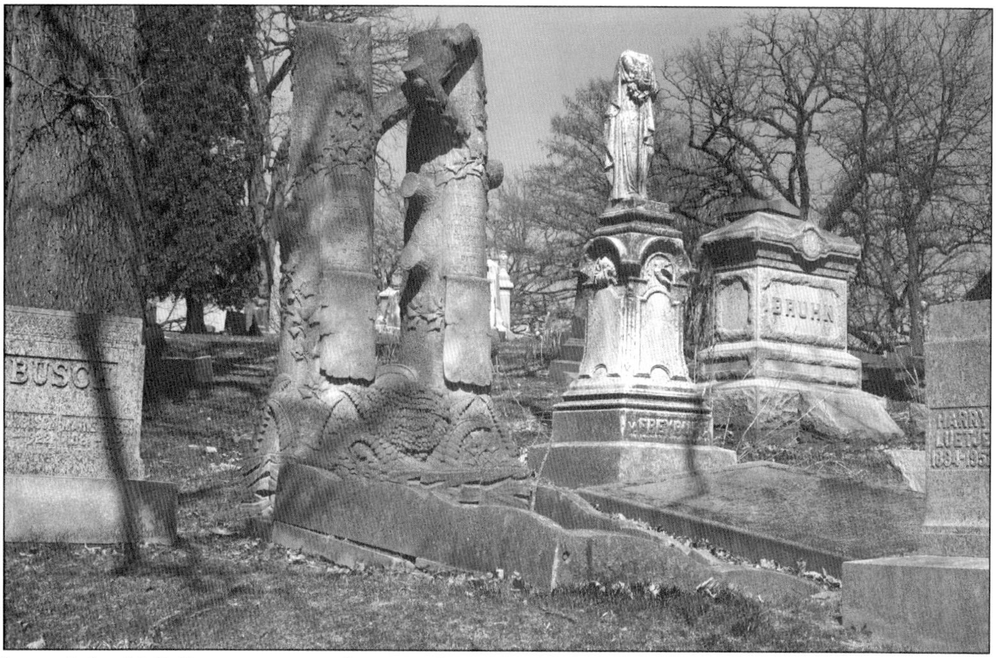

Later, John H.C. Petersen opened a store for general merchandise with Henry Abel on Second Street in Davenport. After this partnership broke up, Petersen established the company of J.H.C. Petersen & Sons with his boys on West Second Street in 1871. They dealt in both wholesale and retail dry goods products and were very successful. In 1889, John retired and gave his part of the business to his three sons.

Robert M. Prettyman was born in Delaware on July 5, 1818. He came to Davenport in 1839 and took a job as a clerk in a hotel for a short time, before working as a bookkeeper for J.M.D. Burrows, an early Davenport businessman. Prettyman eventually became Burrows's business partner in 1844, and the two ran a dry goods business together.

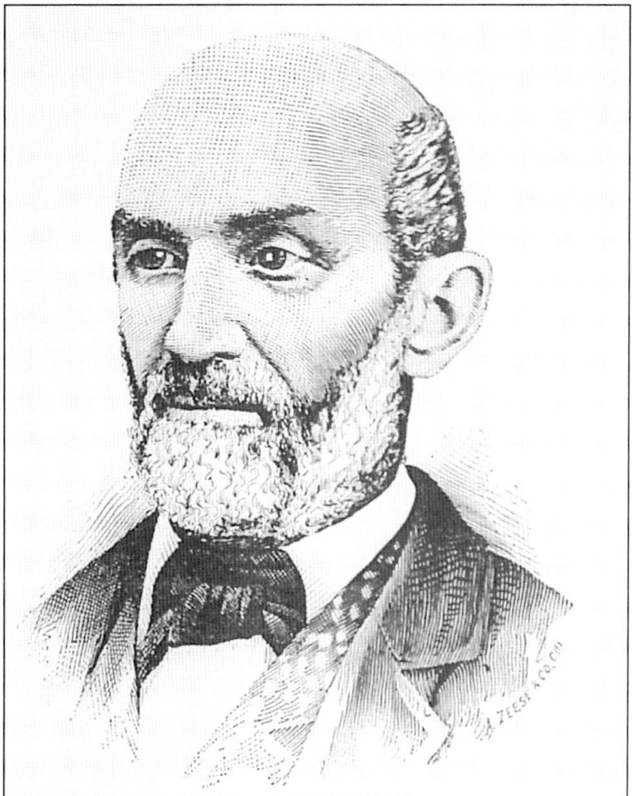

R. M. PRETTYMAN.

In 1846, J.M.D. Burrows and Robert M. Prettyman bought a mill from A.C. Ambrose. At its highest capacity, the mill produced around 300 barrels of flour per day. Over time, the partners pursued different business ventures. Prettyman left his partnership with Burrows to run a steamboat agency on the Upper Mississippi. He died in 1873.

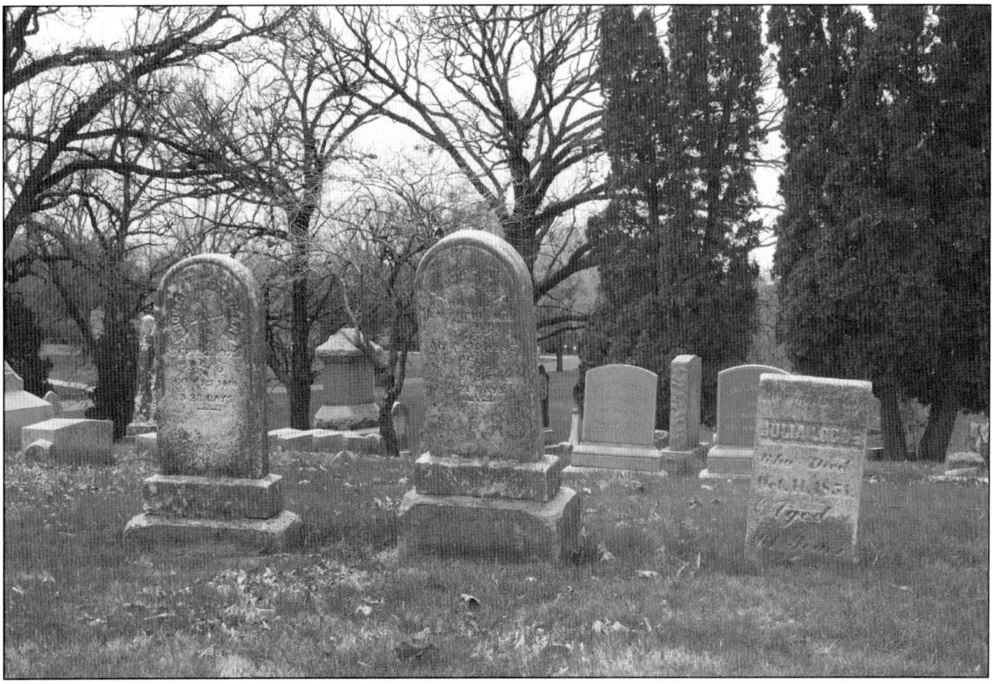

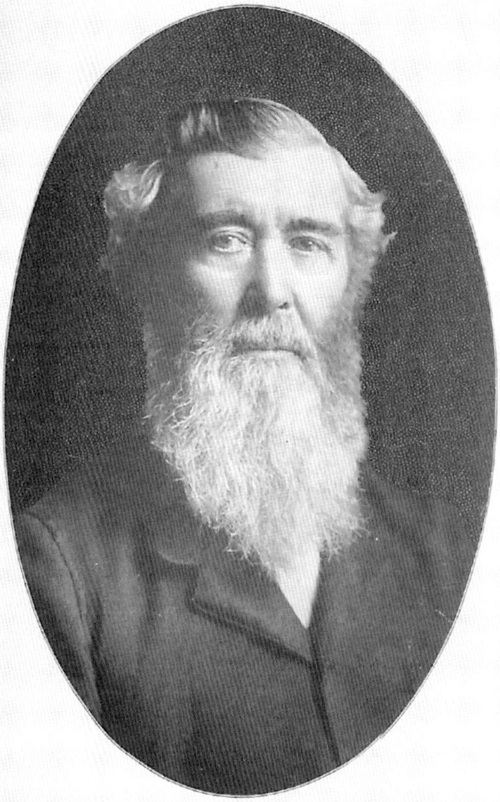

A. W. BROWNLIE

A.W. Brownlee was born in Canada in 1837. The following year, his parents moved to Long Grove, Iowa. At this time, Davenport was only a small Native American trading post. Brownlee received his early education at home and at local log cabin schools. He became a farmer and married in 1862.

A.W. Brownlee eventually gave up farming and moved to Davenport, raising and shipping livestock along with his brothers. They were very successful in this endeavor and were one of the best-known dealers in that business. Brownlee died from complications of a stroke at his home at 634 East Fourteenth Street in Davenport. He is buried in Long Grove, Iowa.

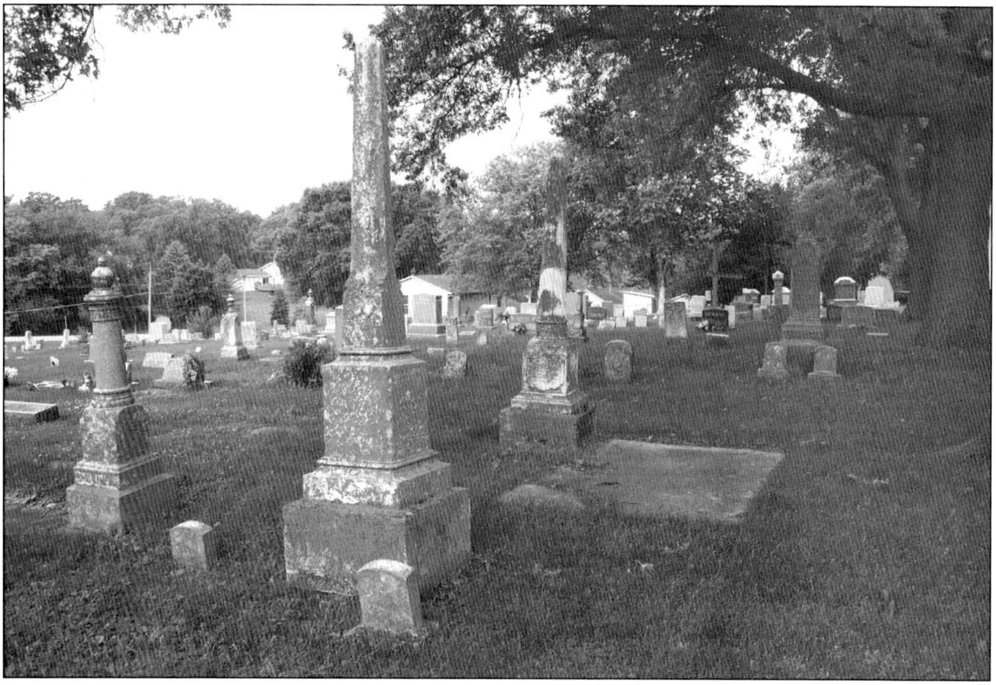

Edward Savage Crossett was born in New York. He began his working life in a printing shop and then as a clerk for several years. When he was about 20, Crossett and his brother bought a store in Schroon Lake, New York. About two years later, Crossett left the business to his brother and moved west, settling in Wisconsin. Upon arriving there, he began working in a lumber supply store.

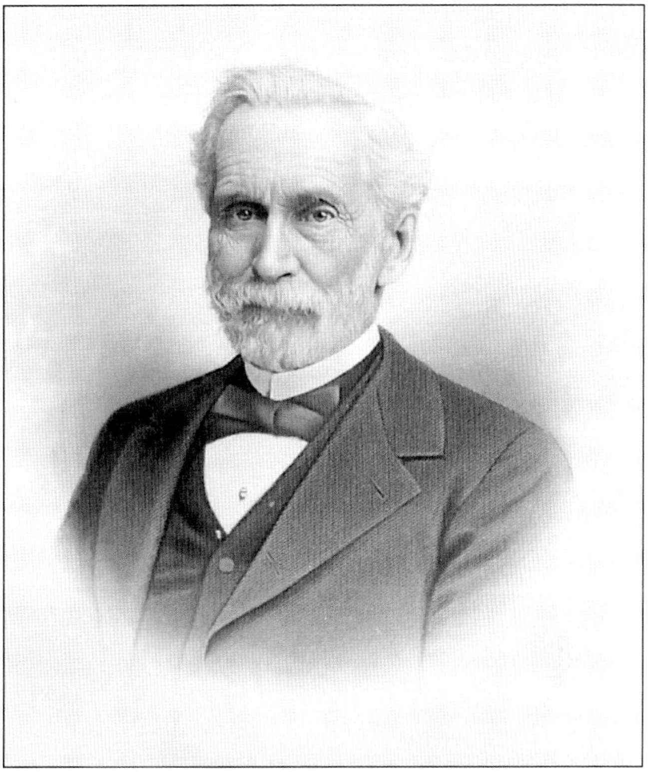

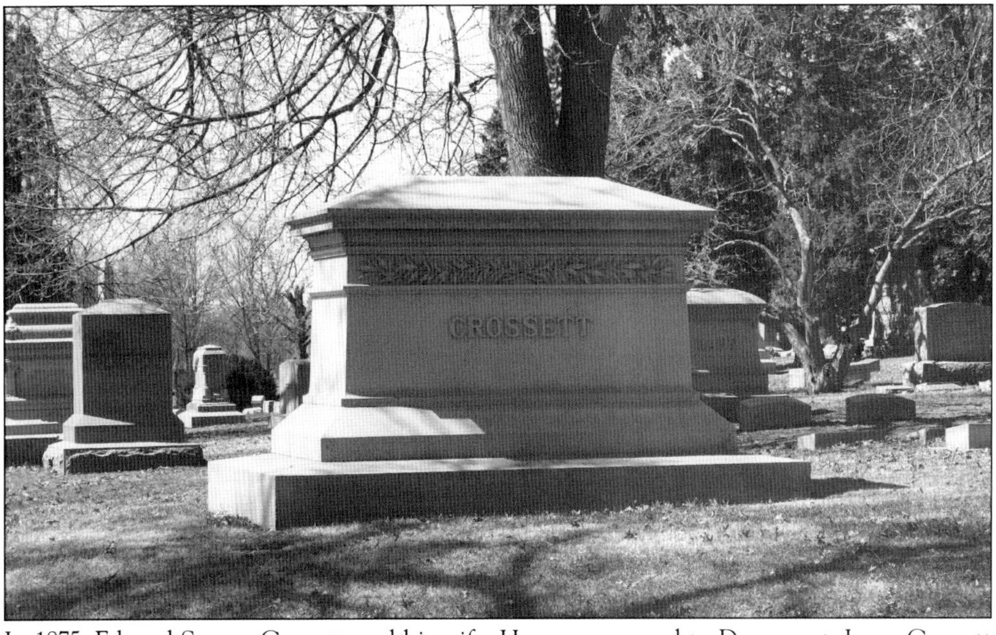

In 1875, Edward Savage Crossett and his wife, Harmony, moved to Davenport, Iowa. Crossett joined the business of Renwick, Shaw, and Crossett, a successful lumber company. He was a very generous man, donating several thousands of dollars to the Davenport YMCA and the construction of St. John's Methodist Episcopal Church, which still stands at Fourteenth and Brady Streets in Davenport. It was his preference that his donations were kept private.

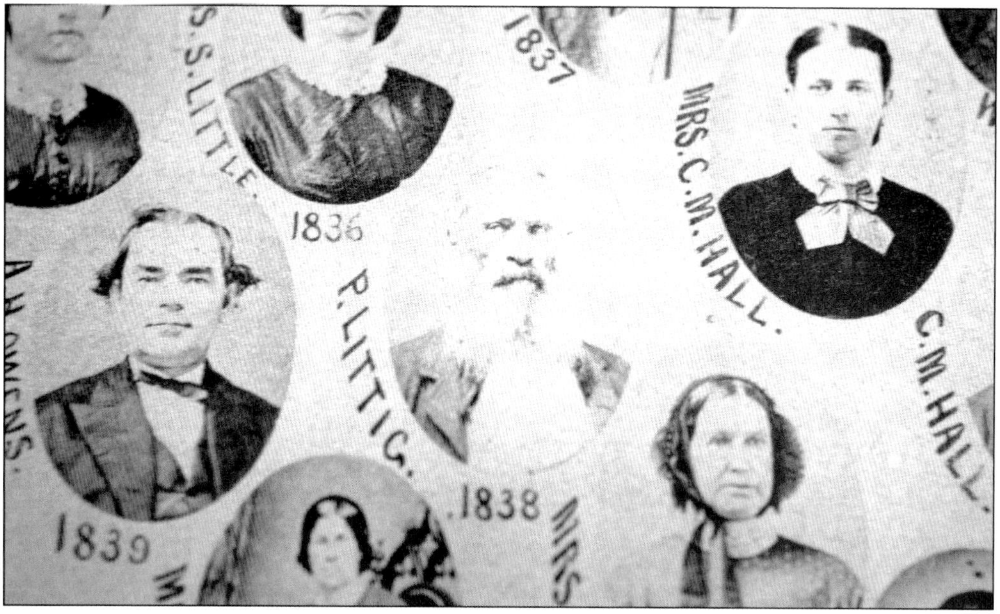

Peter Littig was born in Lorraine, France, in 1794. He joined the French Army at the age of 19. A supporter of Napoleon Bonaparte, he was a member of the escort that joined Napoleon after his exile in Elba. Littig fought at the Battles of Waterloo and Leipzig and personally watched Marshal Poniatowski fall in combat.

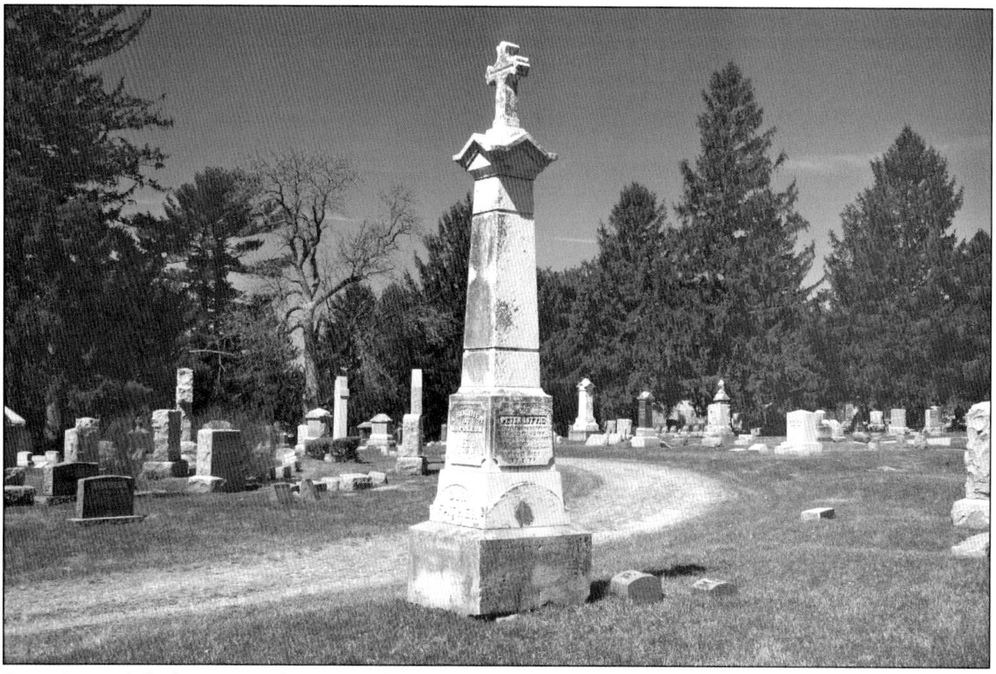

Peter Littig left the army after Waterloo. Moving to Paris in 1826, he worked as a marble cutter. In 1835, Littig immigrated to New Orleans, and then later to Stephenson, or Rock Island, in 1837. He worked as a stonemason, and built the first stone house in Rock Island. Littig eventually quit stonework and became a successful brewery owner, building the Eagle Brewery in Davenport. He died in 1881.

Born in 1823 in Paris, France, John Littig immigrated to New Orleans with his parents when he was a young teenager. After residing there for two years, Littig moved up the Mississippi from New Orleans and came to St. Louis, Missouri. In 1837, Littig and his parents moved to Rock Island and then to Davenport, where he would eventually become a farmer.

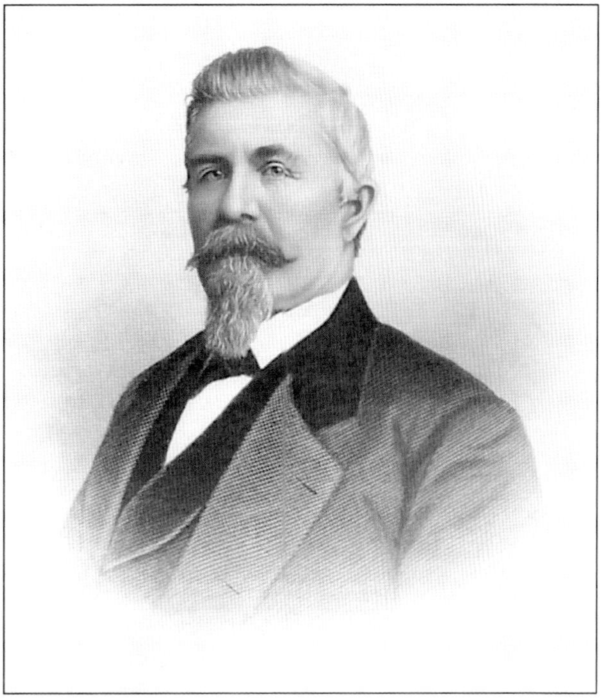

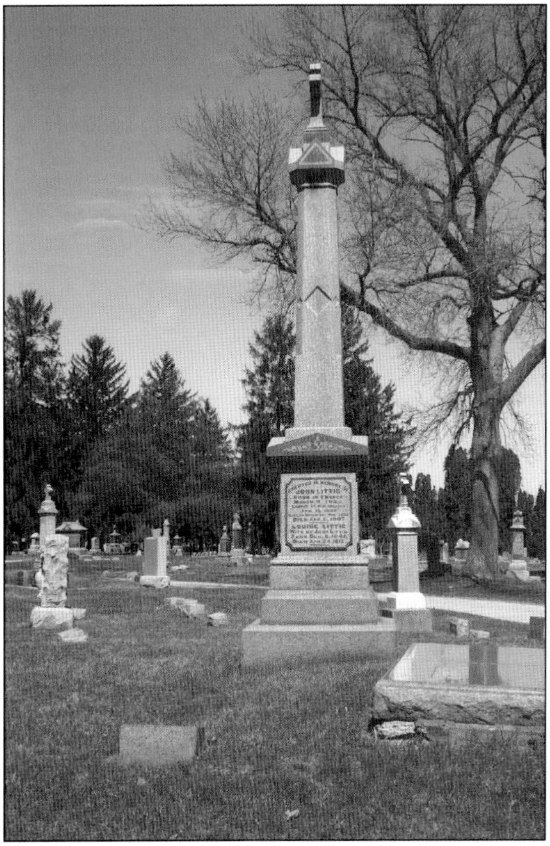

John Littig spent several years with Antoine Le Claire. During this time, he saved his money and eventually purchased land around nearby Gilberttown. Littig continued to invest his money in real estate, eventually holding around 560 acres of land. In addition to his real estate holdings, Littig was a farmer. He married Margaret Stovir in 1844. After her death, Littig married again in 1858, this time to a Louise Roggie.

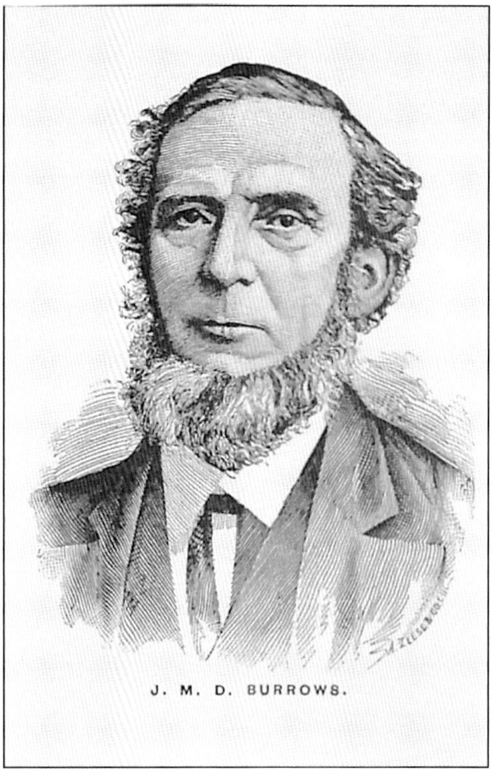

Born in 1814, J.M.D. Burrows was a successful businessman in Davenport. He was a cofounder of Oakdale Cemetery in Davenport. Eventually becoming the richest man in the city, Burrows was ruined financially during the Panic of 1857. He tried to rebuild his fortune by focusing on the milling business but was unsuccessful after both the mills he bought burned down. He died in 1889 from heart disease.

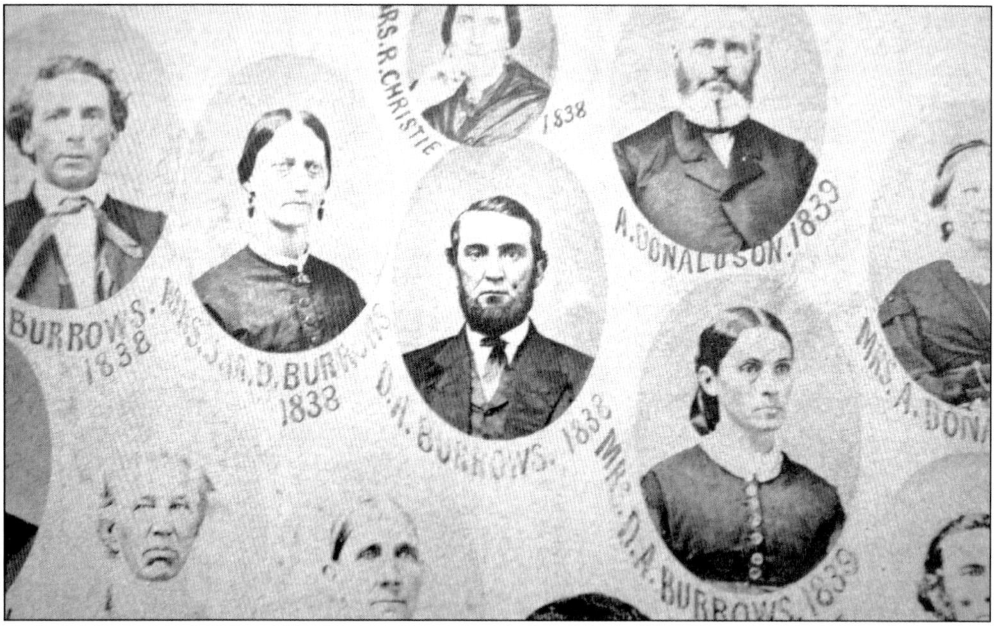

David Alvord Burrows was born in New Jersey in 1825. In 1838, he came to Iowa with his brother J.M.D. Burrows. David helped his brother in his produce business but went back home to New Jersey a year later when he was 13 years old. He eventually came back and became wealthy through the milling business. Unfortunately, David suffered financial losses after the Civil War. He died in 1910 from apoplexy.

E.B. Hayward was born in New York on October 25, 1842. In 1861, when he was only 19, he joined the 5th New York Cavalry during the Civil War. Hayward started as a private but was eventually promoted to brevet major in the Union army. Serving for four years, he received an honorable discharge at the conclusion of his service.

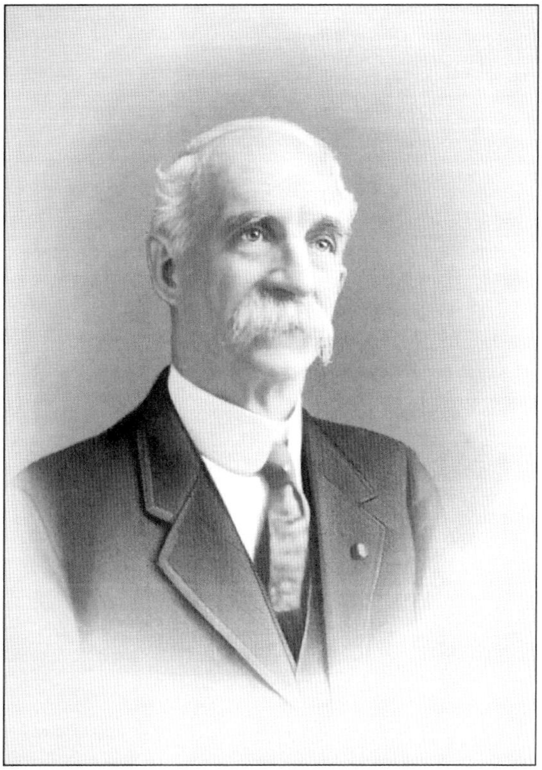

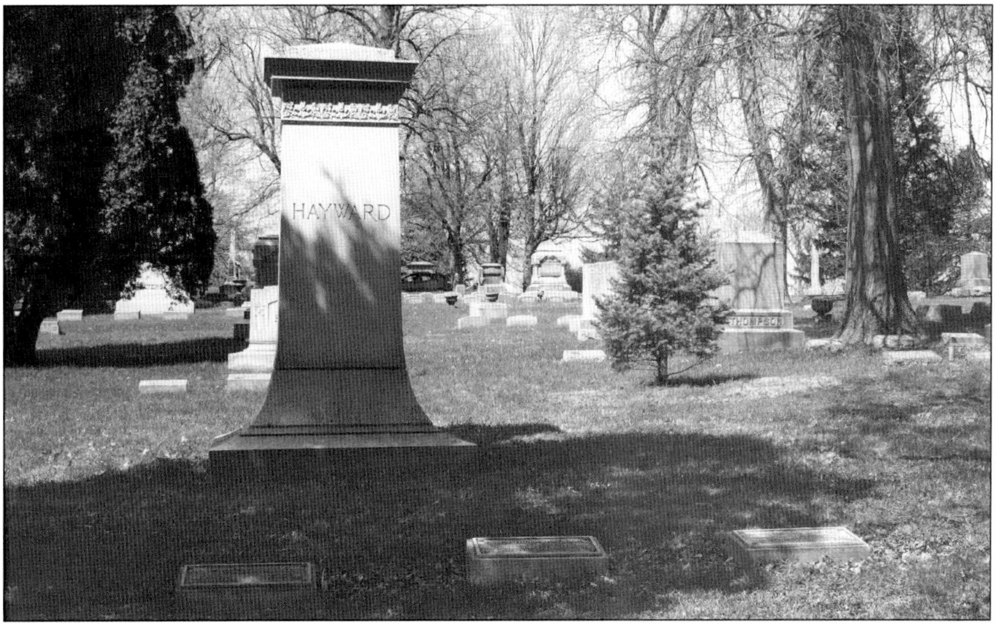

E.B. Hayward came to Davenport in 1869. He worked in the lumber industry at the Lindsay and Phelps Sawmill and Lumber Mill. He later assisted in organizing the Eagle Lumber Company and the Hayward Timber Company of Texas, as well as the State Lumber Company of Vancouver, British Columbia. Hayward was also an active member of St. John's Methodist Episcopal Church. He died at his home at 902 Bridge Avenue.

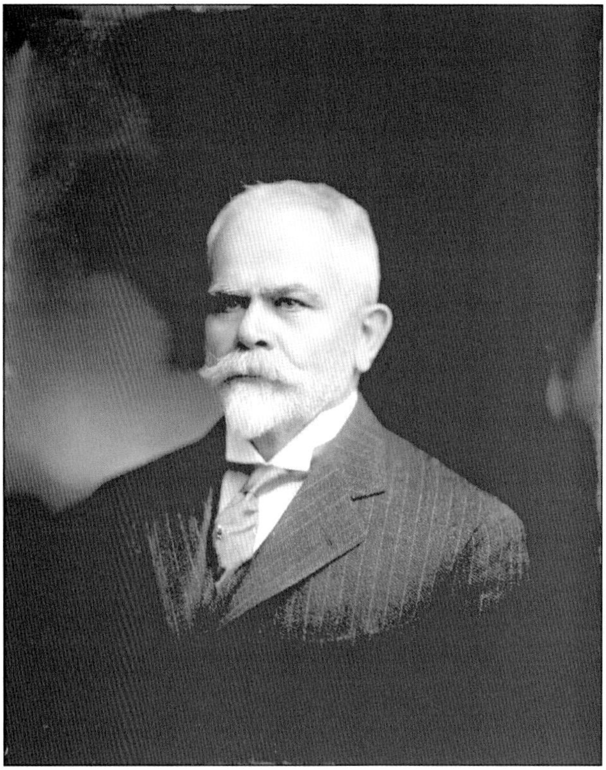

Born in Germany in 1848, time would see L.P. Best grow into a successful businessman. After coming to the United States in 1869, he became a chemist in New York. In 1874, he made his way to Davenport, being called to this city to take charge of the works of the Glucose Manufacturing Company. He guided the company to great success until he retired in January 1898.

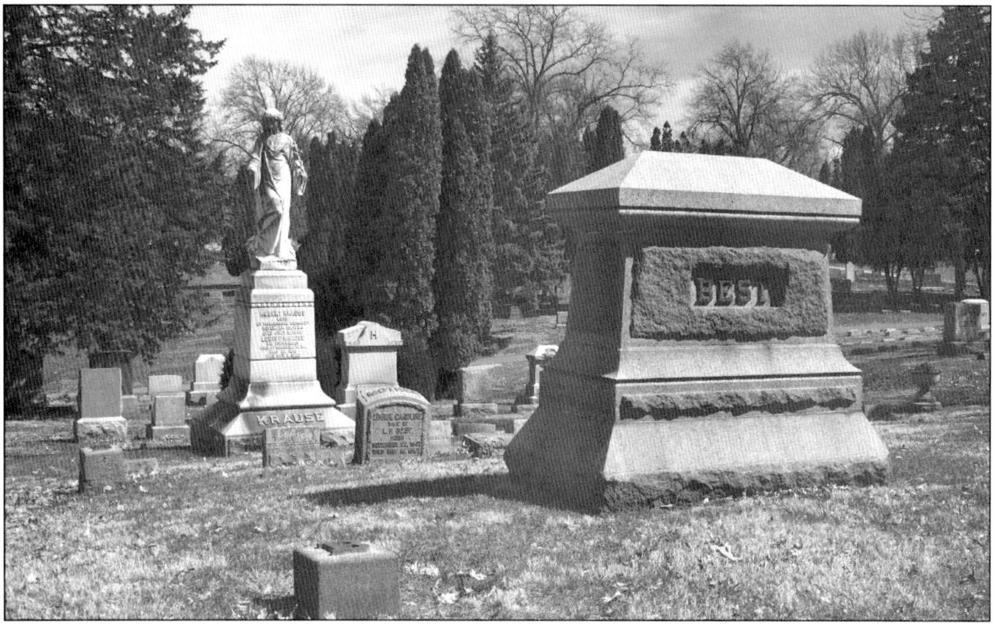

L.P. Best built another successful plant in Granite City, Illinois, named the Best-Clymer Company, and later became a director at the Bettendorf Company, the Davenport Foundry and Machine Company, and the Davenport Water Company. He also served four years as president of the Davenport school board. He died in San Diego, California, from pneumonia and was cremated at the Davenport Crematorium in 1926.

Henry Kohrs, who would rise from mere butcher to millionaire pork processor, was born in Germany in 1830. Having learned the butcher trade in his native land, he immigrated to America while in his early 20s and ended up in Davenport in 1854. In 1855, he opened a market. Kohrs worked in different businesses, and by the following year, he had saved enough to open a butcher shop on Harrison Street.

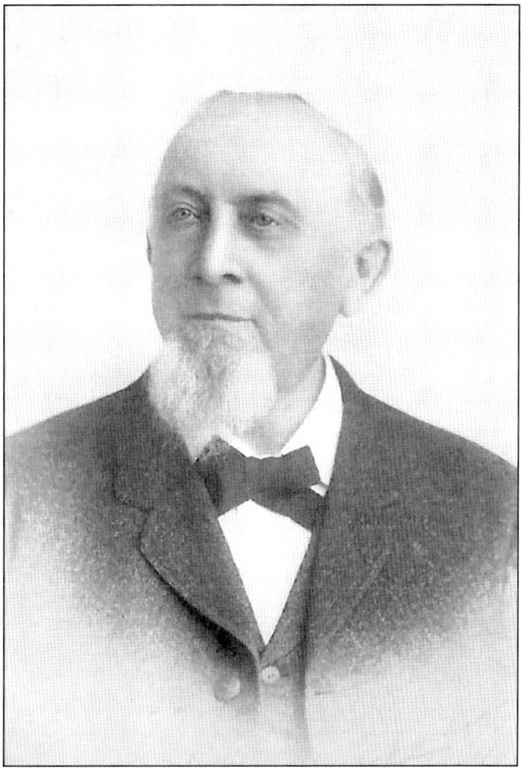

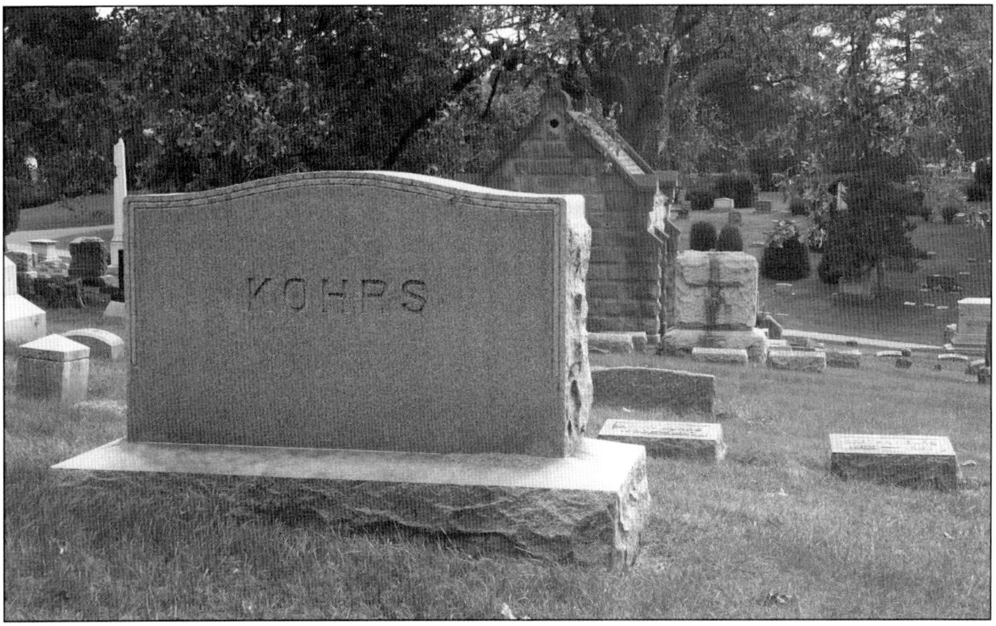

Over the next several years, Henry Kohrs continually expanded his business. By 1874, he entered into the pork-packing industry and built his plant into an extremely lucrative business that sold his products all over the world, known as the Kohrs Packing Company. Eventually, his sons joined the business, and he let W.H. Gehrmann, a partner, handle the company. Kohrs died on New Year's Eve in 1917.

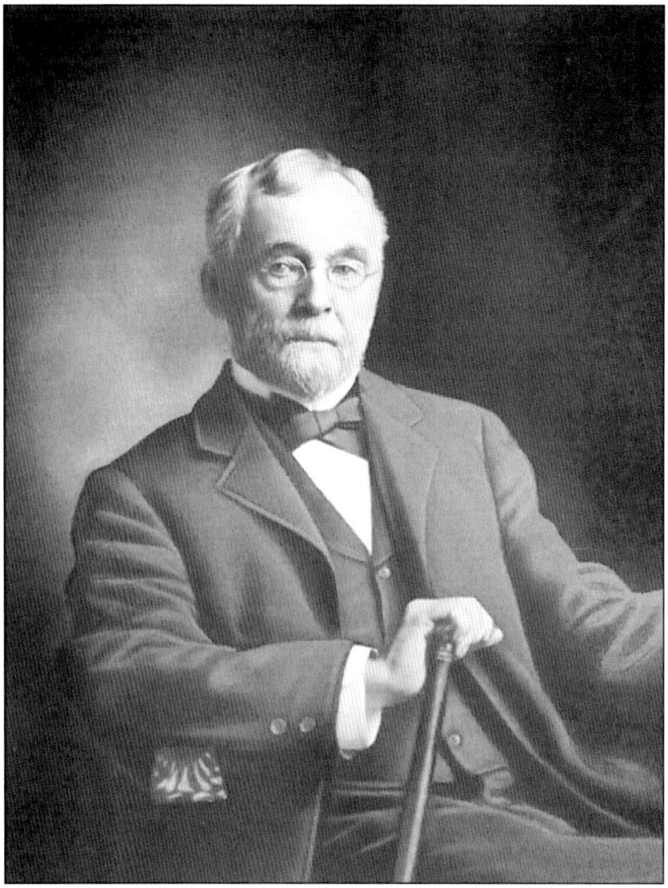

James Edwin Lindsay was born in 1826 in New York. As a young man, he worked in his father's sawmill. By the time he reached the age of 21, he had entered into the logging business with his brother-in-law John Tompkins. In 1861, Lindsay moved to Davenport, Iowa, and leased the Renwick logging mill.

In 1866, James Edwin Lindsay built a sawmill in Davenport and processed timber rafted downriver from lands he owned in Wisconsin. In 1882, he personally located the first holdings of the Lindsay Land & Lumber Company in Arkansas and later served as a director of the Cloquet Lumber Company. He died from chronic myocarditis at his home at 211 College Avenue on October 13, 1915.

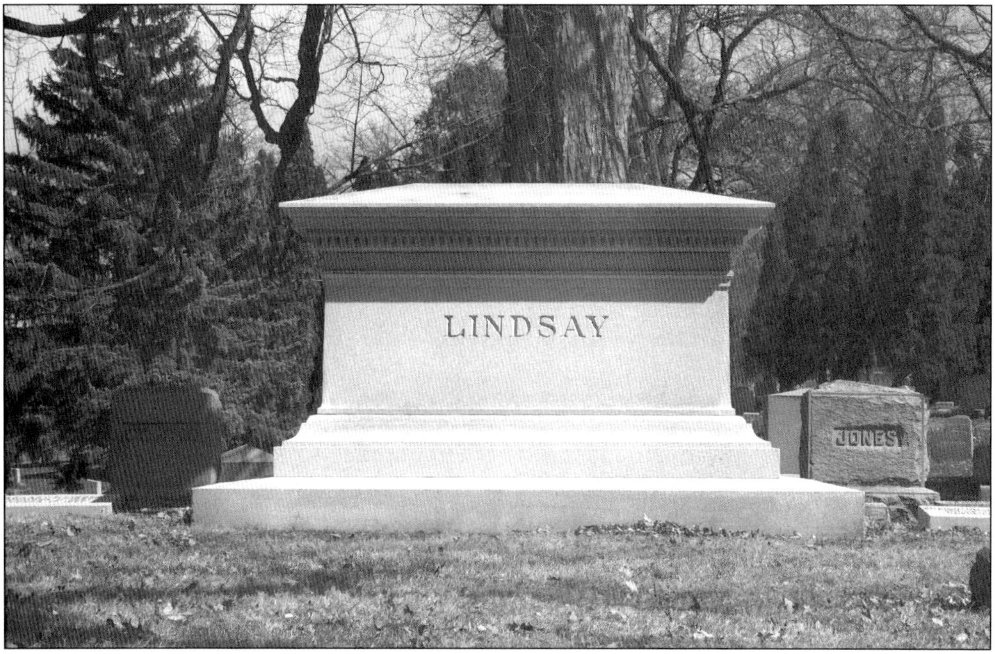

A prolific inventor, William P. Bettendorf was president of the Bettendorf Axle Company. Born in Mendota, Illinois, on July 1, 1857, he had at least 42 patents and invented the first power-lift sulky plow in 1878. Bettendorf came to Davenport in 1886 and established the Bettendorf Metal Wheel Company, which manufactured metal wheels. He died during surgery in his new home in Bettendorf in 1910.

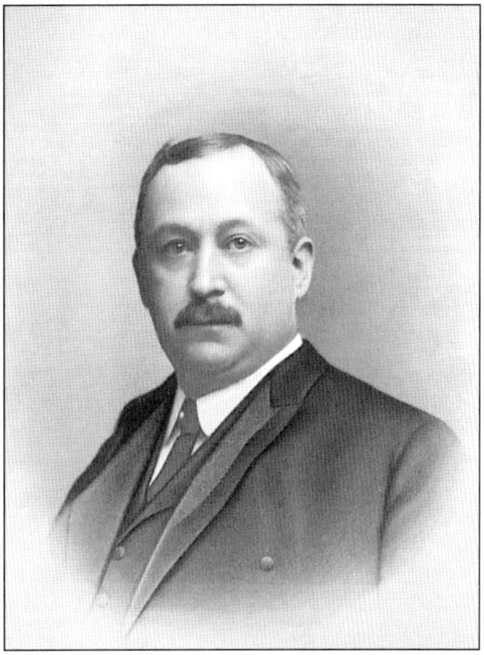

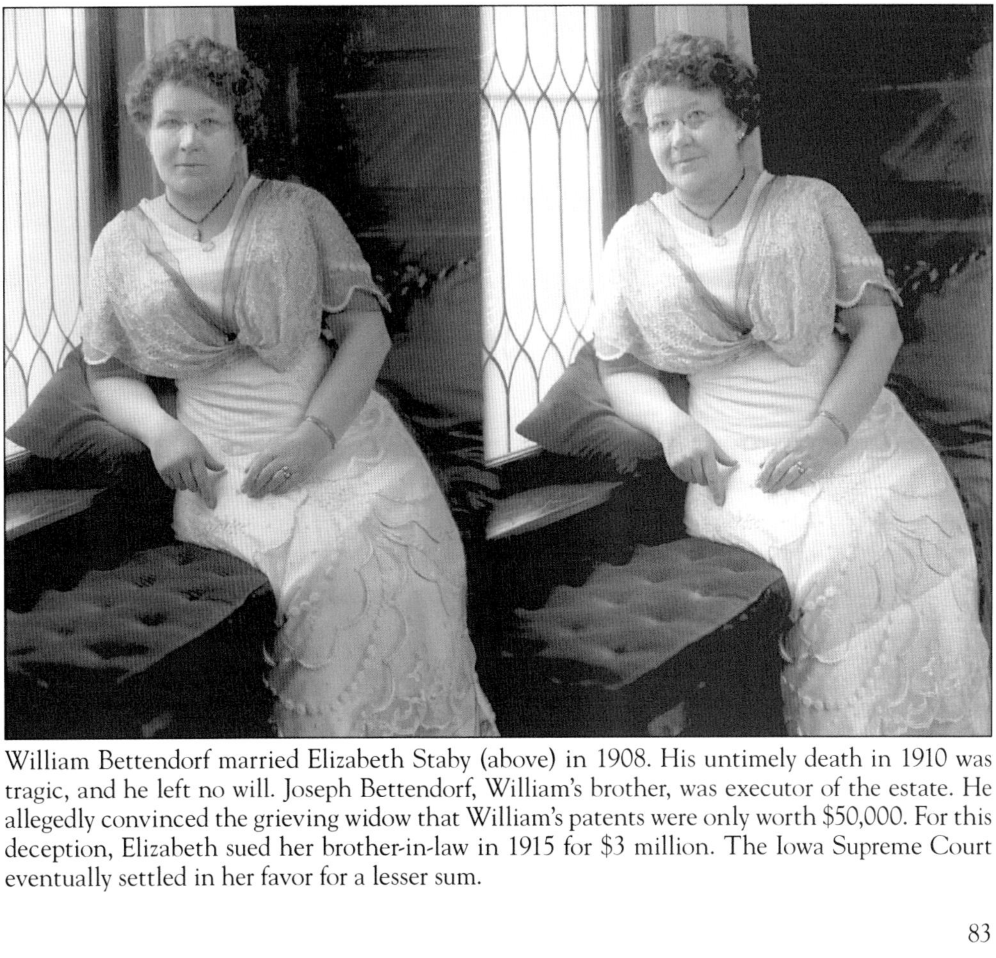

William Bettendorf married Elizabeth Staby (above) in 1908. His untimely death in 1910 was tragic, and he left no will. Joseph Bettendorf, William's brother, was executor of the estate. He allegedly convinced the grieving widow that William's patents were only worth $50,000. For this deception, Elizabeth sued her brother-in-law in 1915 for $3 million. The Iowa Supreme Court eventually settled in her favor for a lesser sum.

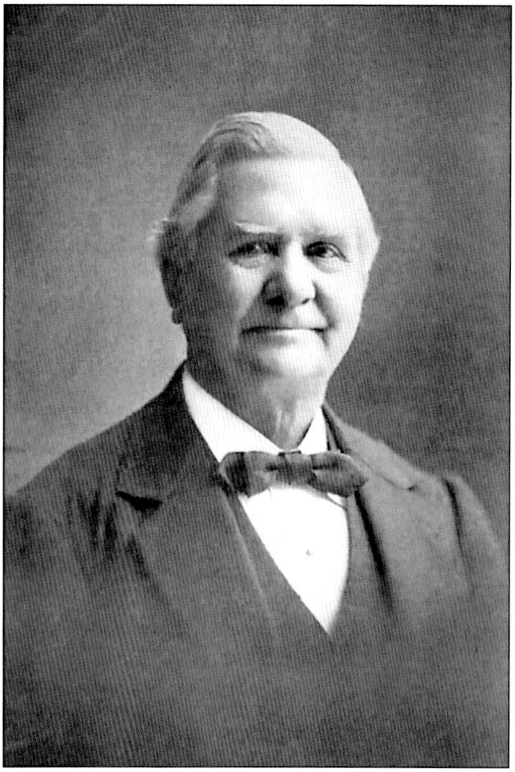

Jacob Eldridge was born in Haddonfield, New Jersey, in 1824. After his mother died when he was only four years old, Jacob's father, D.C. Eldridge, sent the boy to live with his grandmother. Jacob returned to Davenport in 1846 to settle permanently. He first bought land northeast of Davenport and entered into real estate, becoming very successful. He was one of the first land agents of the city.

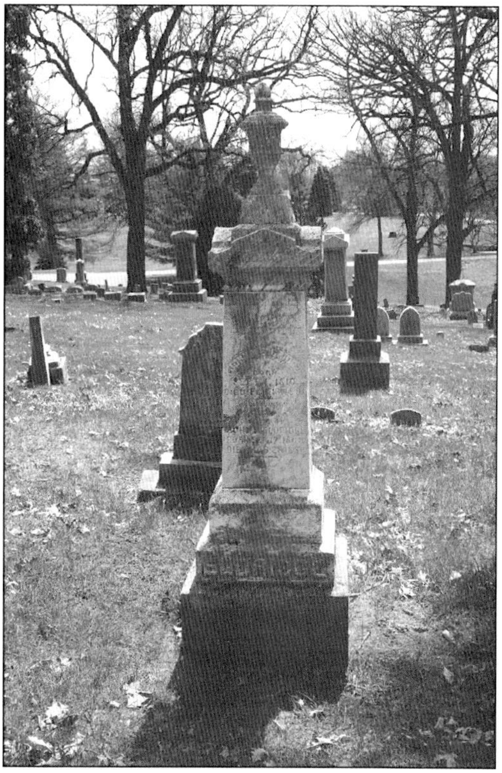

Named after Jacob Eldridge, the town of Eldridge, Iowa, was built and owned by him and located a few miles north of Davenport, Iowa. Eldridge Town in Dakota Territory was also named after him. Eldridge owned more than 10,000 acres in Iowa, Nebraska, and Dakota. He was married three times, the last time being to Agnes Smith in 1866. He died in the summer of 1892.

Jens Lorenzen was born in 1833 in Lueglumkloster, Germany. He arrived in Davenport in 1856 and eventually founded the Jens Lorenzen Crockery Company. Lorenzen opened a store that sold porcelain, stone, and glassware at Harrison Street and Second Avenue. As he grew more successful, he kept moving around the downtown area, finally ending up on West Third Street.

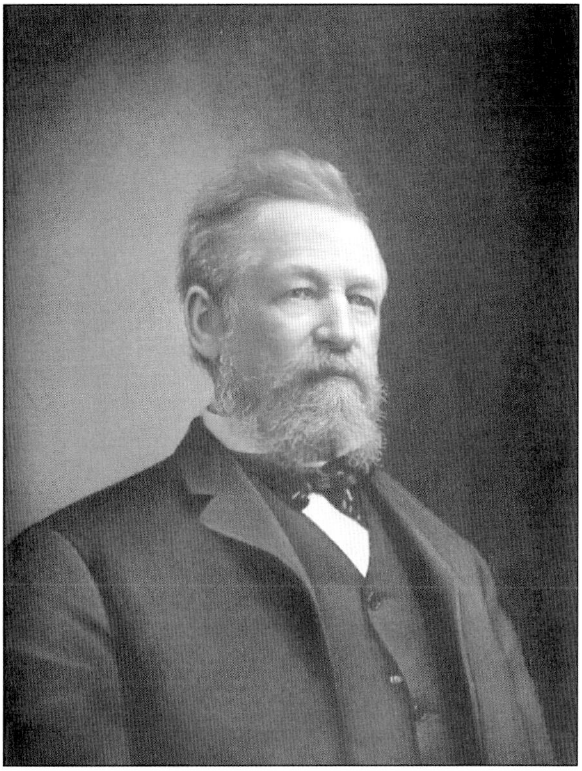

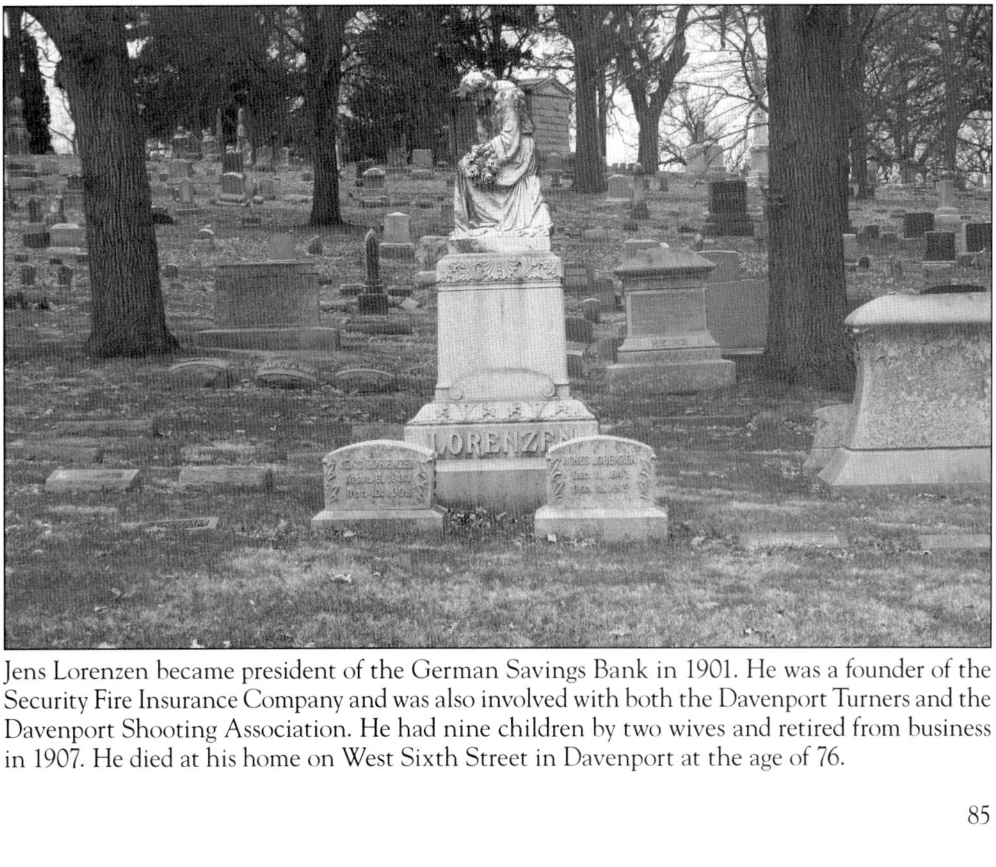

Jens Lorenzen became president of the German Savings Bank in 1901. He was a founder of the Security Fire Insurance Company and was also involved with both the Davenport Turners and the Davenport Shooting Association. He had nine children by two wives and retired from business in 1907. He died at his home on West Sixth Street in Davenport at the age of 76.

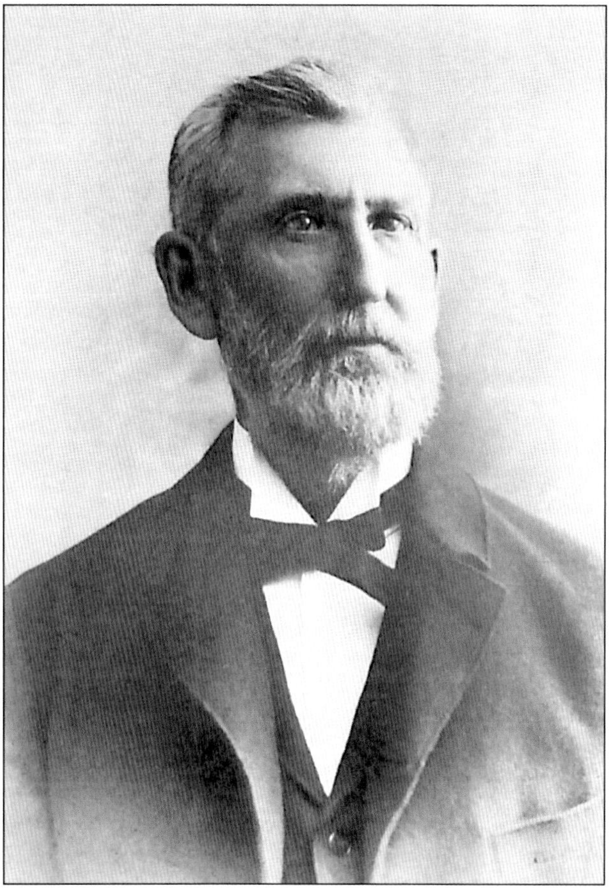

Jesse Armil was born in Pennsylvania in 1833. He and his family relocated to Iowa in 1827 and settled in the Davenport area. Armil's father was a successful farmer that had greatly invested in farmland. While growing up, Armil was educated in Catholic school and assisted his father on the farm.

Later in life, Jesse Armil became involved with dairying. He married Joanna Barrett in 1857. Armil had a 70-acre farm, the land of which is now within the city of Davenport. An early resident of the county, he was a respected member of the Pioneers Society of Scott County. Armil moved to 628 West Locust Street and retired in 1905. That same year, he died of cancer.

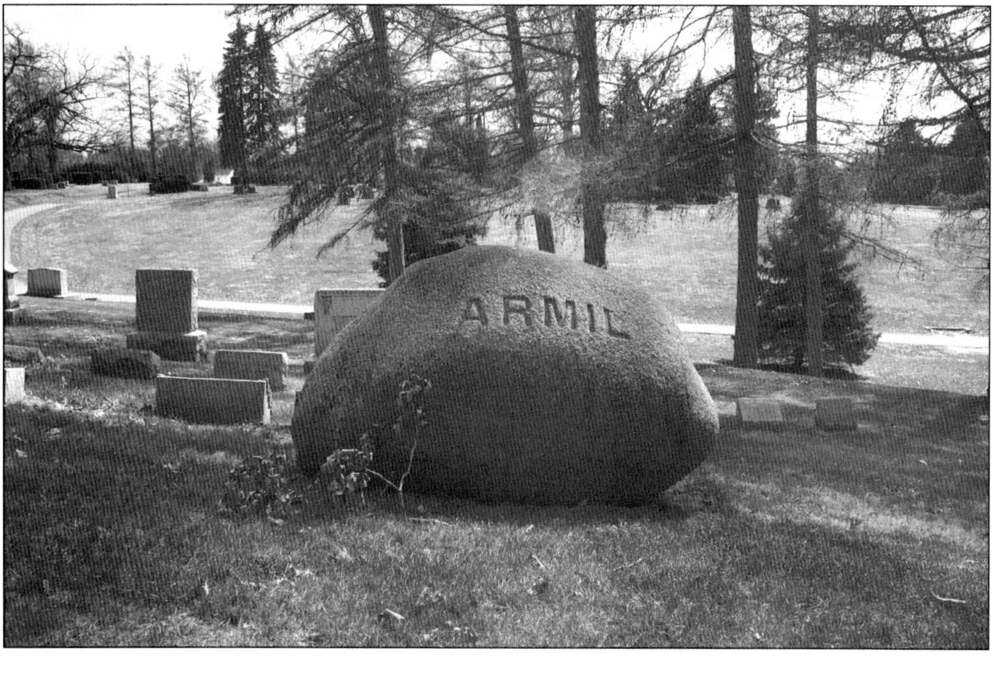

Lorenzo Schricker was born on November 12, 1825, in Bavaria, Germany. He served a four-year apprenticeship in a dry goods store and later worked as bookkeeper for a railroad. Schricker took a contract to build a railroad when he was 19. He immigrated to America in 1848 and moved to Davenport, Iowa, the following year, where he had interests in several general stores.

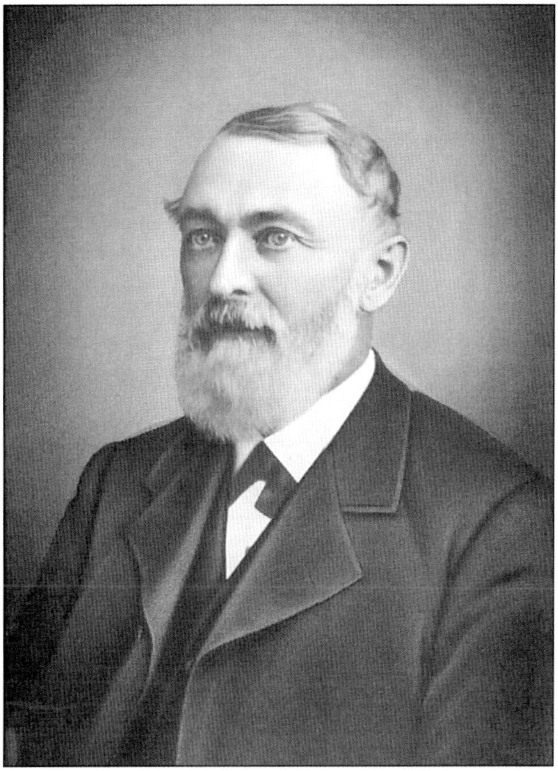

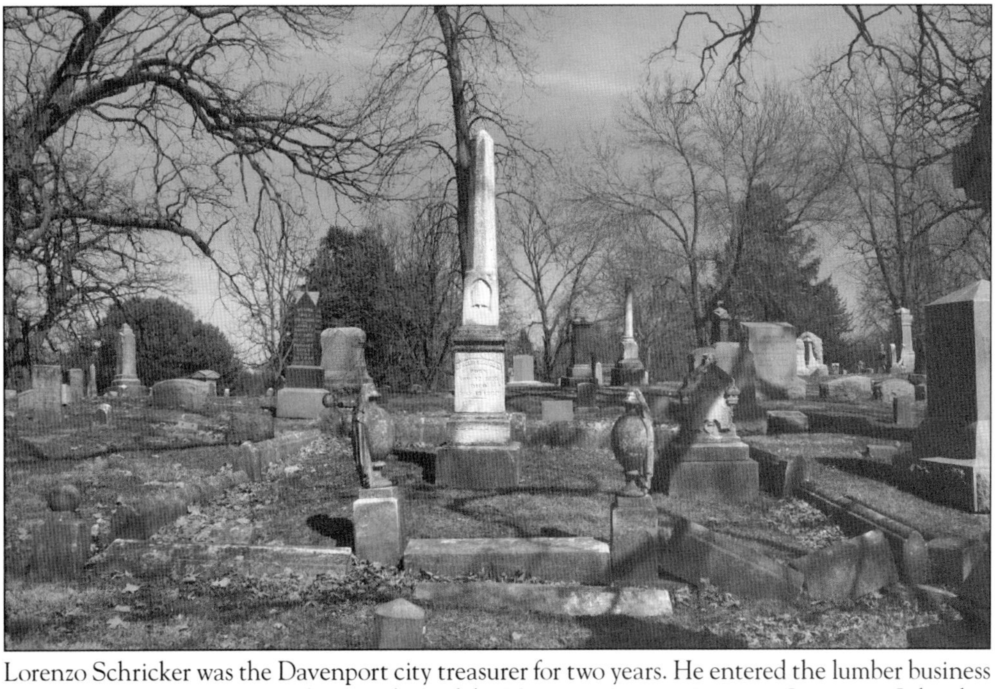

Lorenzo Schricker was the Davenport city treasurer for two years. He entered the lumber business in 1864, and by 1871, he was the president of the Upper Mississippi Logging Company. Schricker owned and managed large tracks of pine trees in Wisconsin. He was also vice president of the First National Bank. He was married three times and died in 1883 from apoplexy.

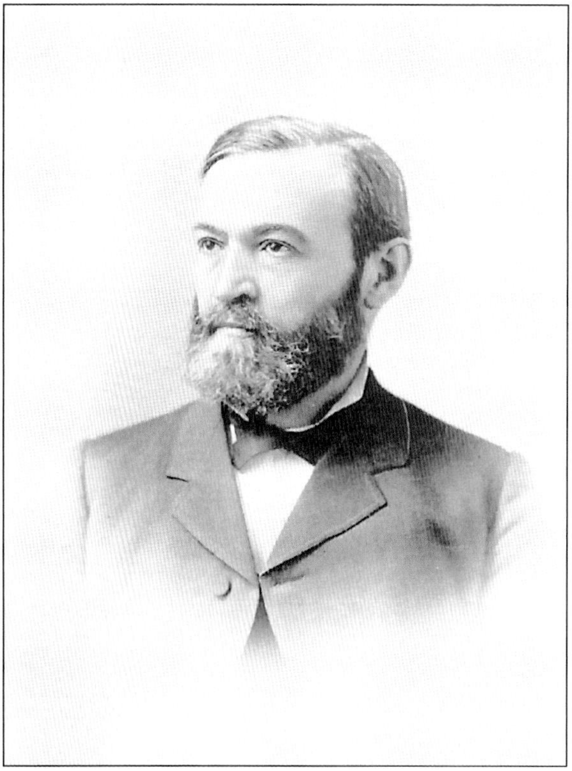

Robert Krause was born in Germany in 1834. He came to America with his parents in 1848, settling in Ohio. Krause came to Davenport in May 1852, where he first worked as a grocery store clerk for two years and then as a clothing house salesman for a little over a year. In 1854, Krause and his brother partnered up and opened their own business.

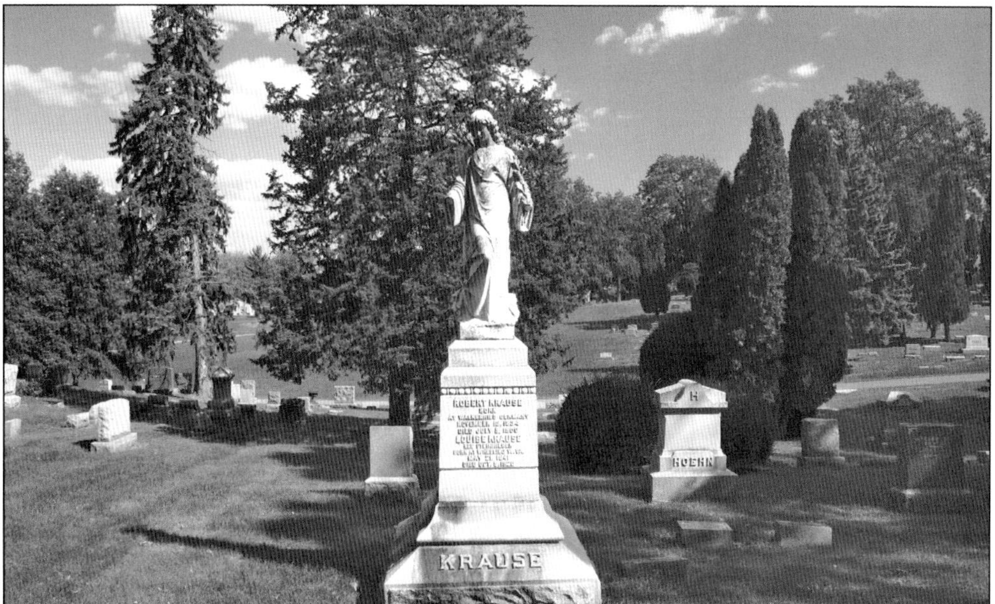

Robert Krause's store was located on East Second Street in Davenport. Krause ran the business himself after his brother left their partnership in 1858. On New Year's Day in 1860, he married Louisa Steinhilber. He helped organize the German Savings Bank, the Davenport Glucose Company, and the Phoenix Mill Company. He died from peritonitis in the summer of 1900.

William Renwick was born in Liverpool, England, on June 24, 1829. In 1846, his family came to Iowa, where he attended college. In 1850, he joined his father in the grain and commission business. Two years later, William and his father began dealing in the lumber industry, and by 1855, they had devoted all of their time and money to it.

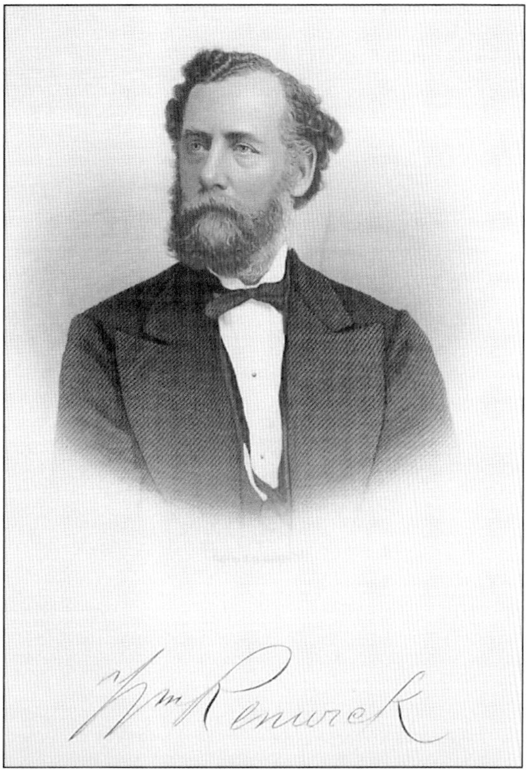

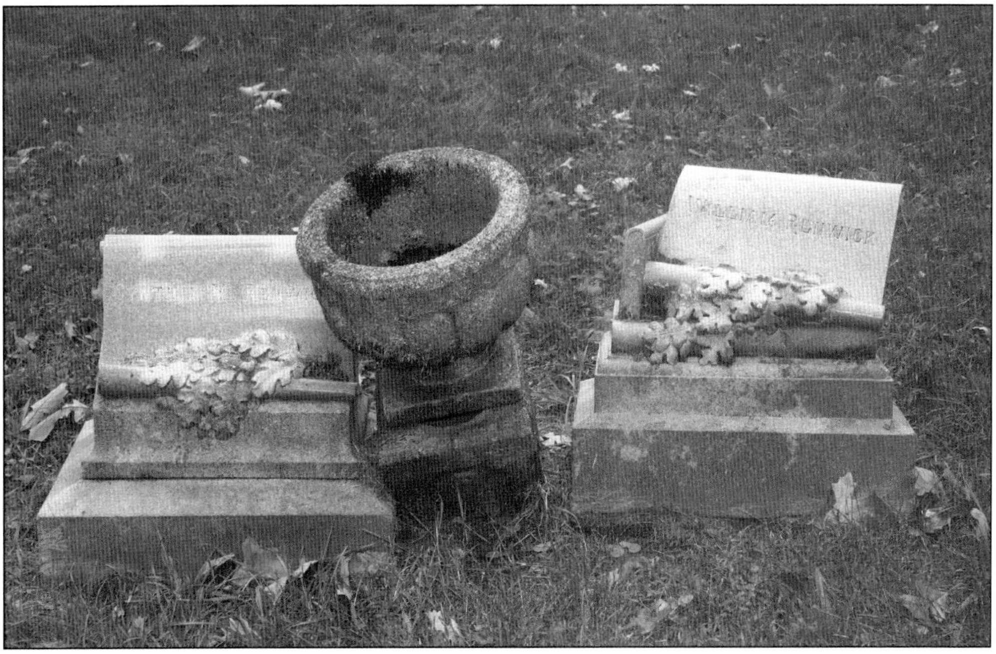

William Renwick ran the business himself until 1875, when he and some associates formed the company of Renwick, Shaw & Crossett. For 22 years, he was a member of the Scott County Agricultural Society and was also an owner of the Davenport City Street Railway Company. Renwick died from kidney disease on January 10, 1889.

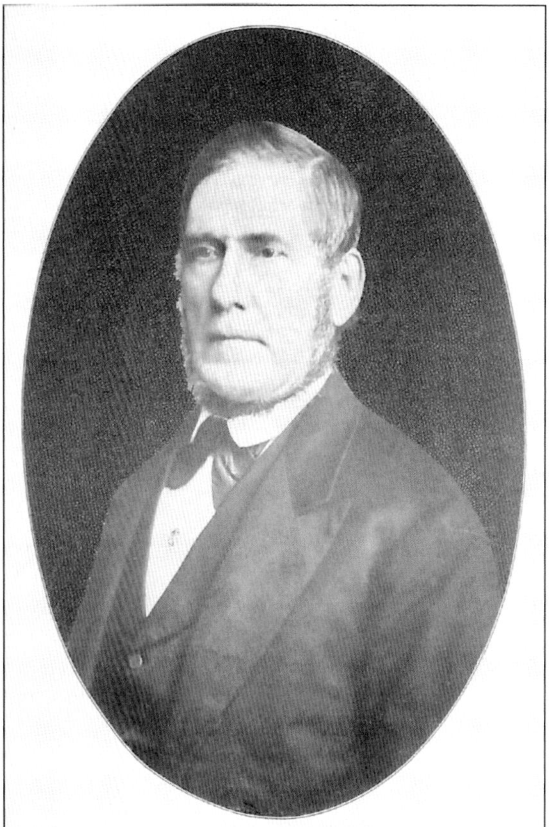

WILLIAM BRAITHWAITE

Born in Lancaster, England in 1814, William Braithwaite began learning to be a blacksmith when he was 14. He came to New York in 1852, working as a blacksmith for almost two years before moving to Susquehanna, Pennsylvania. While there, Braithwaite again worked as a blacksmith, this time for the Susquehanna Railroad.

William Braithwaite came to Davenport, Iowa, in 1856. He began working for the Rock Island Railroad and eventually became the foreman of the blacksmithing department. Braithwaite bought the lot at the corner of Fourteenth and Farnam Streets from Antoine LeClaire in 1857. He died on December 18, 1857, from old age.

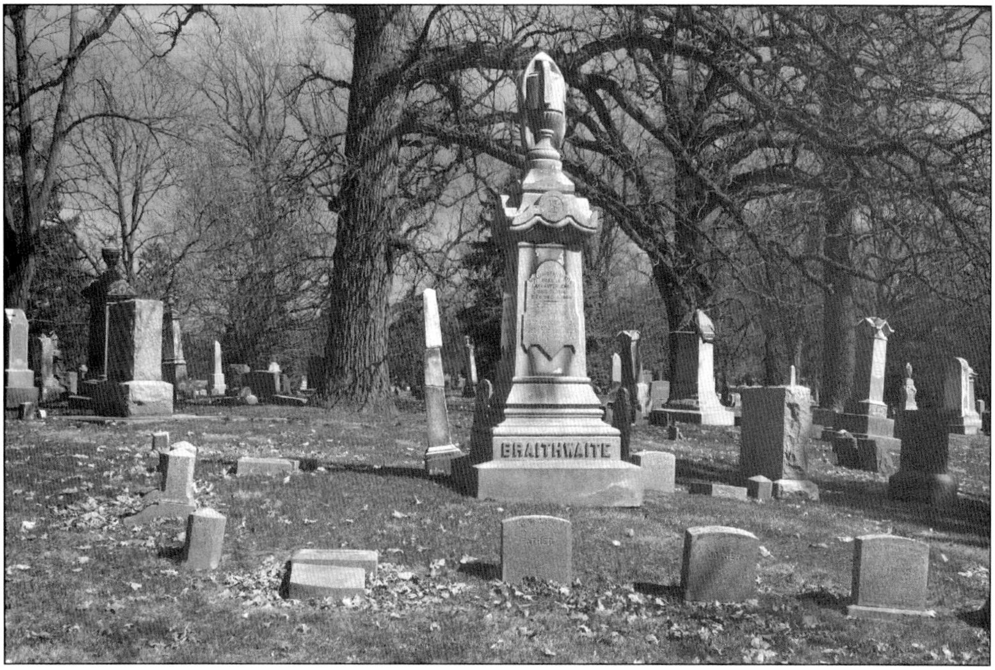

Six

Killings, Murders, and Suicides

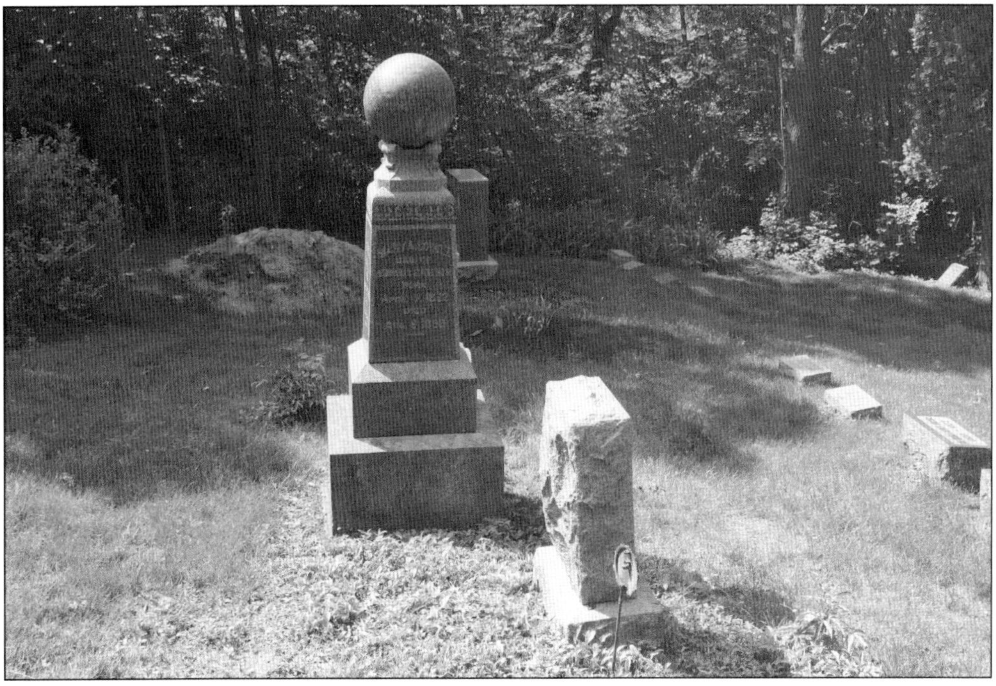

On August 6, 1898, Mary Shultz was shot and killed by her estranged husband, Henry. She had left Henry prior to this event because he was abusive. Mary was staying in the neighborhood around Brady Street and Kirkwood Boulevard in Davenport when he shot her. After shooting her, he killed himself, leaving their two children orphans.

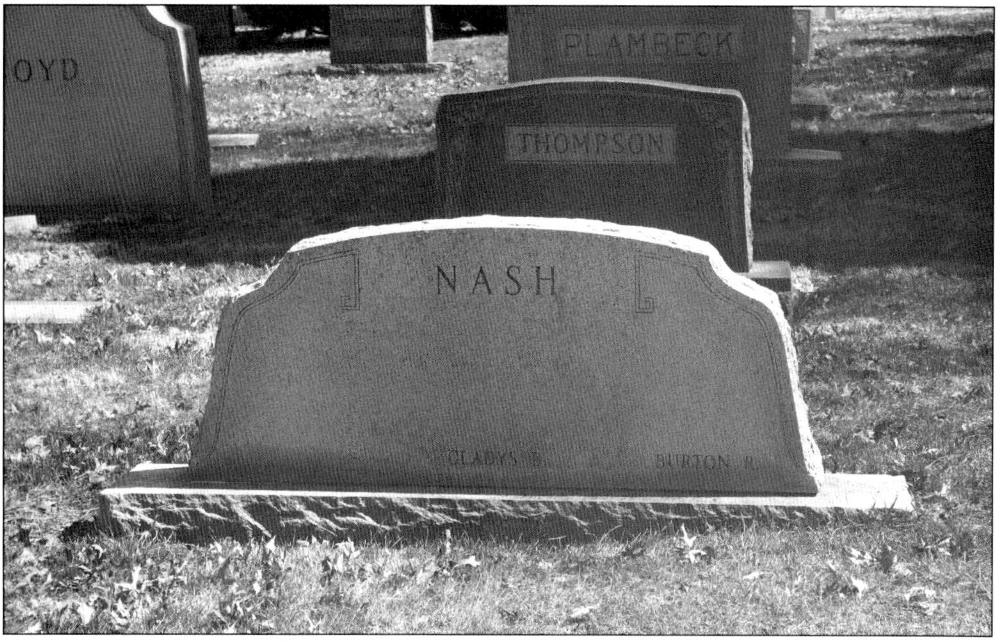

In 1938, Gladys Nash and her 14-year-old son Burton died at their home at 148 Forest Road in Davenport. They were the wife and son of C.A. Nash, the vice president of the United Light and Power Company. Gladys had been shot behind the right ear and in the chest and stabbed in the stomach. Her clothing was torn, exposing the upper front portion of her body.

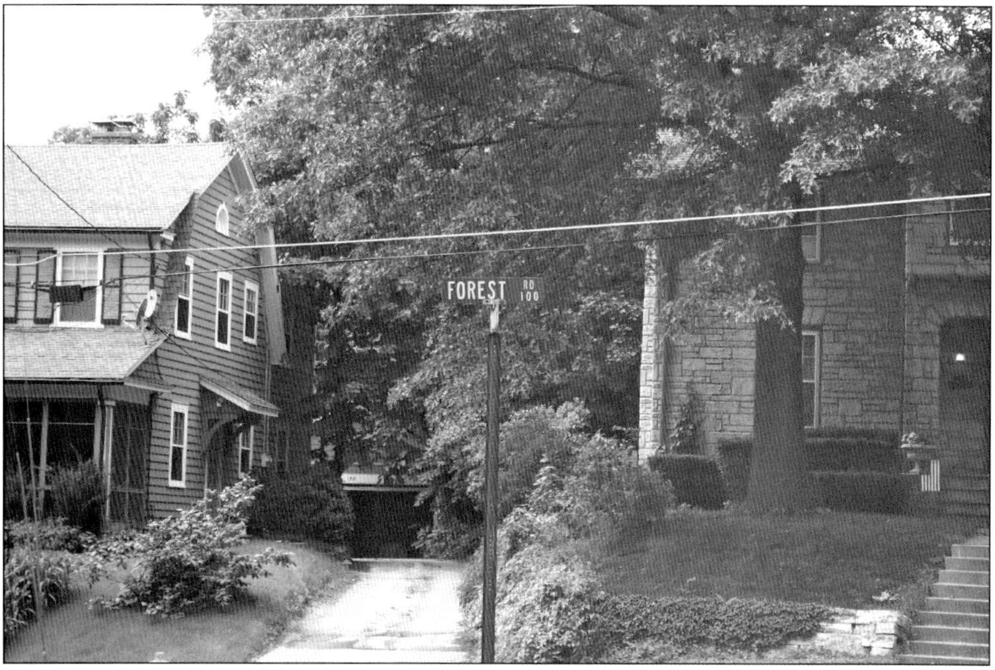

Reed Philips, the Davenport chief of police, expressed the opinion that Burton Nash had shot his mother in the head by accident and that she fell on a knife after the shooting. Panic-stricken, Burton had shot Gladys through the heart, then went to the basement and committed suicide. C.A. Nash did not believe the boy was responsible.

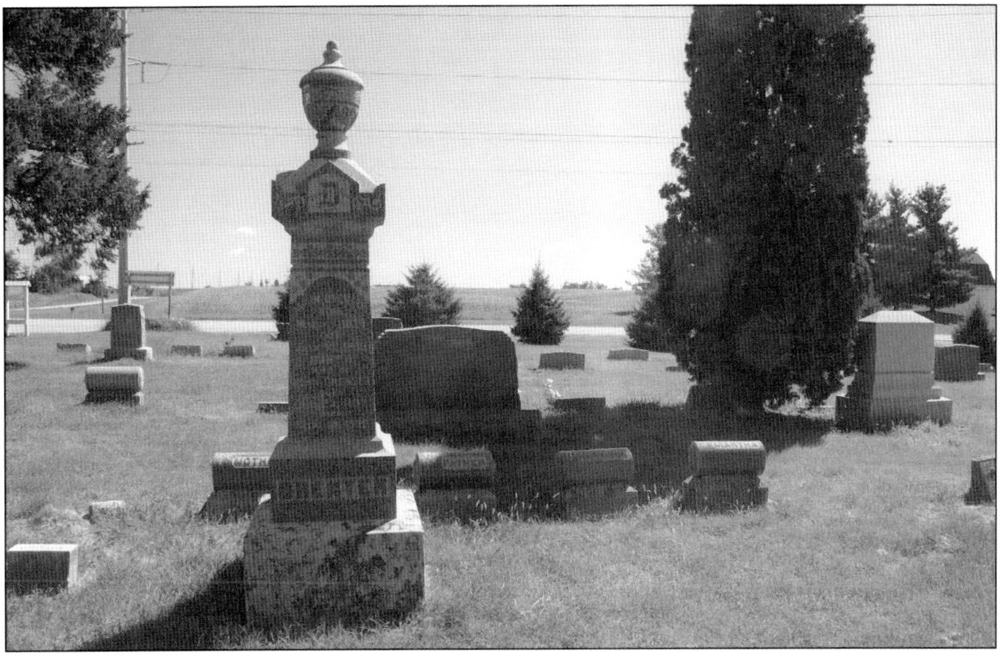

Harry Drenter loved Grace Reed, an orphan that lived with his brother, but she rejected his advances. One Sunday, Grace went to the Summit Church in rural Scott County with Sam Moore in his buggy. Extremely jealous, Harry shot them as they returned home. Half of young Grace's face was blown away, and Sam was severely wounded. Afterwards, Harry committed suicide.

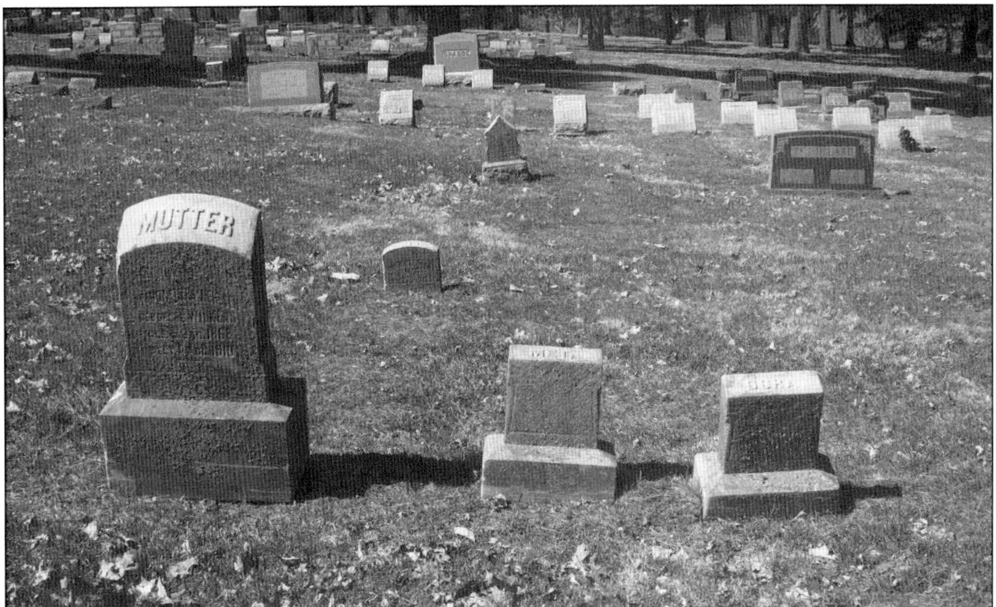

In 1910, the wife of Nick Nehlsen, a local farmer, and two of their daughters were found dead in the family's home. Large amounts of strychnine had been put into candy by Margaretha Nehlsen and then given to Dora, age four, and Meta, age three. The actions of an older daughter had inadvertently led to Margaretha's mental instability. All three were buried at the same time in Pine Hill Cemetery.

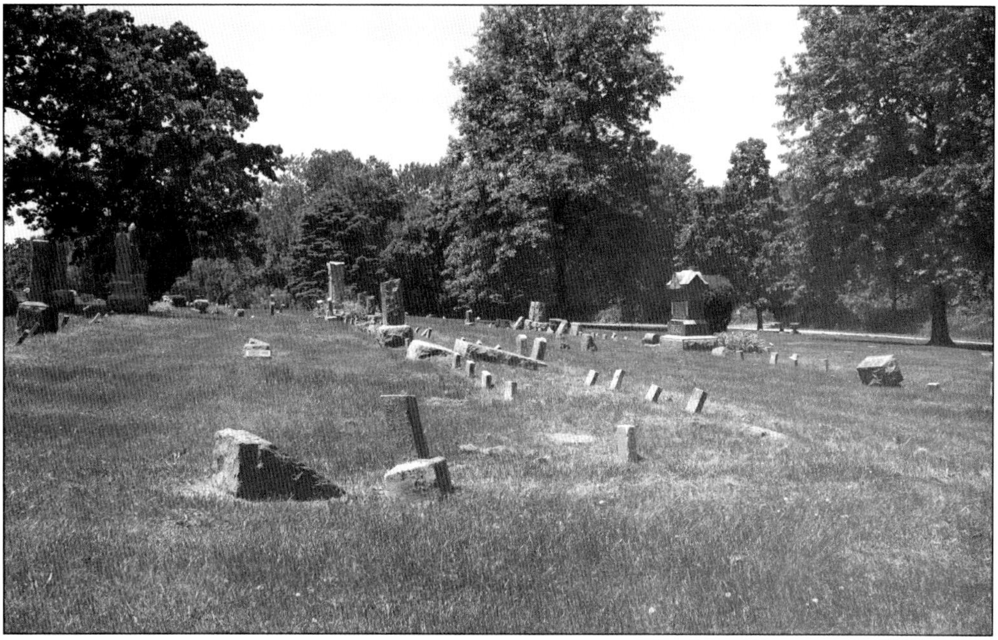

In 1921, Roy Purple, who was a Davenport barber, and Harry Hamilton, decided to rob the Stockman's bank in Long Grove, Iowa. They drove to the bank and tried the front door, but it was locked. They waited and then tried again, and this time found the door open and went inside. A local garage owner had seen the thieves, so he, along with others, grabbed guns and waited for them to exit.

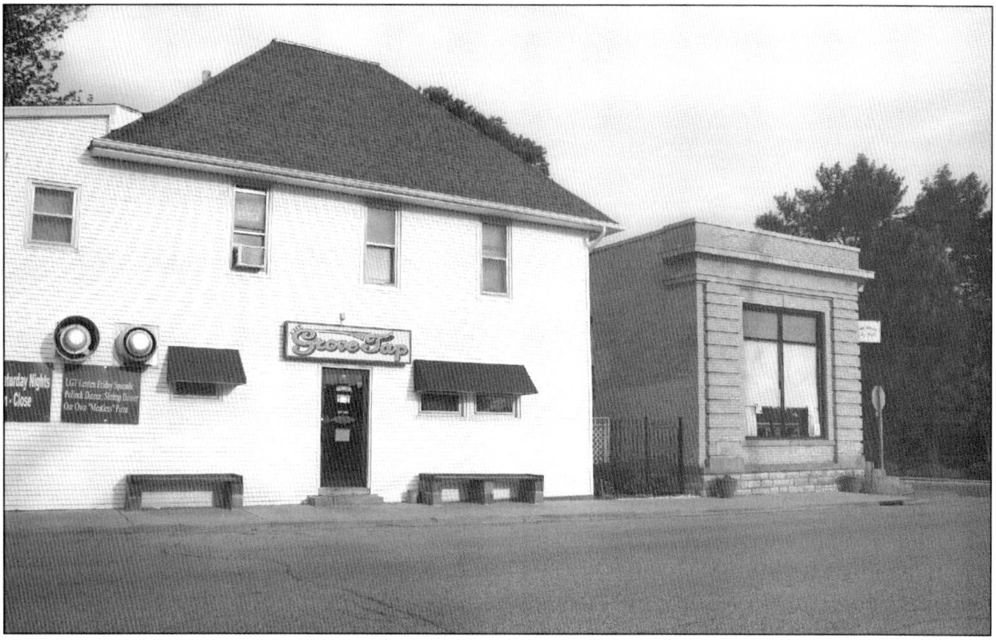

As Roy Purple and Harry Hamilton exited the bank (on the right), they ran directly into citizens' gunfire. A bullet hit Purple in the head, immediately killing him. Hamilton received four bullet wounds altogether with one piercing his shoulder. This bullet traversed the length of Hamilton's body. Understandably, Hamilton staggered and fell.

Seven

Others

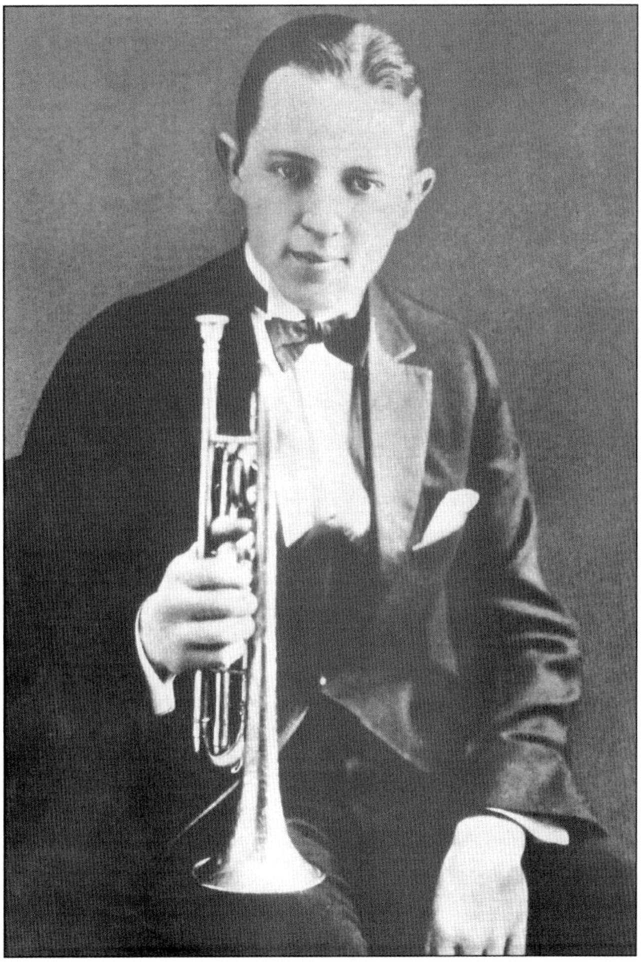

Leon "Bix" Beiderbecke was born in Davenport, Iowa, on March 10, 1903, to Bismark and Agatha Beiderbecke. A musical prodigy, gifted with an amazing memory for music as well as perfect pitch, Bix could play songs on the piano at a young age. After a phenomenally bright—but exceedingly short—jazz music career, Bix died of pneumonia on August 6, 1931. He was only 28 years old.

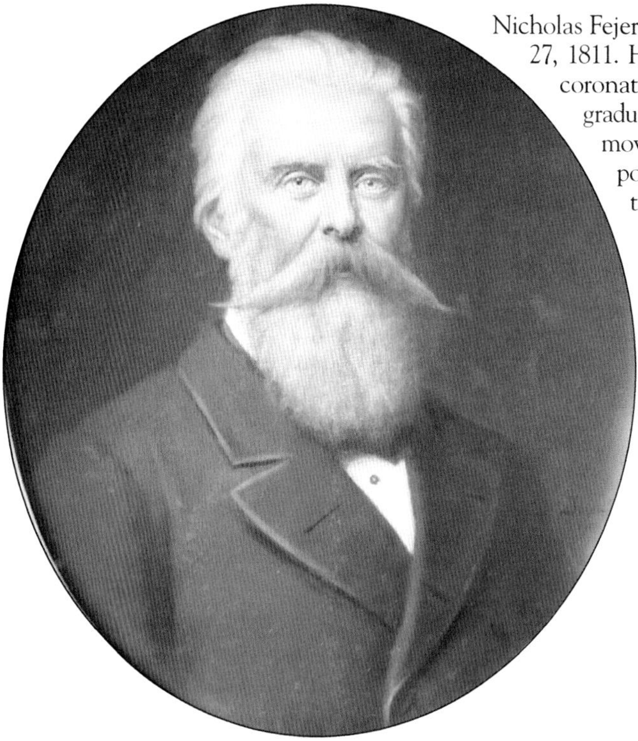

Nicholas Fejervary was born in Hungary on May 27, 1811. He studied law and witnessed the coronation of King Ferdinand. In 1832, he graduated from the University of Pesth and moved to a farm. Involving himself in politics early on, Fejervary was elected to the legislature in Hungary and stayed there for three years. He was later elected to the Diet (the Hungarian parliament) in 1843.

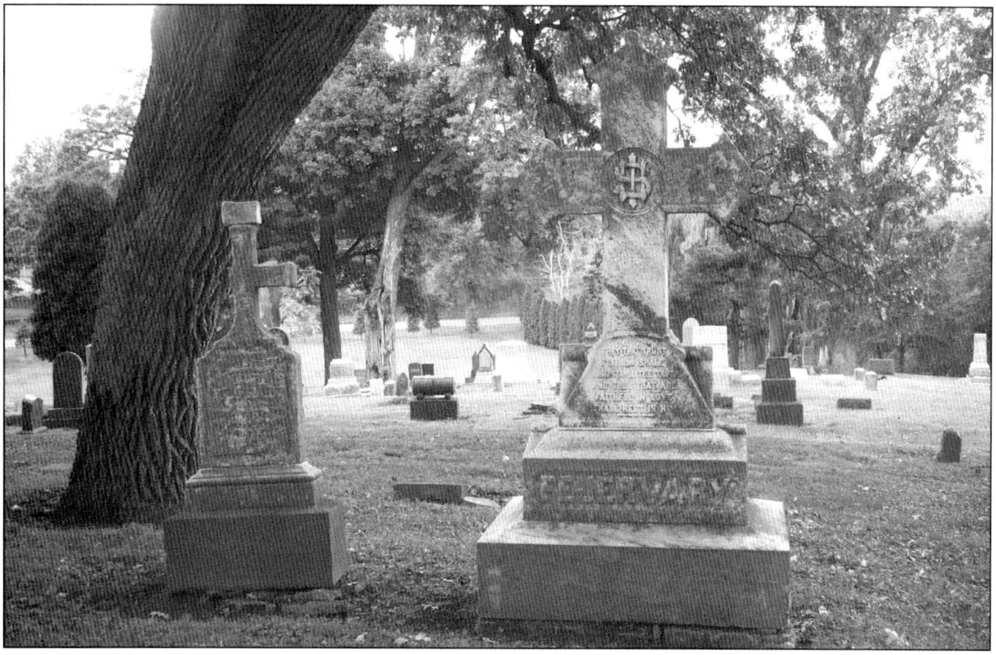

Nicholas Fejervary gave up his political career in 1844 and married Caroline Kars the following year. In 1852, he moved to the United States, specifically Scott County. Fejervary bought up 3,000 acres of land in Scott County and neighboring counties. He was able to make a profit from this land, and in 1853, he and his family moved into Davenport. Fejervary died in 1895 from Bright's disease.

Willard Barrows was born in Massachusetts in 1806. A surveyor and engineer by vocation, he had lived in Connecticut and later taught school in New Jersey. In 1835, he surveyed parts of the state of Mississippi, and in 1837, he was involved in the first Iowa surveys and became acquainted with Col. George Davenport and D.C. Eldridge. He arrived in the town of Rockingham with his family during 1838.

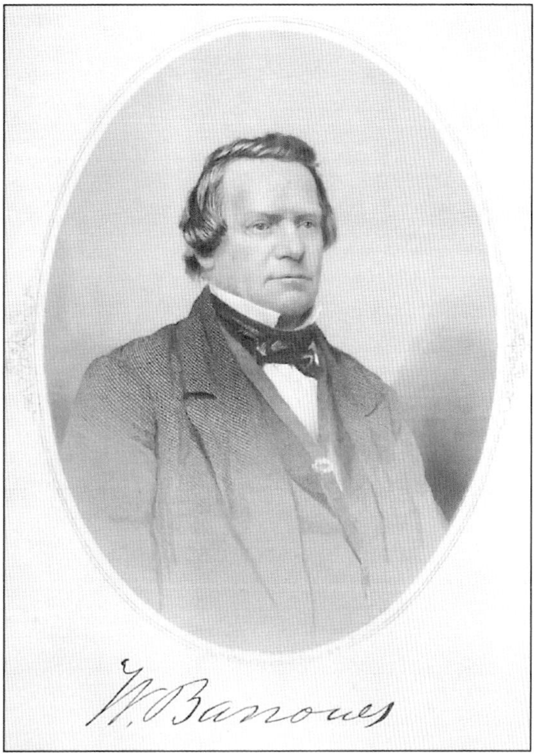

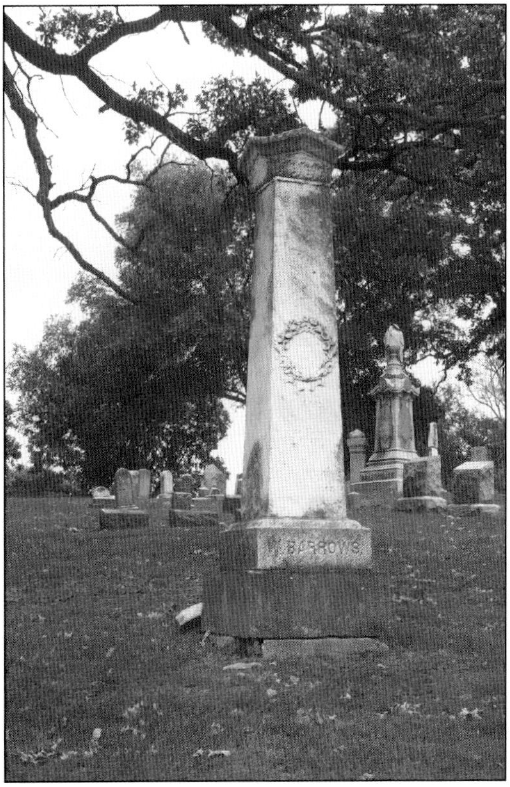

Willard Barrows surveyed the islands of the Mississippi from the Rock River to Quincy, Illinois. He was a justice of the peace, postmaster, and notary republic at Rockingham until 1843. After doing surveys in Wisconsin, he traveled overland to California in 1850. Barrows made the *Barrows New Map of Iowa* in 1854. He wrote a history of Scott County in 1859, earning him the nickname "the Historian of Scott County."

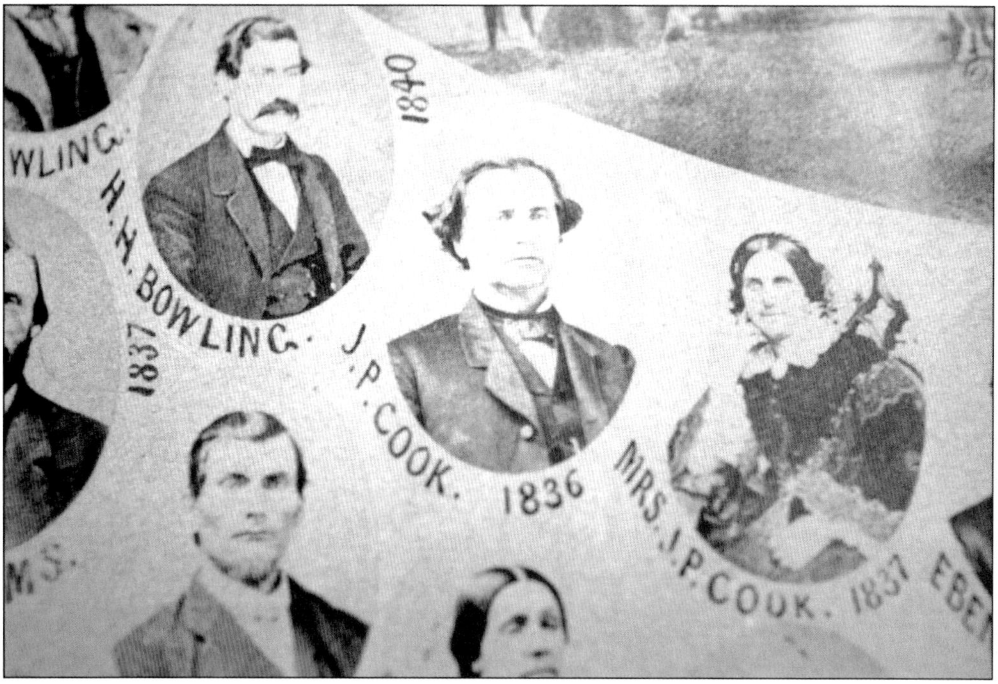

John Parsons Cook was born in August 1817. His great-grandfather Ebenezer was a captain of a company of soldiers at Fort Ticonderoga, serving there with Ethan Allen. When Cook was 19, he came to Scott County and settled there with his father. Their farm, known as the Cook Farm, served as the western boundary of the city of Davenport at that time. This farm was located close to City Cemetery in Davenport.

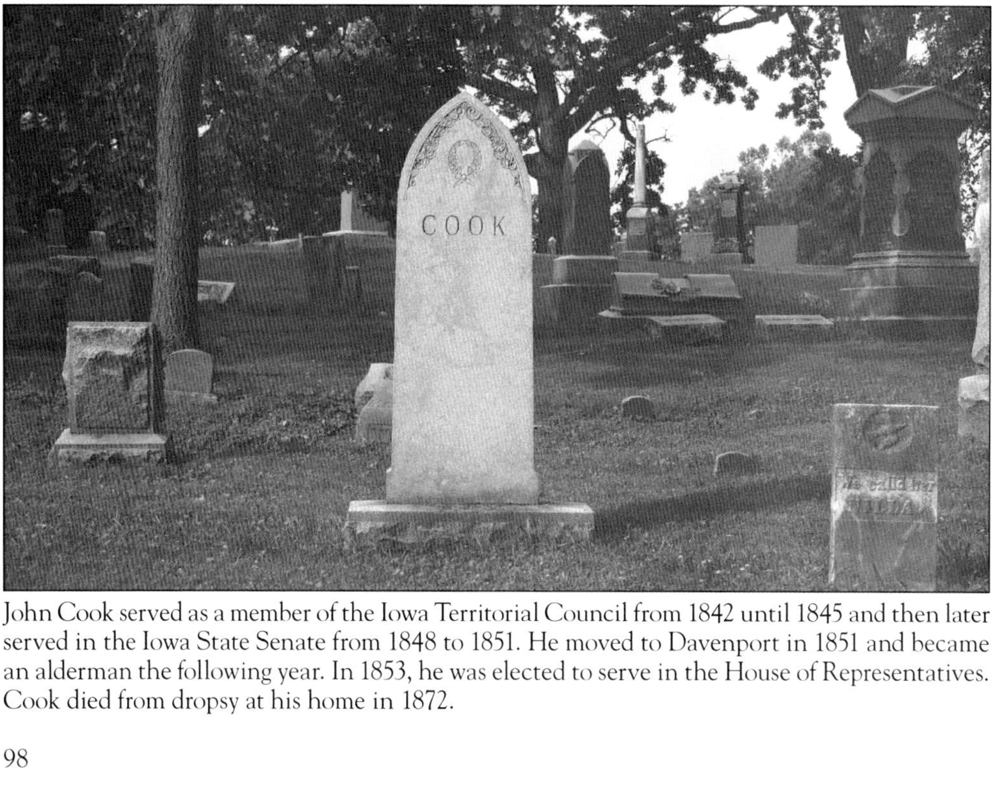

John Cook served as a member of the Iowa Territorial Council from 1842 until 1845 and then later served in the Iowa State Senate from 1848 to 1851. He moved to Davenport in 1851 and became an alderman the following year. In 1853, he was elected to serve in the House of Representatives. Cook died from dropsy at his home in 1872.

Originally from Scotland, James Dyer organized both the first temperance movement in Scotland and the first cooperative business in Southern Scotland. He immigrated to the United States in 1852 and was involved with the Underground Railroad in the state of New York. He moved to Pleasant Valley in 1854 and took up farming and growing fruit, two fields in which he later became known as an expert.

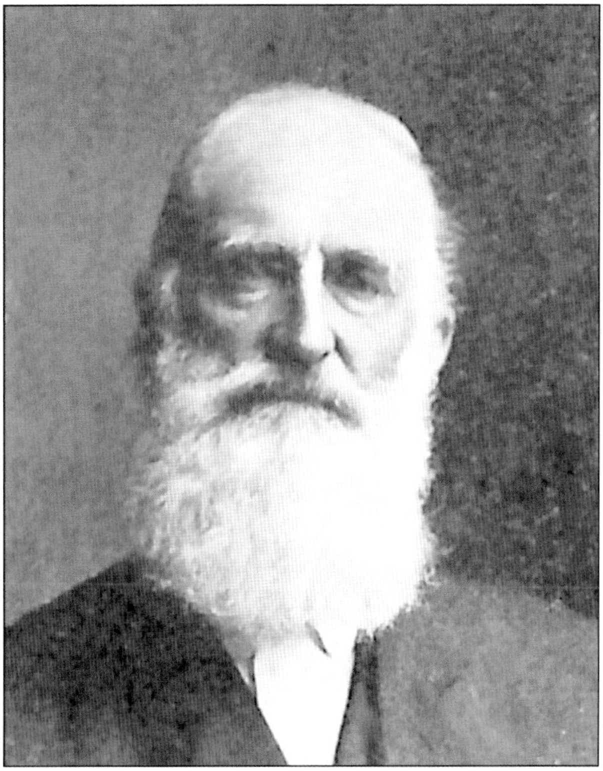

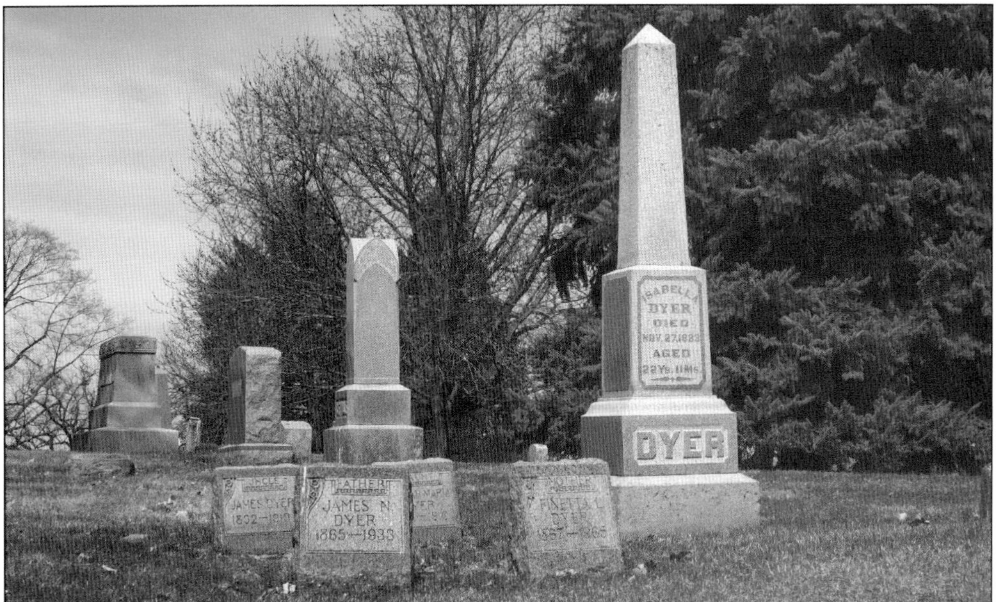

In 1859, James Dyer married Sarah Hedges, who was the first white person born in Pleasant Valley. Family and friends called Sarah by her nickname, "Auntie," because she would take care of sick people. They had no children of their own, though James and Sarah adopted his brother's children and raised them.

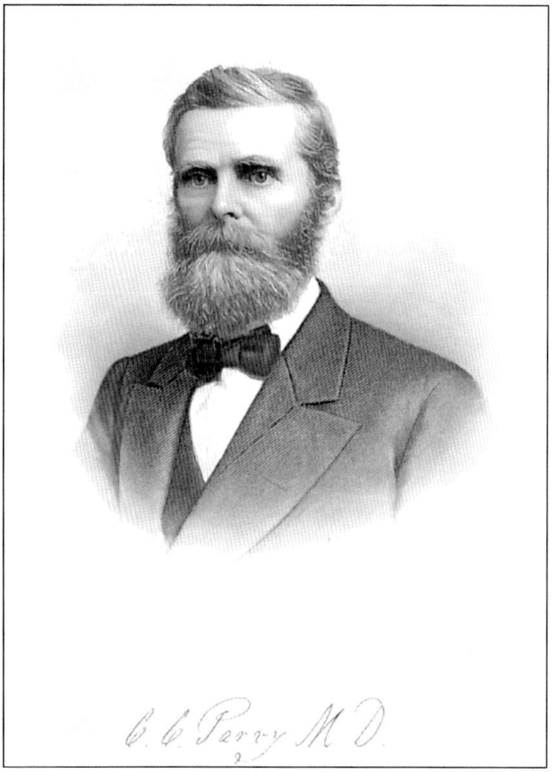

C.C. Parry was born in England in 1823 and came to America in 1832. In time, he earned a degree in medicine from Columbia University. In 1846, he and his family moved once again, this time to Iowa. At first, he practiced medicine in Davenport, but he soon switched his studies to botany. He worked in the field of botany for several years and was a recognized authority on the subject.

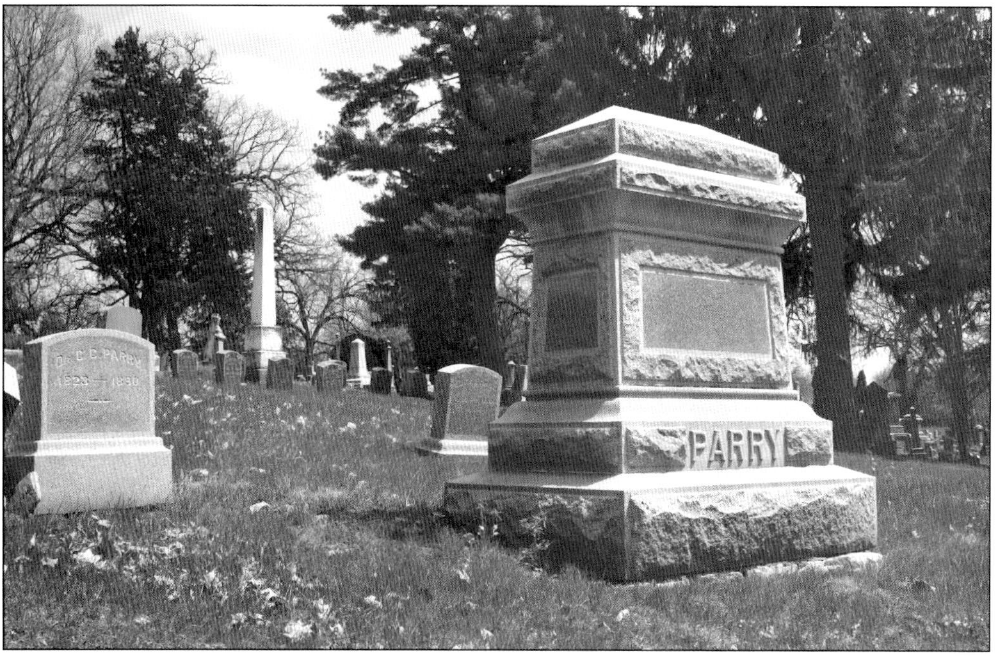

C.C. Parry wrote to many scientific journals, and his botanical work caused him to travel extensively throughout the west. Parry was such an avid supporter of the Davenport Academy of Sciences that he was elected its president in 1858. He was continually reelected to the position until he turned it down in 1875. Parry died in 1890.

Le Roy Dodge was born in New York on December 25, 1811. In 1836, he moved to Scott County, Iowa. He had been a clerk in the post office in Dubuque and was later a clerk on one of the steamboats plying between that point and St. Louis. Eventually, Dodge became a river pilot and owned many boats over the course of several years.

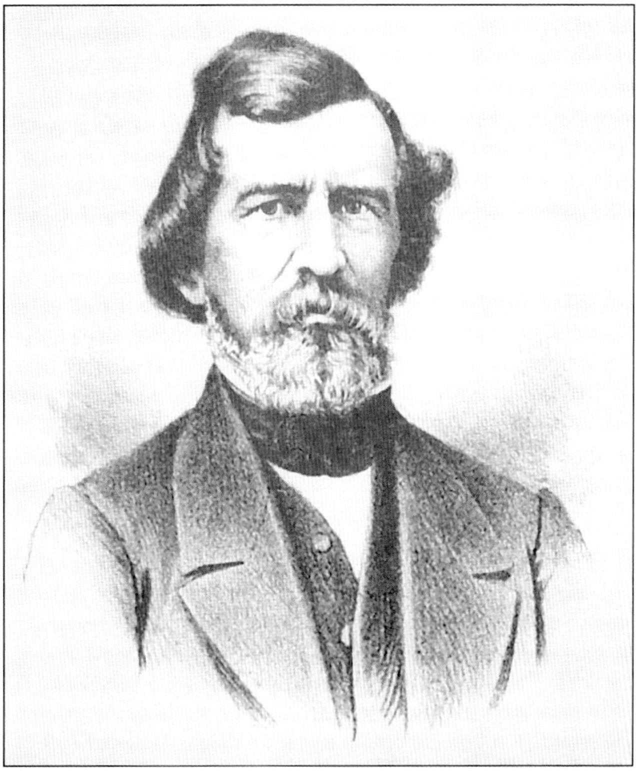

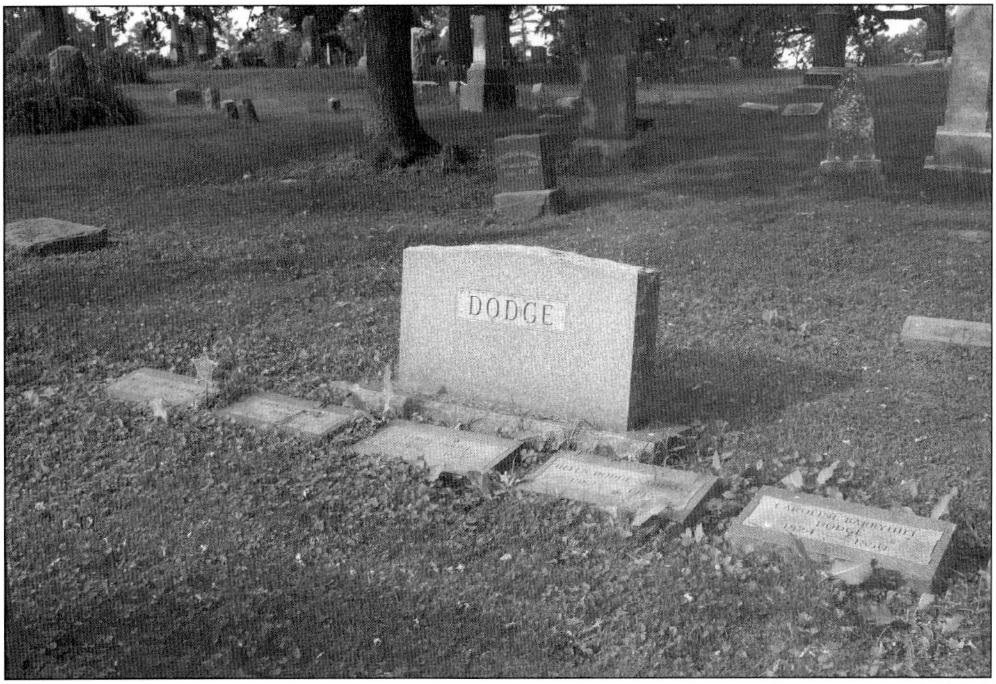

In 1852, Le Roy Dodge represented Scott County in the legislature. He owned 400 acres on the bluff above Buffalo, Iowa, and along the Mississippi River and built his home there. Dodge retired to his farm a wealthy man in 1859. He died in 1871 from complications of a mowing machine accident.

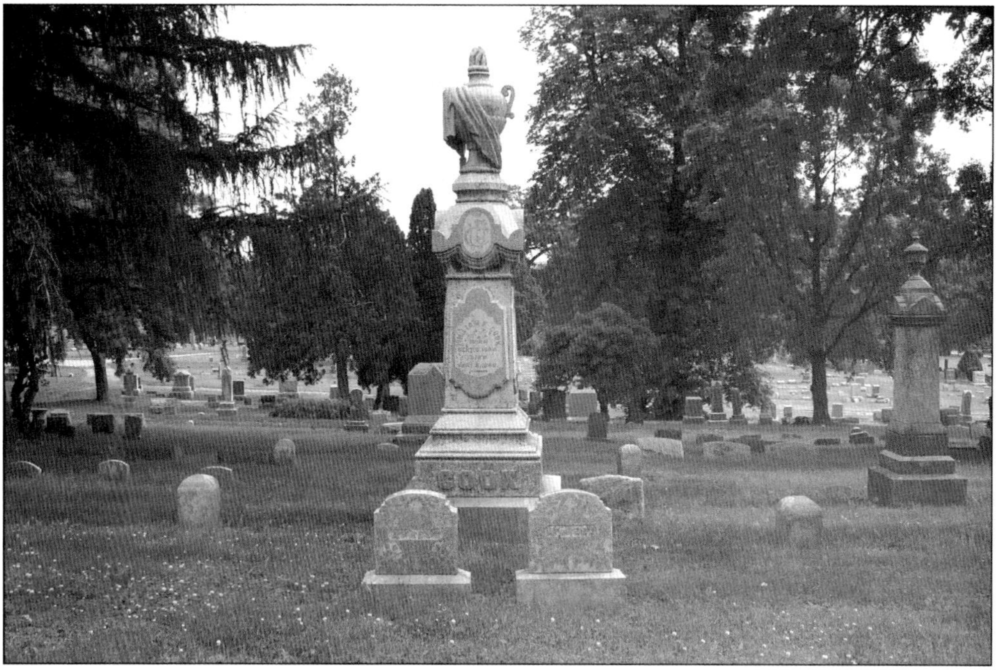

Amanda Cooke was born in England in 1847 but eventually came to America. While traveling west on a wagon train from Illinois to California in 1865, about 300 Cheyenne Indians attacked the party. Cooke saw her mother speared to death. She and her sister were captured, and she never saw her sister again. A year later, Cooke was purchased from the Indians and returned to her home in Illinois.

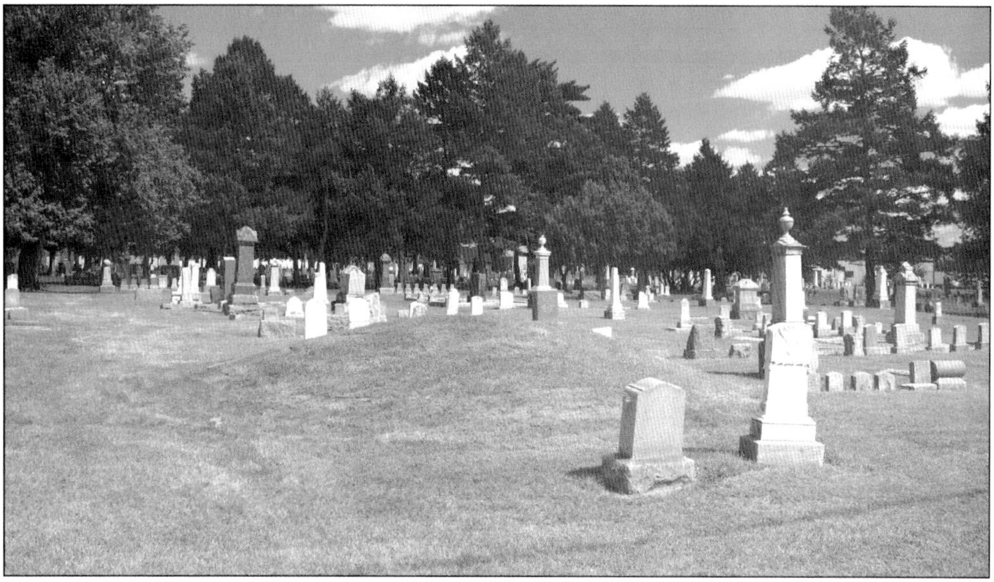

The unusual mound in City Cemetery has been a local curiosity for a long time. It has been theorized that victims of a cholera epidemic in 1873 are buried in mass there. The authors' research found that it is the grave of Heindrich Oldendorf, a Davenport gardener who died from asphyxiation in Chicago in 1890. However, this does not explain the mound itself, leaving the question open for more speculation.

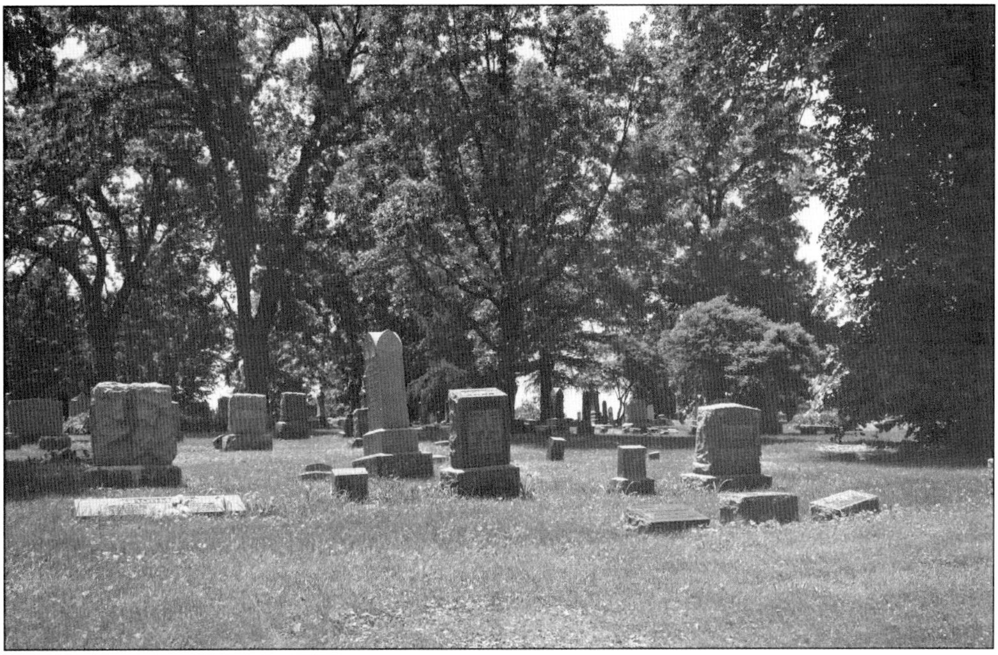

John Henry was born to slave parents in Montgomery, Alabama, in 1856. When he was only six, Iowa troops took him north, where he eventually settled on a farm near Vinton, Iowa. He was educated by a local farmer and eventually attended Davenport Business College. Over time, Henry worked as a farmhand, yard worker, and carpenter.

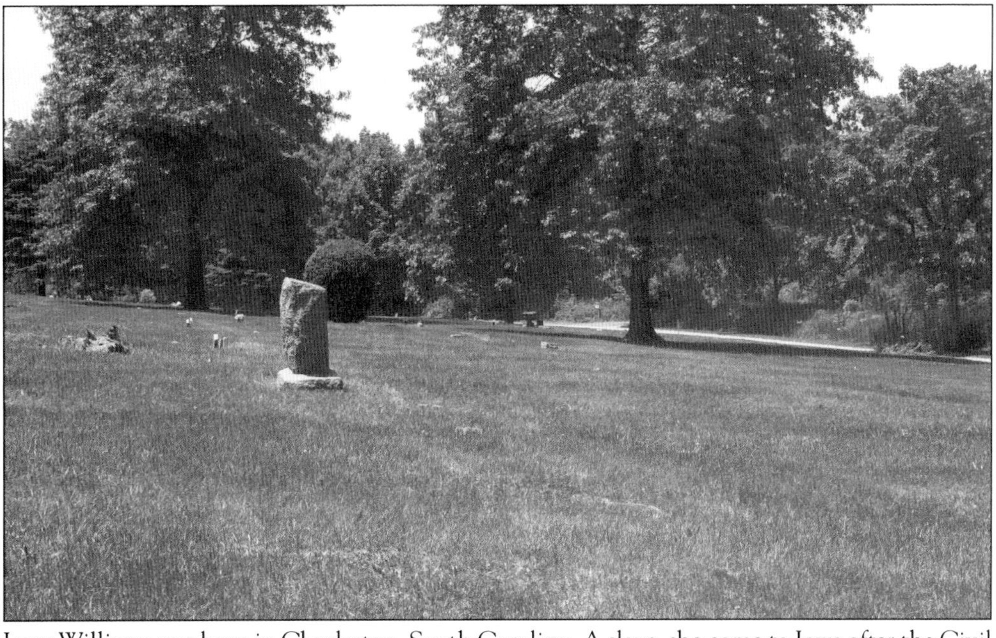

Lucy Williams was born in Charleston, South Carolina. A slave, she came to Iowa after the Civil War with the 10th Iowa Infantry. She lived in the basement of the African Methodist Church on West Fourth Street in Davenport. Williams was active in her church and provided services as a nurse. At the end of her life, while claiming to be more than 100 years old, she died at the county infirmary.

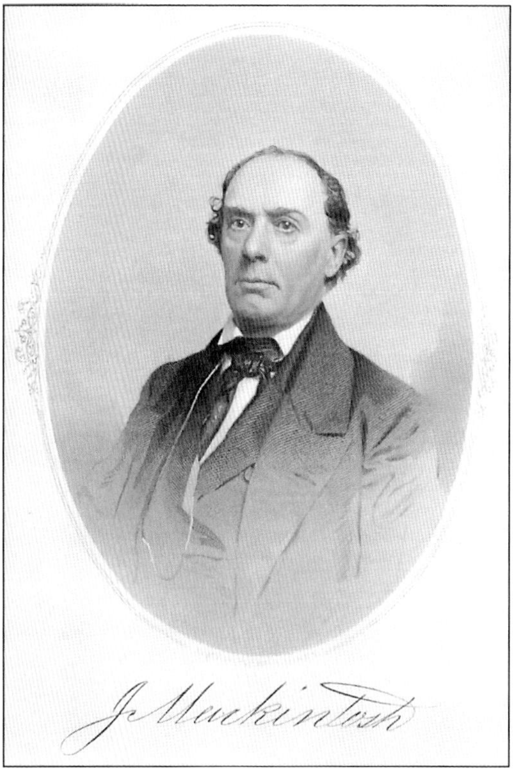

James MacKintosh eventually settled in Davenport, opening a general store in 1836. He took a very active role in various aspects of public life, including the battle for the county seat between Davenport and nearby Rockingham. He was an alderman in 1858 and 1859. MacKintosh also invested large amounts of money in city improvements. He died in October 1862 from a brain disease.

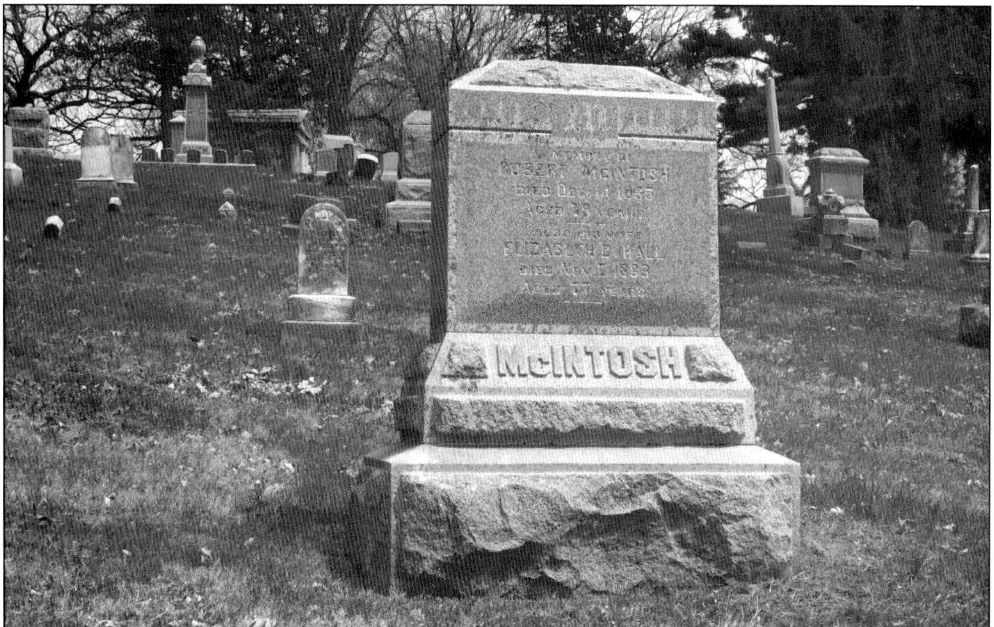

Henry Lee was born in Connecticut in 1815. He became an ordained minister in the Episcopal Church in 1839 and became a rector of a church the following year, which he stayed at for three years. Lee was elected bishop of the Diocese of Iowa in 1854, making him the first Episcopal bishop of Iowa.

After visiting the major churches in Iowa, Henry Lee moved to Davenport in 1855. He invested in more than 6,000 acres with money he raised and was key in the founding of Griswold College (below). Bishop Lee also helped in having Grace Cathedral built. He died on September 26, 1874.

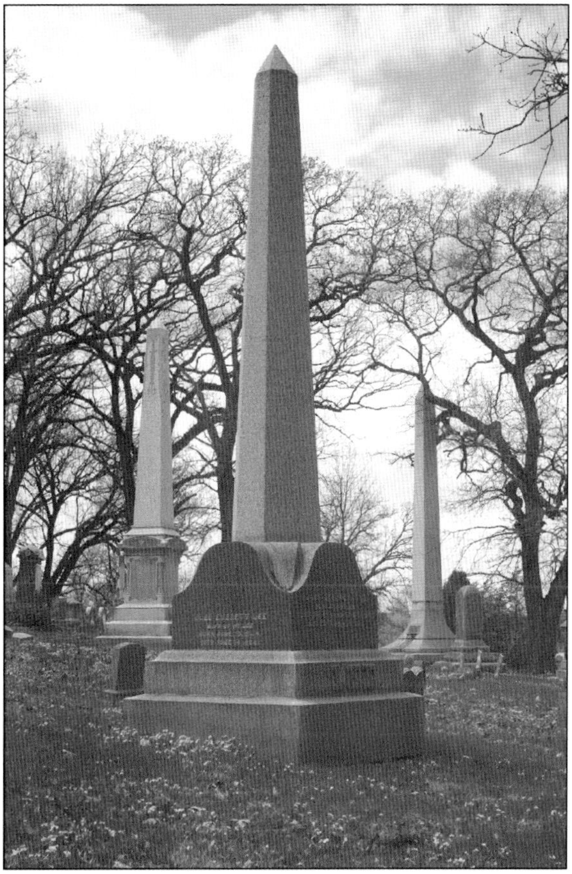

Jonathan S. Slaymaker was born in Pennsylvania in 1835. When he was 18, he began working as a civil engineer with a railroad. This job eventually brought him to Davenport. During the Civil War, Slaymaker joined the 2nd Iowa Regiment of Volunteer Infantry as a first

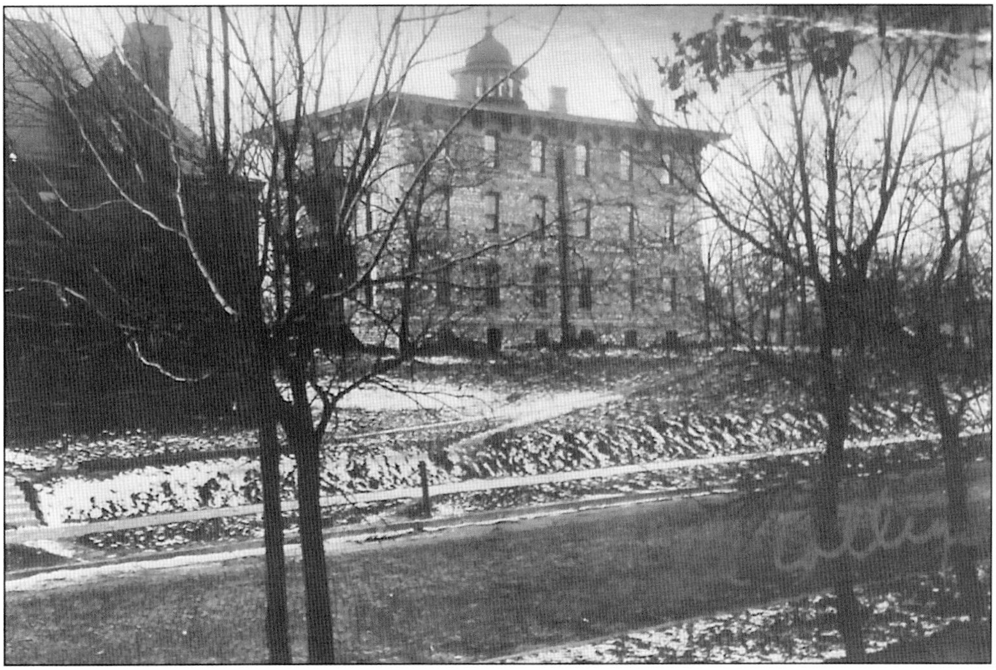

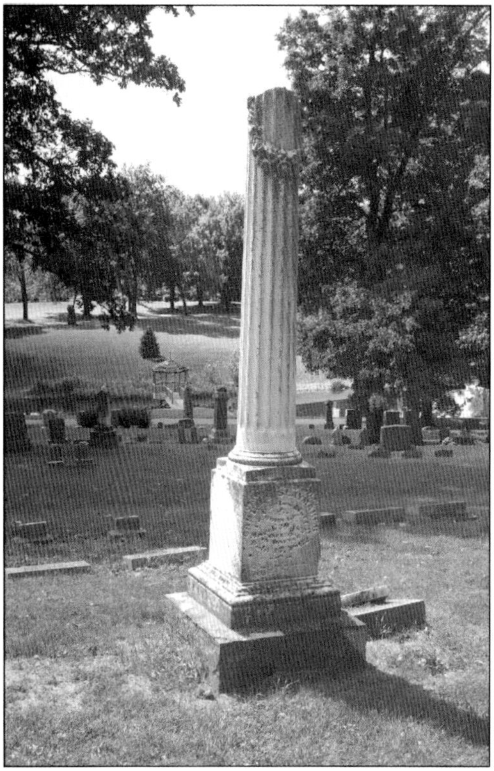

lieutenant. Eventually, he would achieve the rank of captain. In 1862, Slaymaker and the 2nd Iowa Infantry faced the Confederate forces at Fort Donelson.

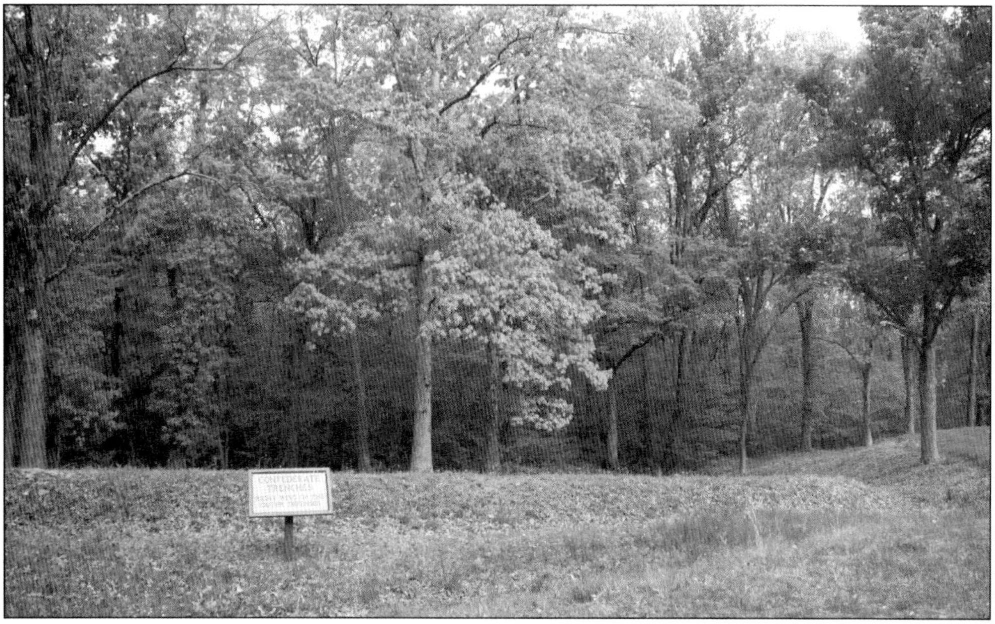

On February 15, 1862, Jonathan S. Slaymaker and the 2nd Iowa Infantry were ordered to charge at Fort Donelson. They took the Confederate breastworks, but Slaymaker was shot through the thigh. Falling to the ground, Slaymaker raised himself to his side, waved his sword, and said, "Go get them, boys!" He then sank to the ground and died, having bled to death from a severed artery. His body was returned to Davenport, Iowa.

Joseph B. Leake was born in New Jersey on April 1, 1828. He graduated from Miami University in 1846 before studying law in Ohio. Leake joined the bar in 1850 and moved to Iowa in 1856. He opened a law office in Davenport and was elected a member of the House of Representatives in 1861.

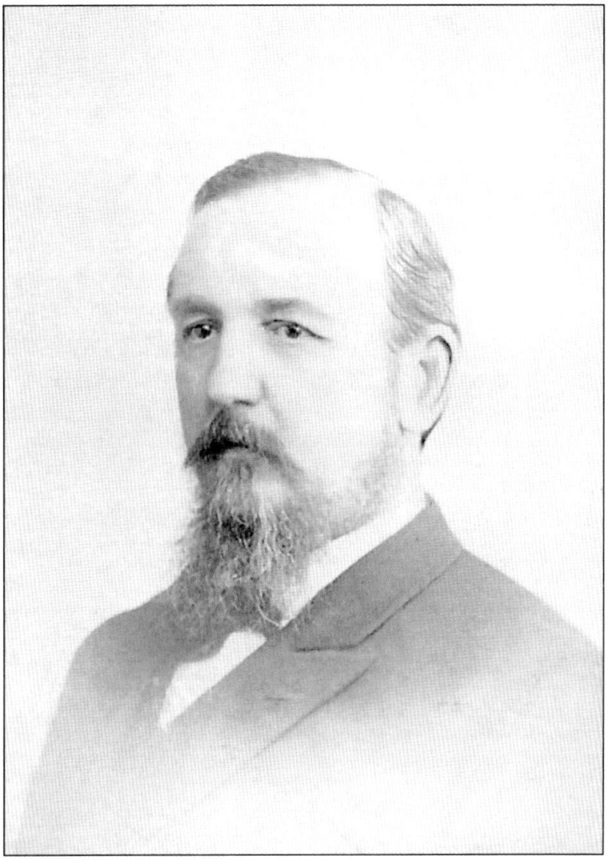

Joseph Leake joined the Union army and fought in several engagements. He was captured at the Battle of Bayou Fordoche and taken to Camp Ford, a Confederate prison in Texas. He was released in 1865. After leaving the army, he returned to Iowa and was elected to the state senate. Leake died from a heart attack in 1913.

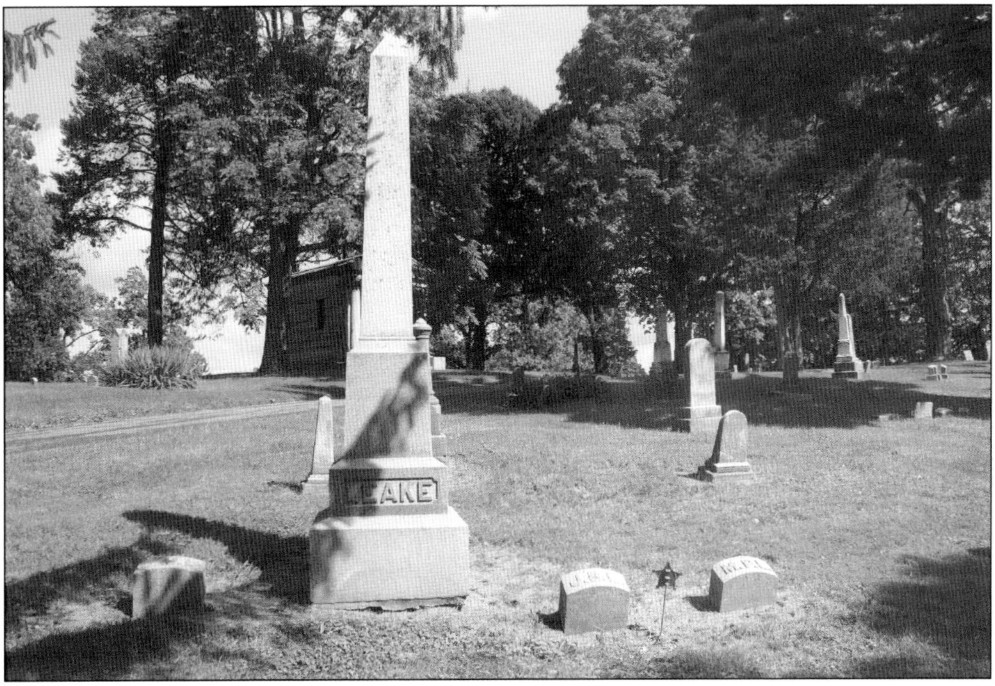

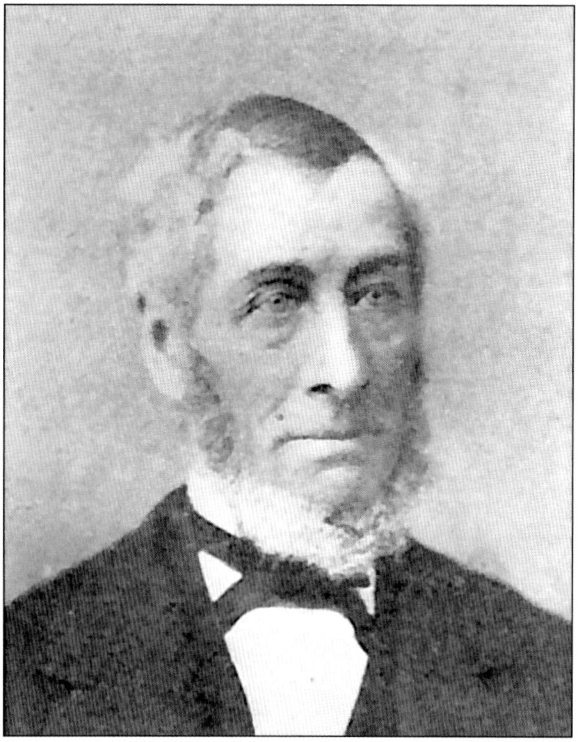

Enoch Mead was born in Connecticut in 1809. He graduated from Yale in 1830 and entered the seminary in the same year. Upon graduating, his first assignment was in Lockport, New York, followed by an assignment to a church in New Haven, Vermont, in 1834. During this time, he was also made chaplain to the 3rd Brigade of Vermont Militia. Mead later became a veteran of the War of 1812.

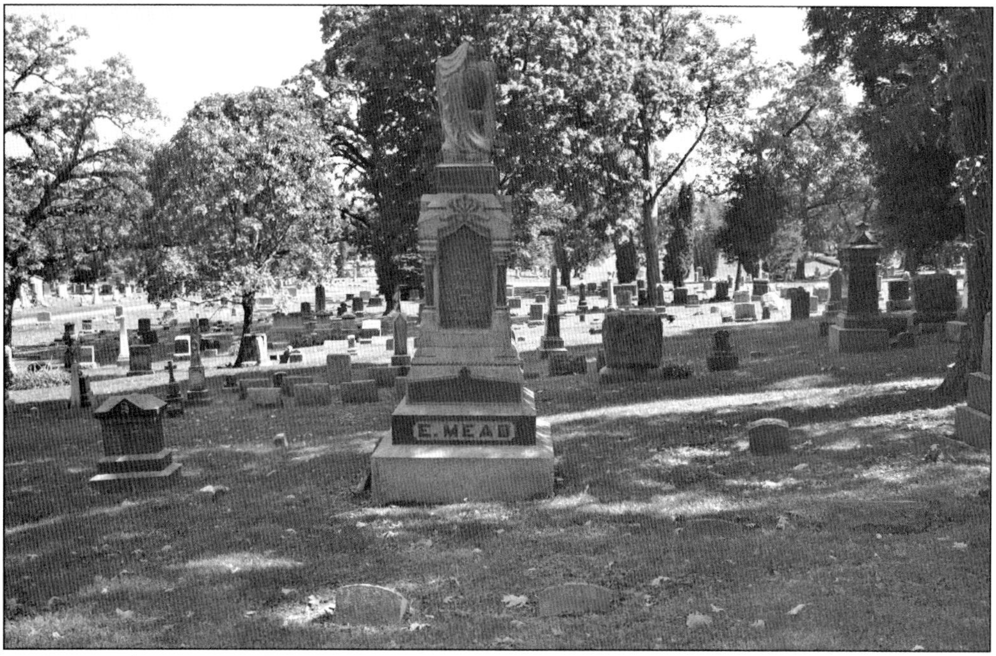

Seeking a place to preach in the West, Enoch Mead set out traveling in that direction and eventually came to the town of Rockingham, then just a short distance away from Davenport. Mead began missionary work in Scott County and other surrounding counties, doing so for several years until failing health caused him to stop. He retired himself to agricultural and horticultural work. Mead died in 1892.

In 1856, Henry Lischer, a Mexican-American War veteran, moved upriver from St. Louis to Davenport. He and another man, Theo Olshausen, purchased a German language newspaper, *Der Demokrat*. They ran the paper for four years, then sold it in 1860 and bought another newspaper in St. Louis. While here, Lischer served in the Home Guards during the Civil War.

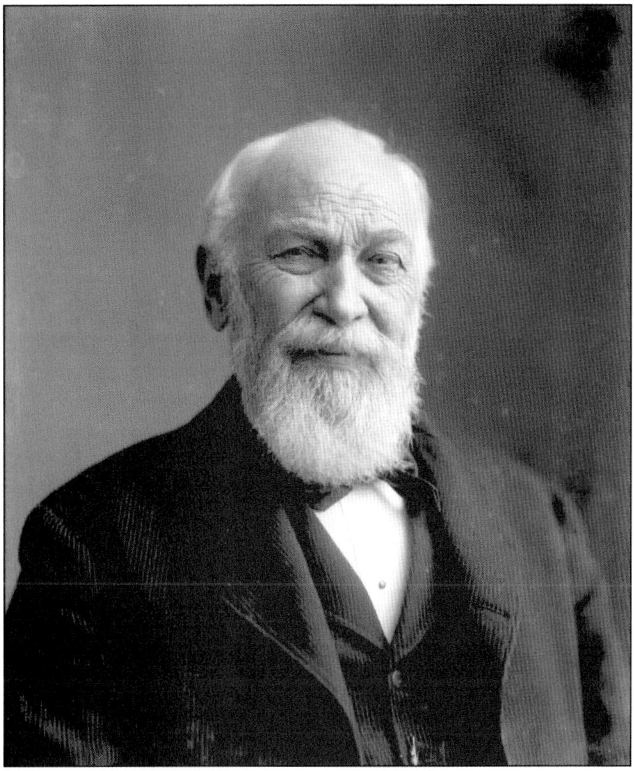

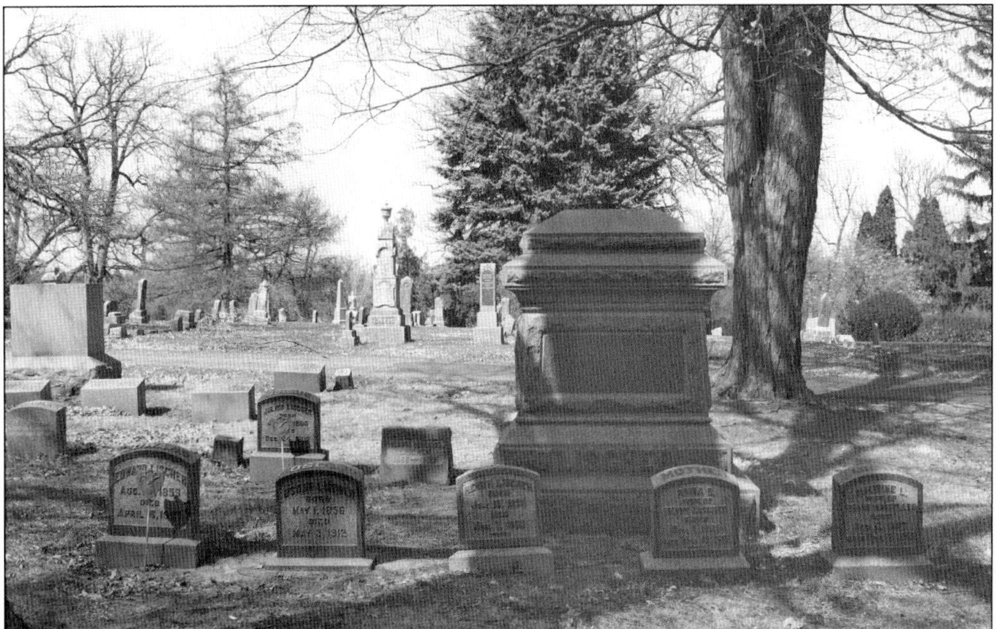

When his term was over, Henry Lischer sold his interest in the St. Louis newspaper and returned to Davenport and *Der Demokrat*. Lischer served as a director the German Savings Bank in Davenport from its inception in 1868 and then served as its president for 23 years. He died of a stroke in 1903.

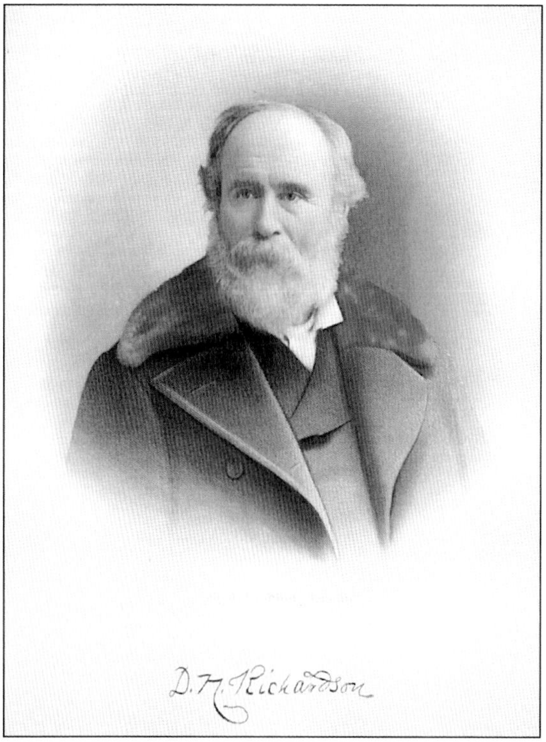

D.N. Richardson was a professional newspaperman who originally came to Peoria, Illinois, from his native New England in 1854. He began his career there working for the *Peoria Morning News*. The following year he traveled to Davenport and became editor of what would be the *Democrat* for 43 years. His brother J.J. Richardson came to Davenport in 1859 and became the publisher of the *Democrat* for 58 years.

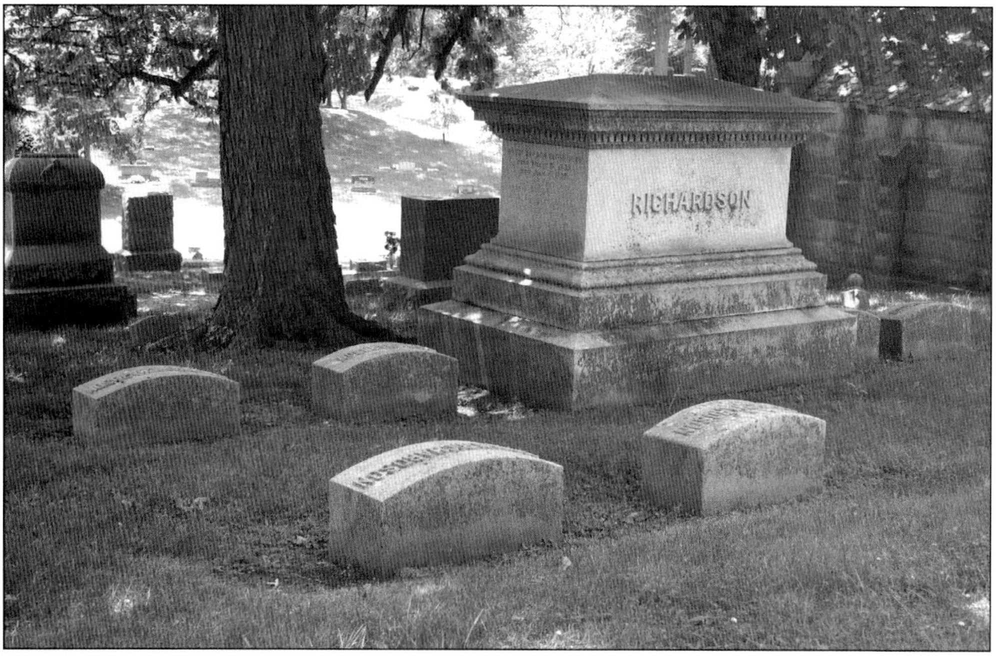

Together, D.N. and J.J. Richardson formed the company Richardson Brothers in 1863. Times were very hard in the early days of the *Democrat*. David did many jobs at the newspaper himself and was an excellent writer. Because there was not much money, J.J. would trade advertisement in the newspaper in return for an actual product instead of monetary compensation. He had a profound interest in the local history of Davenport and wrote several articles about it.

John Forrest was born in Russia, New York, on July 14, 1807. In his youth, Forrest worked on his father's farm and was educated in local schools. He eventually became a store clerk. After two years, Forrest decided to continue in the mercantile business as his own employer. In 1837, he moved west and settled in Davenport, Iowa.

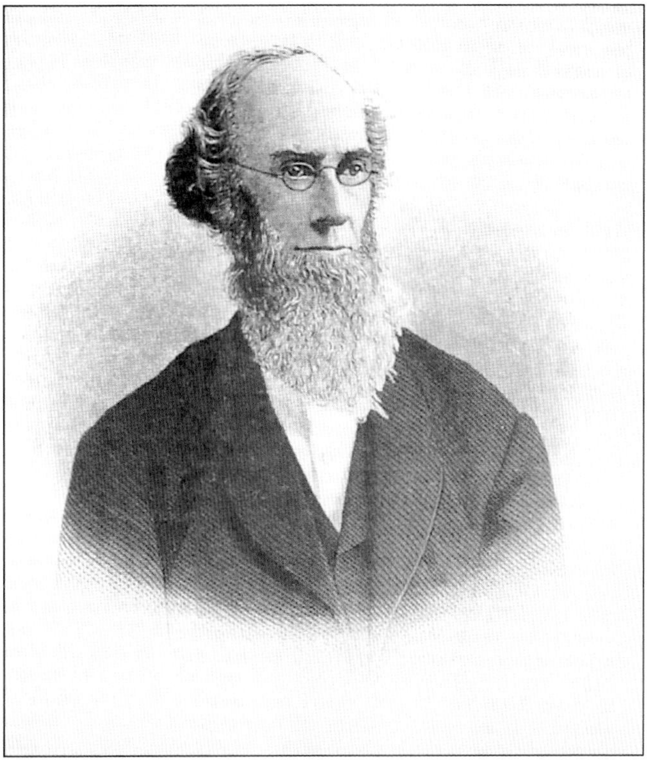

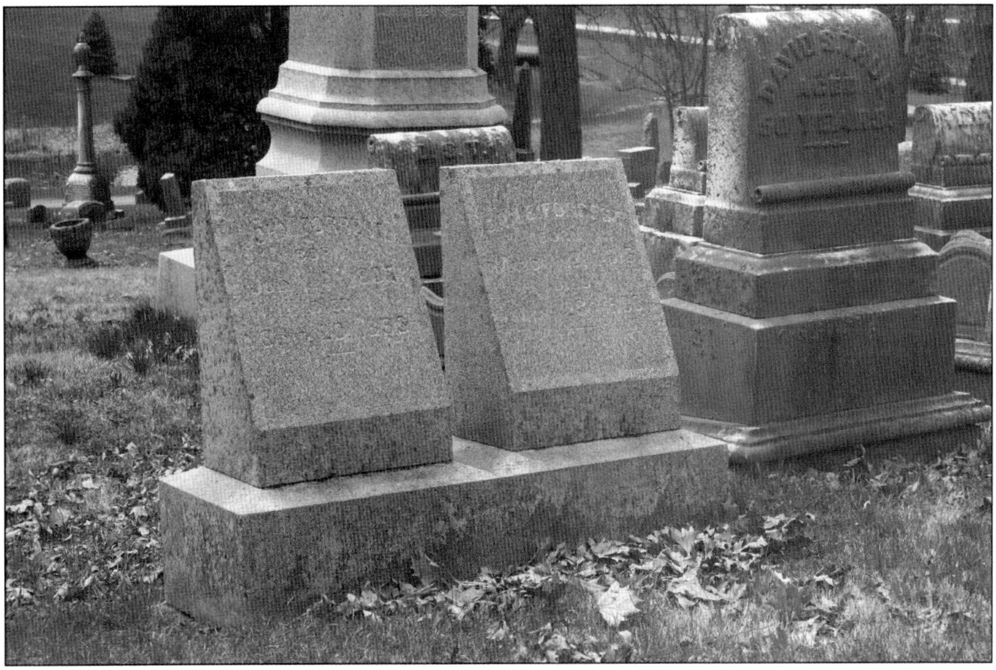

In Davenport, John Forrest was elected justice of the peace. In 1845, he was made postmaster for four years. Forrest was also a city alderman and the mayor of Davenport for a single term in the absence of George Sargent, who was the mayor elect. Forrest was involved in the contest between the towns of Rockingham and Davenport to become the county seat of Scott County.

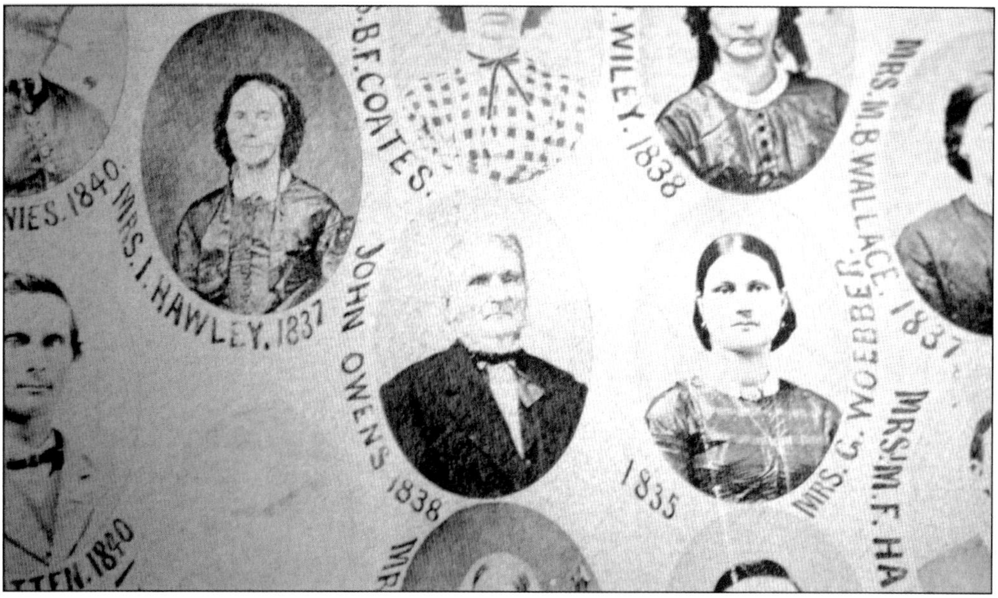

Born in Wales in 1793 but raised in New York City, John Owens spent several years living in Cincinnati, Ohio. Owens came to Davenport with his family in 1838 after visiting the area with J.M.D. Burrows, another man who would become a notable early Davenport resident. He ran a successful general store there for more than 30 years and served as the director of the Davenport National Bank.

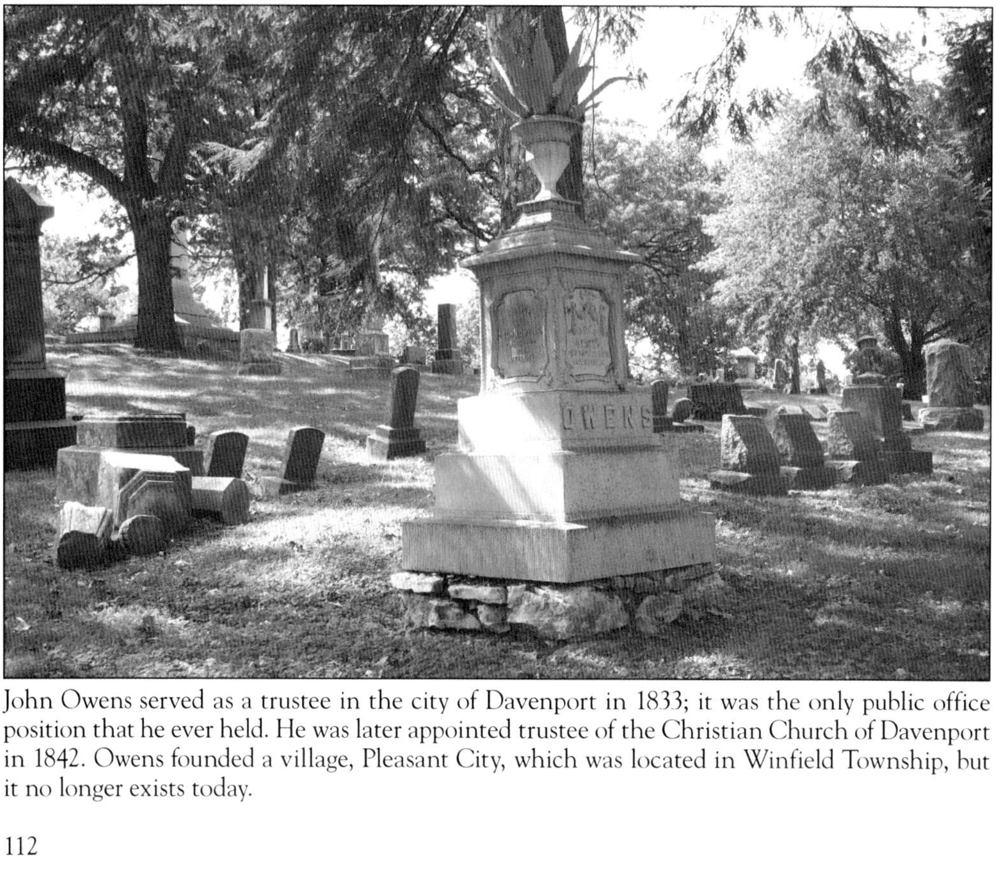

John Owens served as a trustee in the city of Davenport in 1833; it was the only public office position that he ever held. He was later appointed trustee of the Christian Church of Davenport in 1842. Owens founded a village, Pleasant City, which was located in Winfield Township, but it no longer exists today.

Alice French was born in 1850 in Andover, Massachusetts. Her aunt was married to Bishop Henry Lee, the first Episcopal bishop of Iowa. Based on his description, the French family moved to Davenport in 1856. Alice attended Vassar College in 1866 but dropped out after a semester. She returned to Davenport two years later after having attended Abbott College.

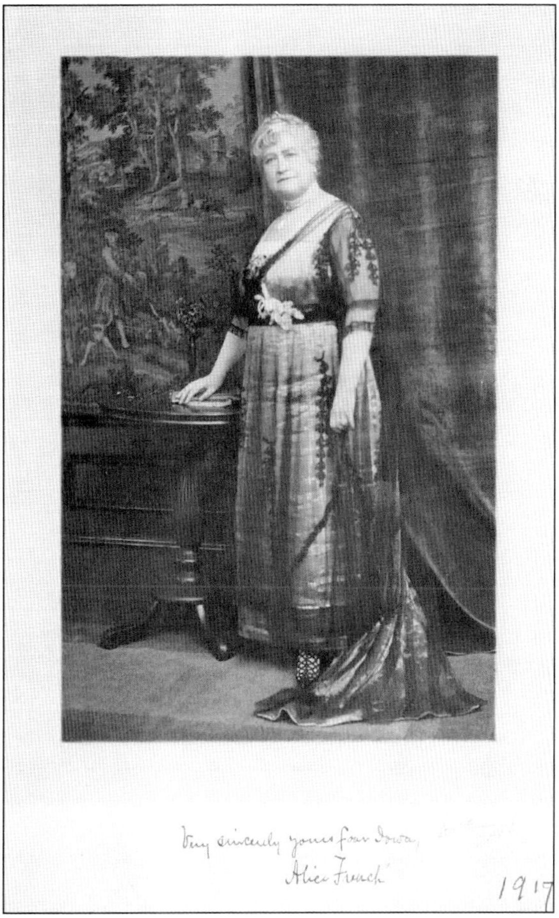

Alice French began writing her first book in 1904. She would go on to write several more books and magazine articles. French helped organize the anti-suffrage movement in Iowa and had an interest in orphans' homes in Russia. When she was 32, she decided to not get married because she did not want to give up her lifestyle. French died from complications of diabetes in 1934.

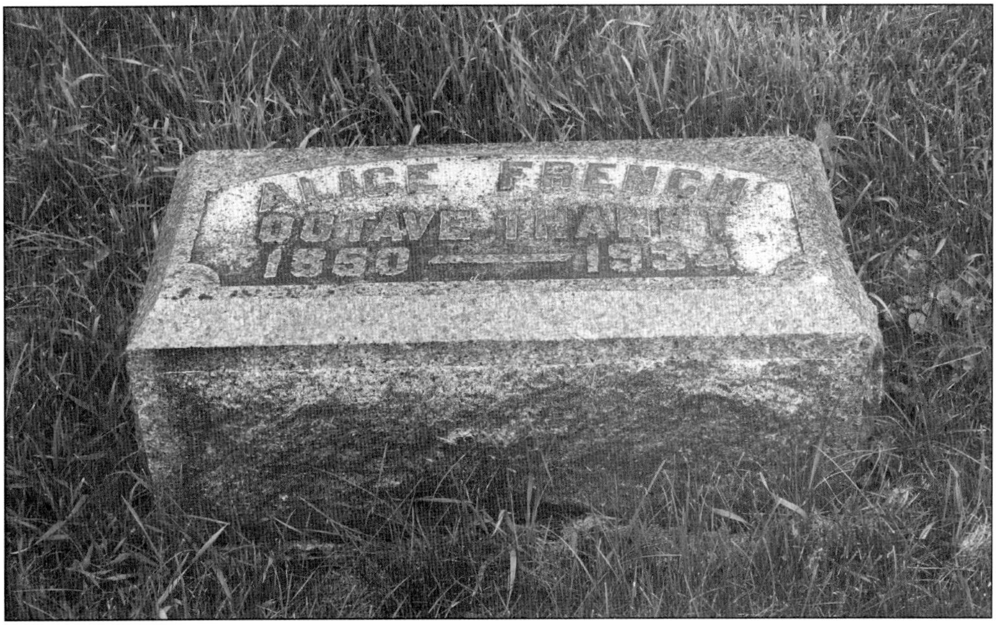

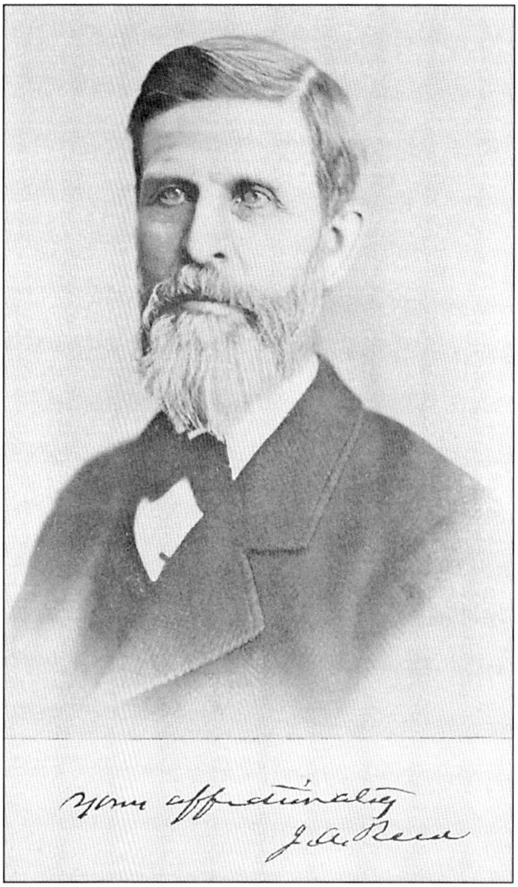

Dr. Julius A. Reed, a descendant of Gov. William Bradford of Plymouth, Massachusetts, was born in Connecticut in 1809. He attended Trinity College in Hartford, Connecticut, and graduated from Yale in 1829. Reed worked as a private tutor for a while and also assisted in organizing the First Congressional Church. Reed also became one of the first three Congregational ministers in Iowa.

In 1845, Dr. Reed moved to Davenport with his family. For 24 years, he was the superintendent of the American Home Missionary Society. He helped select a site for Iowa College. After withdrawing from this position, he moved to Nebraska. Reed died in 1890 at his daughter's home in Davenport.

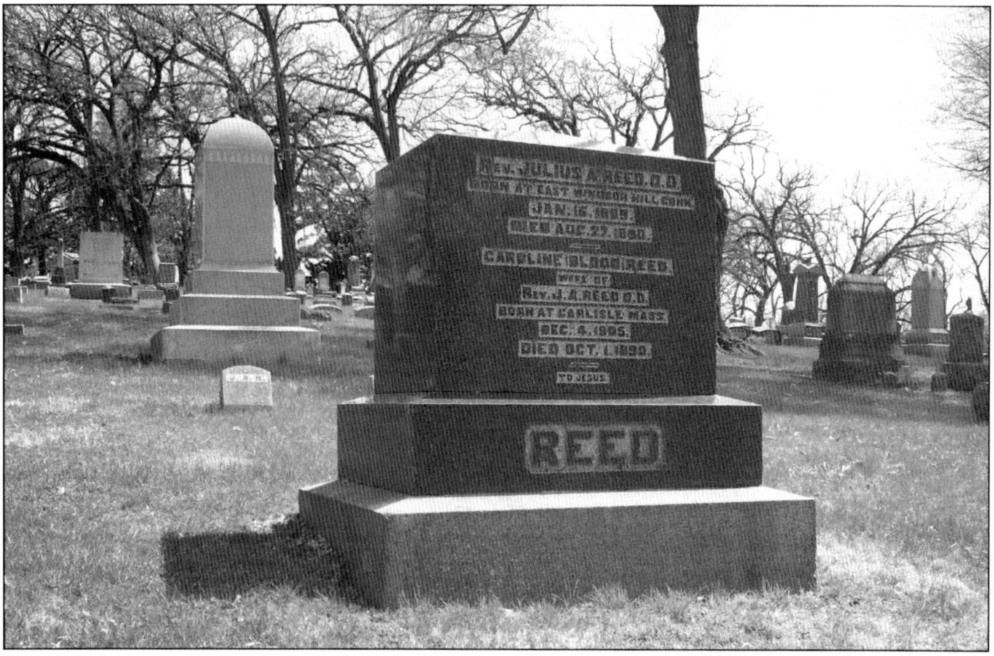

Born in Pennsylvania on May 24, 1834, Mathias Proudfoot worked on a farm and learned how to be a carpenter at a young age. A short time before his birthday in 1861, he came to Iowa with his father and settled in Lincoln Township where he bought a 120-acre farm.

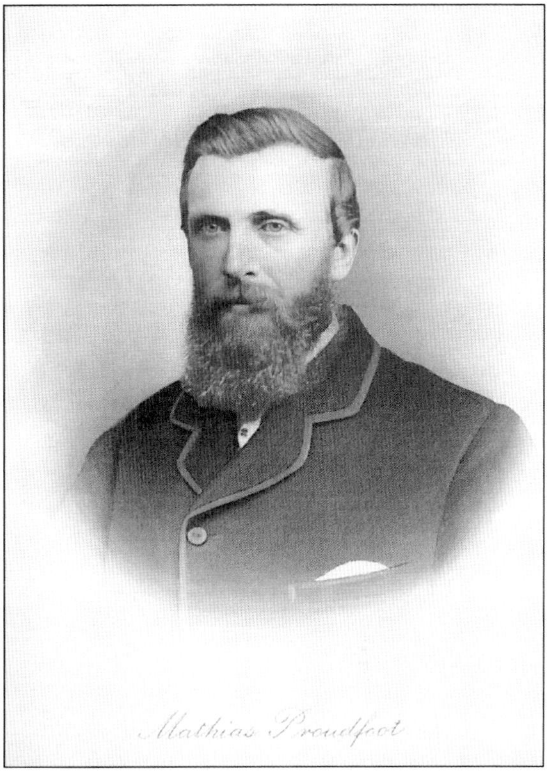

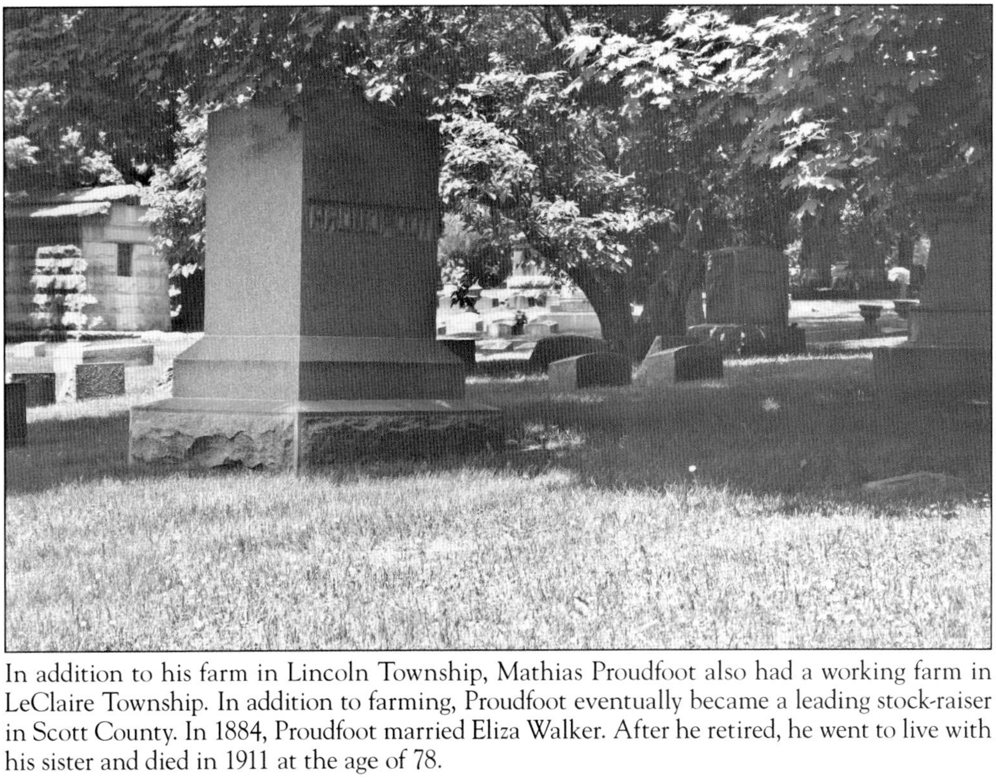

In addition to his farm in Lincoln Township, Mathias Proudfoot also had a working farm in LeClaire Township. In addition to farming, Proudfoot eventually became a leading stock-raiser in Scott County. In 1884, Proudfoot married Eliza Walker. After he retired, he went to live with his sister and died in 1911 at the age of 78.

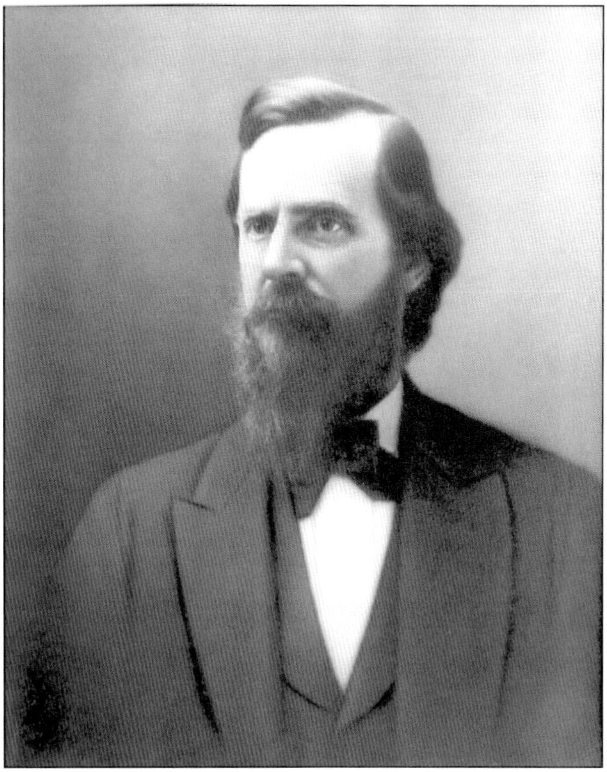

Ira M. Gifford was born in New York in 1834. A president of the First National Bank, he was elected clerk of district court several times in Scott County. Gifford also served on the board of trustees for the Davenport Savings Bank and was secretary for the Davenport Plow Company.

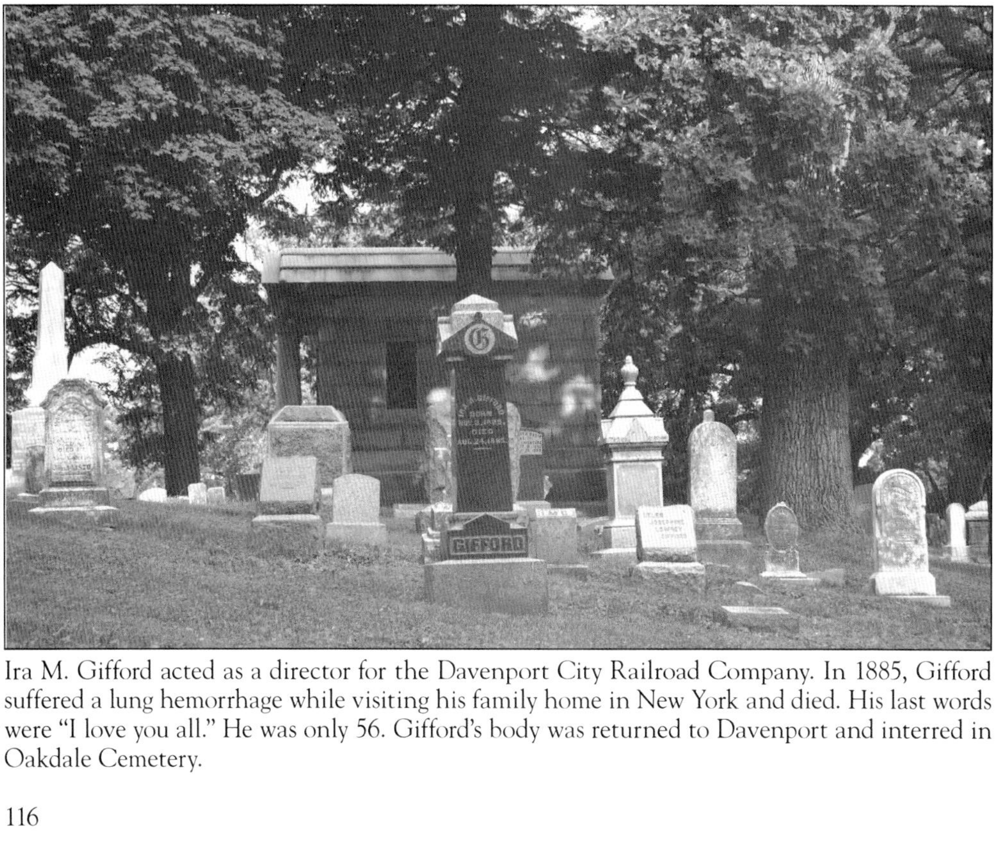

Ira M. Gifford acted as a director for the Davenport City Railroad Company. In 1885, Gifford suffered a lung hemorrhage while visiting his family home in New York and died. His last words were "I love you all." He was only 56. Gifford's body was returned to Davenport and interred in Oakdale Cemetery.

Eight

DAVENPORT AS THEY KNEW IT

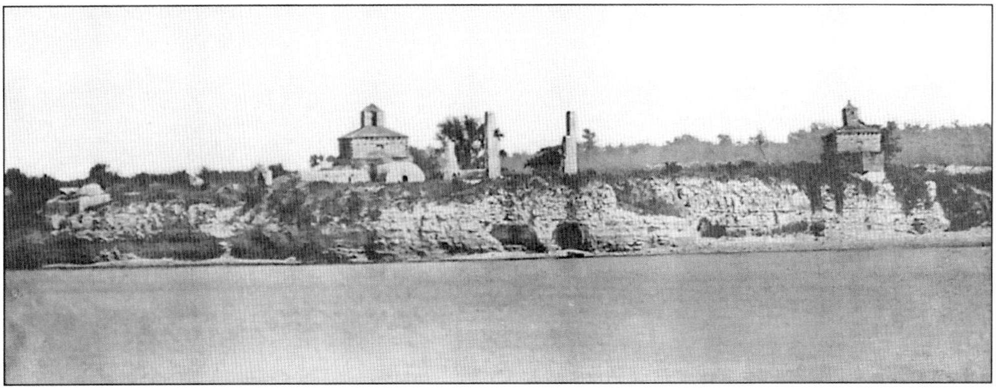

In September 1815, the 8th US Infantry came upriver from St. Louis and landed on Rock Island on May 10, 1816. The soldiers began to build a fort there right away and named it Fort Armstrong, after the late Secretary of War. The fort contained three blockhouses and 30-foot limestone cliffs that protected two of the fort's four sides. This picture shows the fort as it was in 1859.

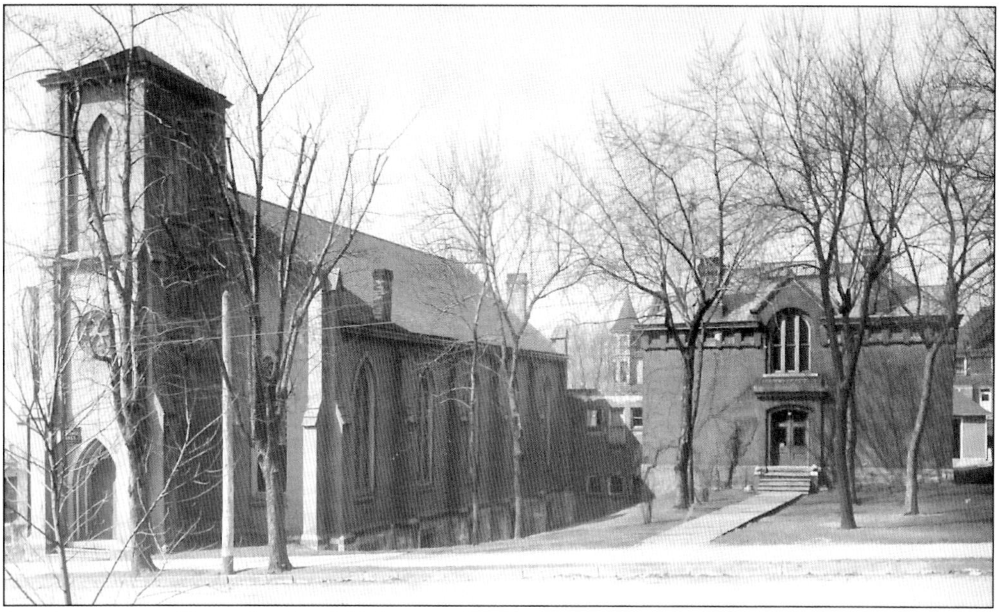

On the evening of December 14, 1867, four people met in a small real estate agency office in Davenport. They agreed upon increased study in the sciences for both themselves and for the community at large. From this humble beginning, the Davenport Academy of Sciences was born.

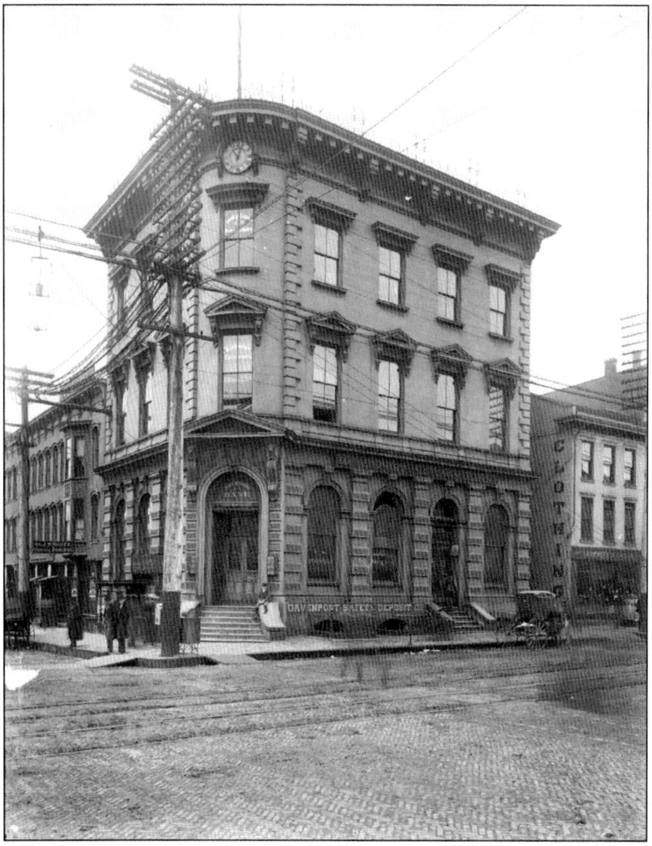

On June 29, 1863, the First National Bank opened with Austin Corbin as president and Ira M. Gifford as cashier. The new bank also secured the first certificate issued under the new banking law in the United States. Gifford would go on to become president of the company. He also served as the clerk of district court in Scott County.

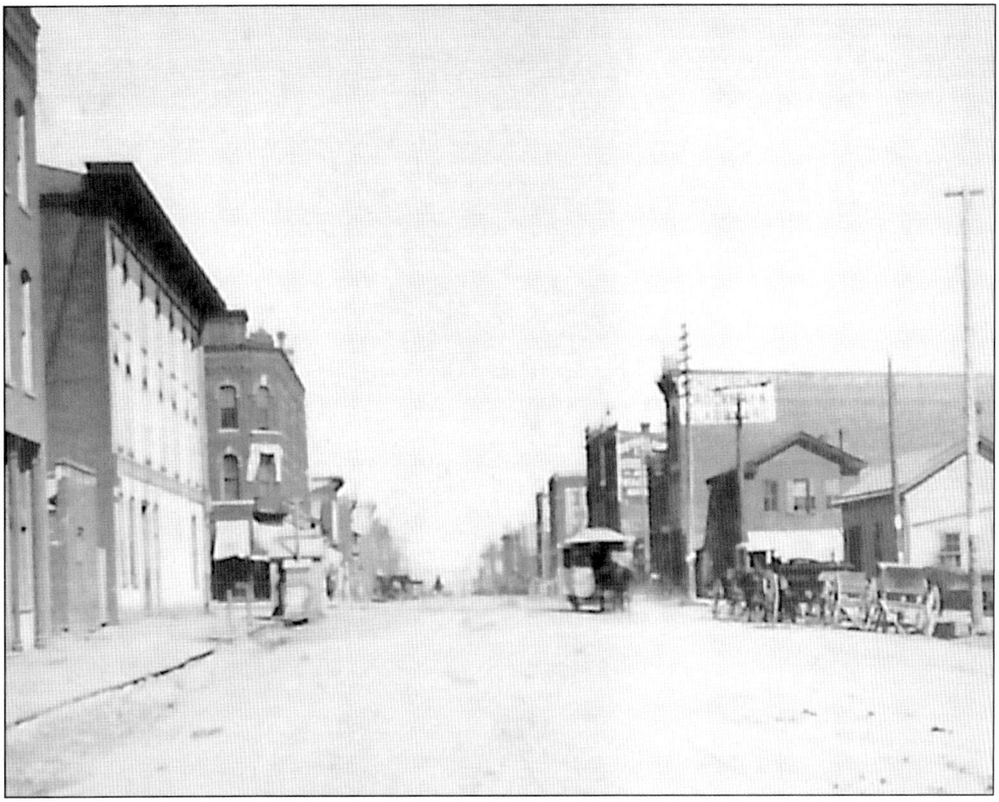

The city of Davenport had two lines of street railway. The first was the Davenport City Railway Company, organized in 1867 and constructed in 1868. The second was known as the Third Street line and ran the entire length of the city. Ira M. Gifford was one of the first directors of this line.

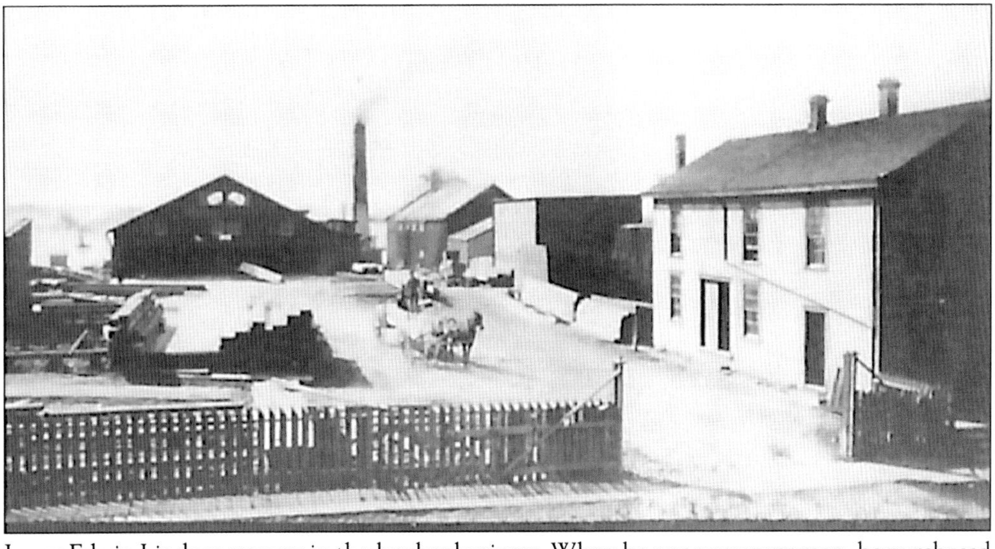

James Edwin Lindsay grew up in the lumber business. When he was a younger man, he purchased timberland in Wisconsin and had the timber sent downriver to the Davenport sawmills. In 1866, he and his partner built a sawmill, the Lindsay and Phelps Sawmill and Lumber Mill, east of Mound Street. That sawmill operated until the end of 1904.

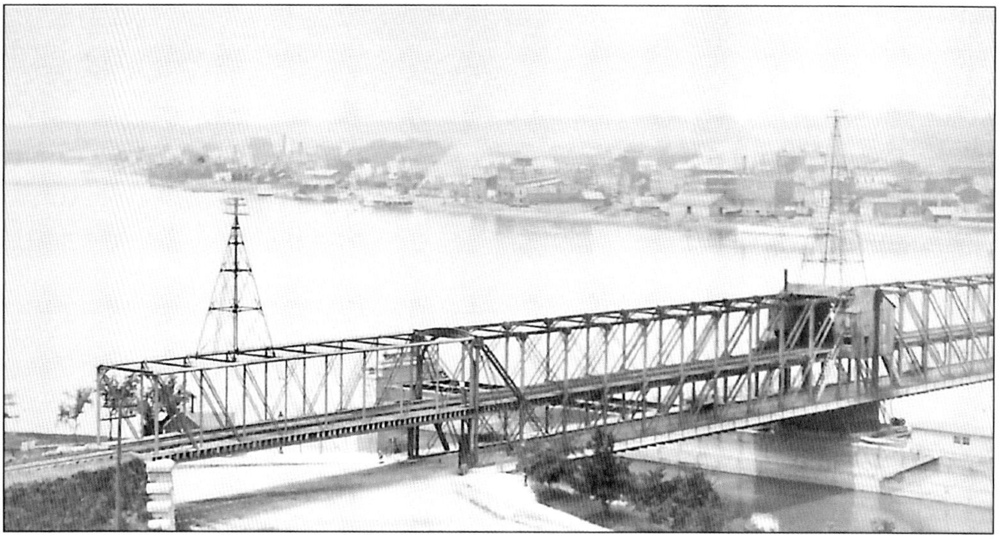

Missing from this photograph is Lock and Dam 15, one of the most prominent features on the Quad City–area Mississippi River. Built in the 1930s, the Lock and Dam system made navigation easier for river travel. In the background is the Davenport Ferry along the buildings of Front Street, the former name for River Drive in Davenport.

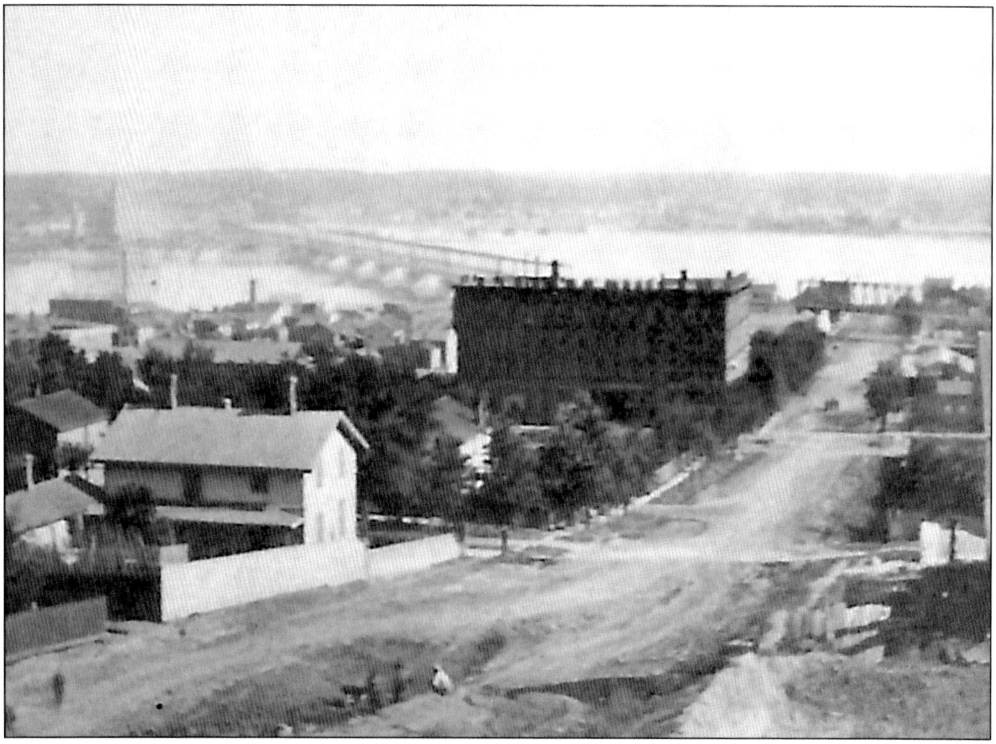

In this picture, taken from Iowa Street and Eighth Avenue, the Mississippi River and the government bridge can be seen. The first bridge across the Mississippi River was constructed in the 1850s, followed by the first railcar crossing the bridge in 1856. After the bridge was destroyed by ice and wind in 1868, a second bridge opened in 1873. Eventually, the third and present bridge was built in 1894.

J.H.C. Petersen moved to Davenport and entered the general mercantile business with a man named Abel Henry. By 1872, Petersen bought out Henry and went into business with his three sons. They steadily expanded and became one of the leading department stores in the area. This is their store, J.H.C. Petersen and Sons Wholesale and Retail Dry Goods, located at 217, 217 1/2, 219, and 221 West Second Street in Davenport.

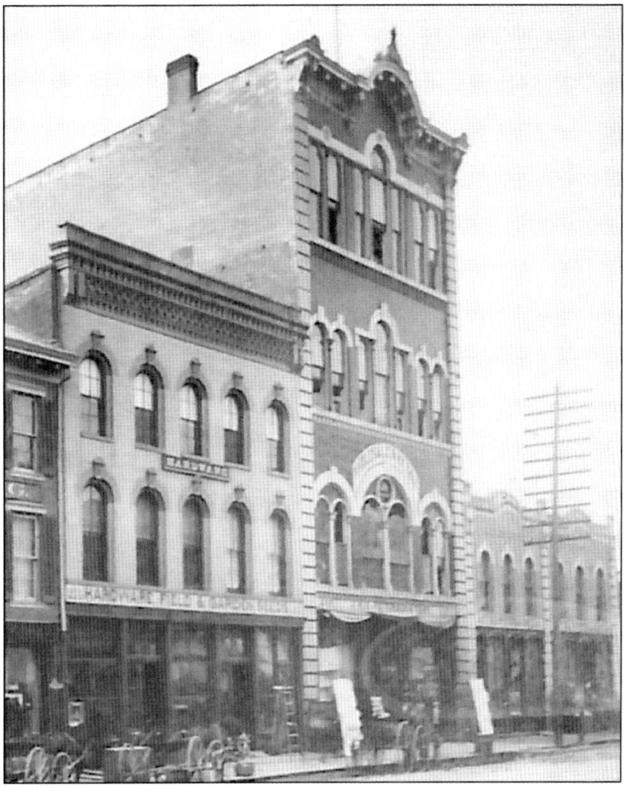

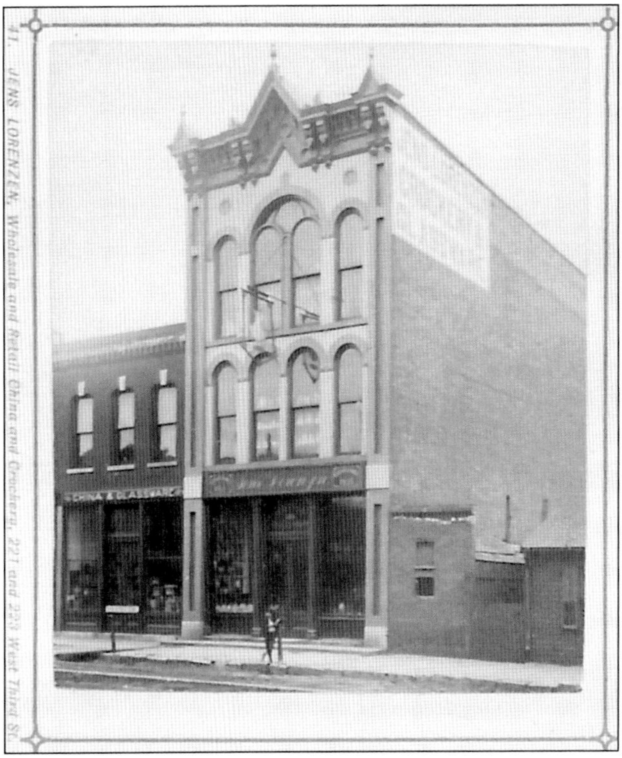

This store owned by Jens Lorenzen was located at 221 and 223 West Third Street in Davenport. The store specialized in stoneware, porcelain, and glass. The business eventually became the Jens Lorenzen Crockery Company, and it grew steadily over the course of several years. By 1882, Lorenzen was earning $100,000 a year. In 1907, he sold his business interests in the company but still owned the property.

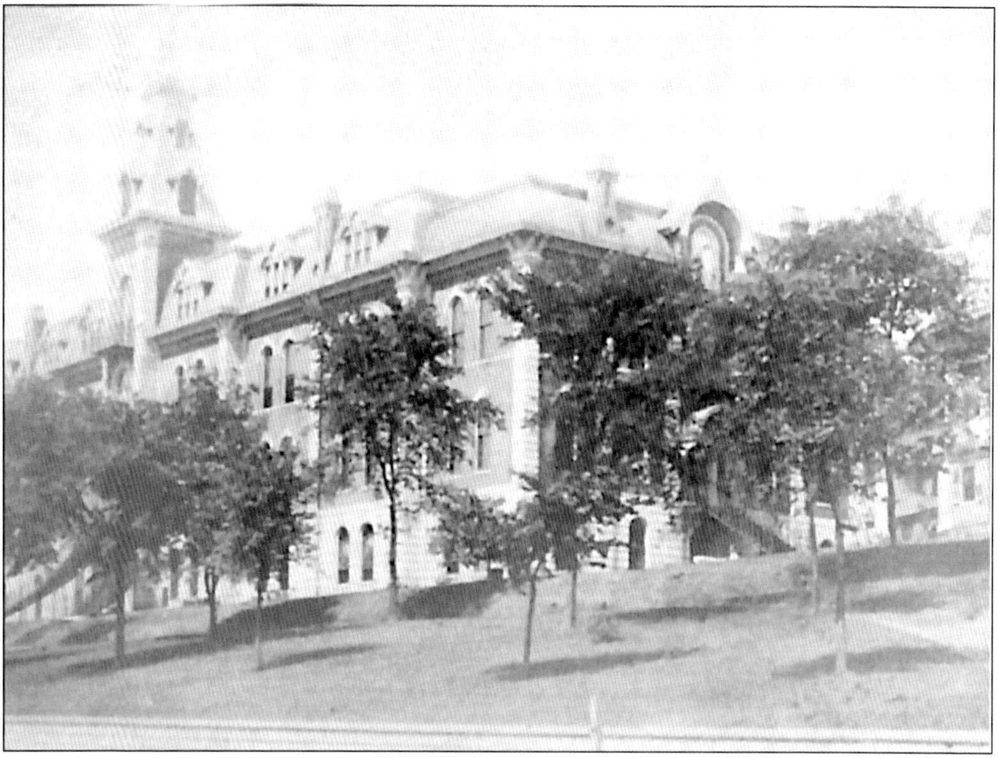

In 1859, the Academy of the Immaculate Conception was opened on the site of Mercy Hospital in Davenport. This Catholic girls school was later moved twice more, the second and final time to Main and Eighth Streets in 1866. Run by Catholic nuns, the school offered up to a 12-year course of study.

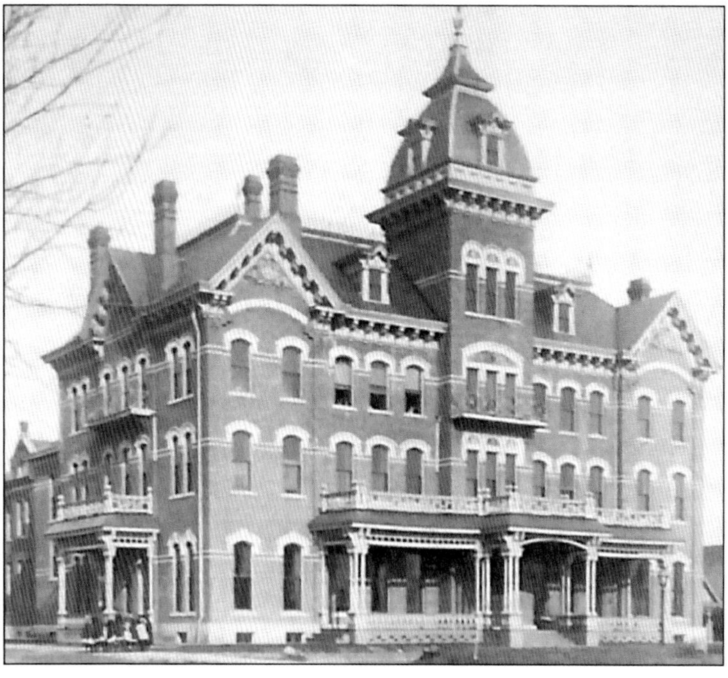

During a convention in Muscatine, Iowa, in 1853, Annie Wittenmeyer asked those present to offer a means to provide for the education and needs of soldiers' orphans in Iowa. People donated tremendous support for the endeavor, and the Iowa State Orphan Asylum was formed. Later, Wittenmeyer founded the Soldiers' Orphans' Home in Davenport for orphans left by the Civil War.

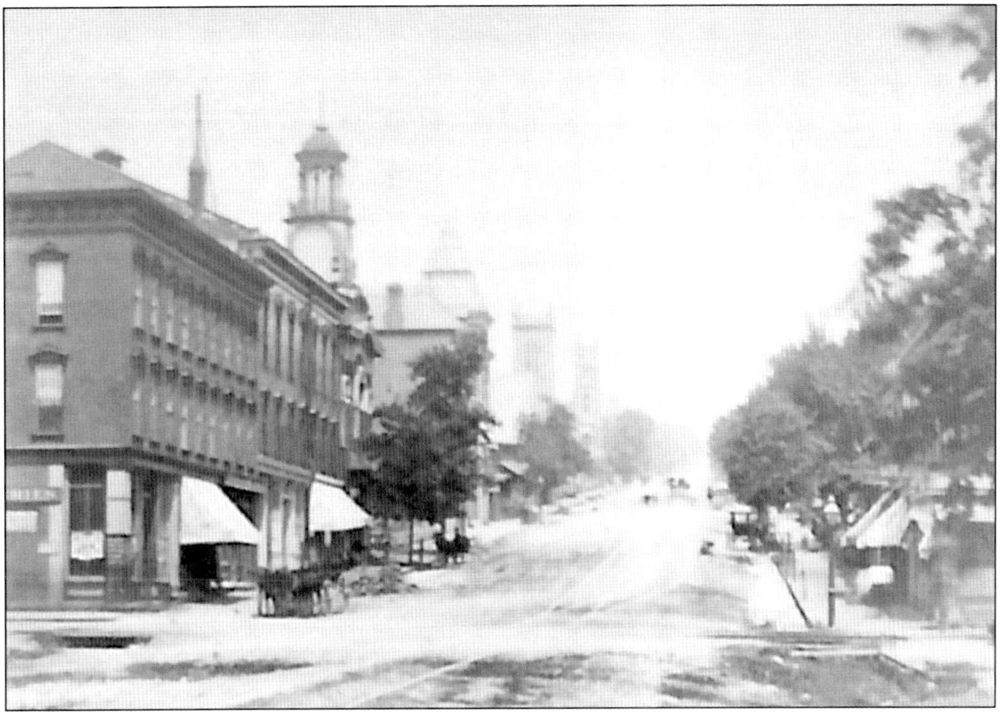

This photograph of Brady Street shows some of the streetcar tracks that ran through the city. The Davenport Central Railway Company was organized and constructed in 1870. In 1871, the streetcars began running from the corner of Second and Brady Streets to the fairgrounds. James Grant was a president of the company. Subsequent branches were built to East Davenport and Oakdale Cemetery, as well as to the Washington Garden in West Davenport.

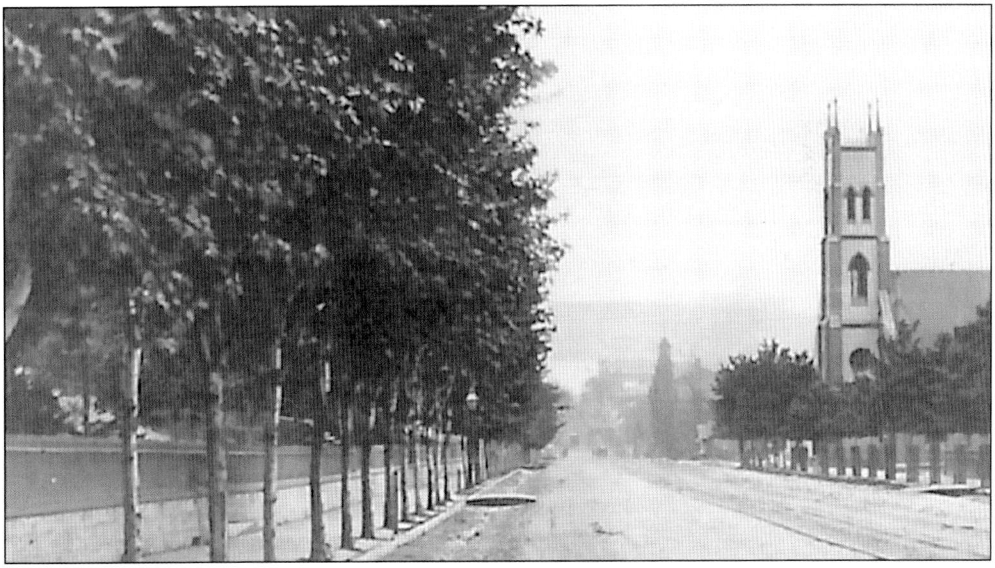

In this scene of Brady Street facing toward the downtown and river area, the tracks for the Davenport Central Railway can be seen. The first line built by the company was the Third Street line, which was first used in early 1869. The Brady Street line came later, and in 1888, it received electric power.

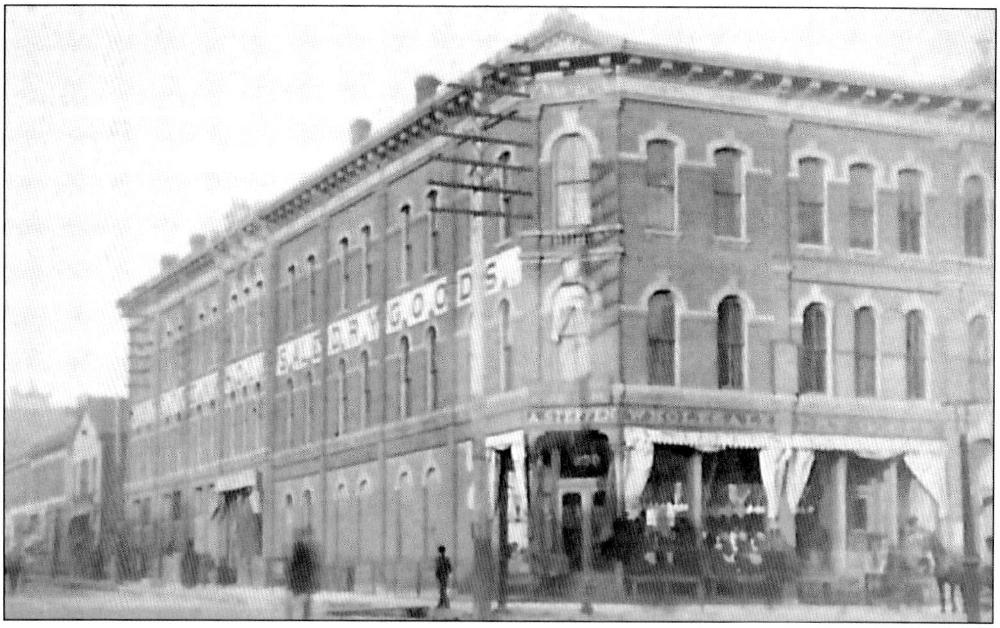

August Steffen, a very successful Davenport businessman, opened this store, August Steffen Wholesale and Retail Dry Goods, at the corner of Second and Harrison Streets in 1878. The building was three stories tall and featured an elevator and basement. The store carried an assortment of both domestic and imported goods. After his retirement, Steffen turned over control of the business to his son and son-in-law.

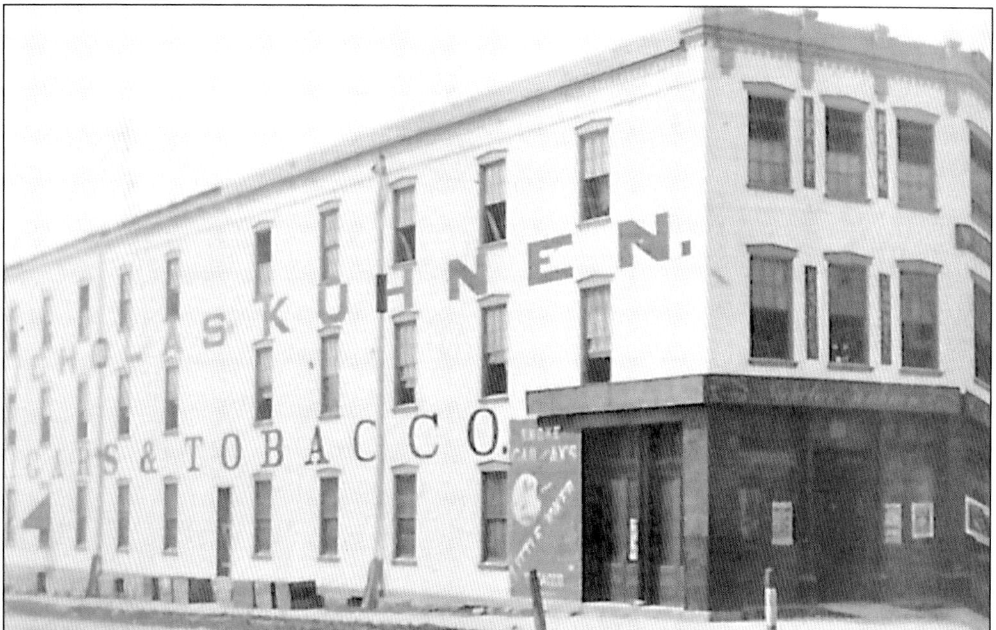

In the 1850s, Nicholas Kuhnen moved to Davenport, Iowa, and opened a cigar and tobacco store. Later, Kuhnen opened a cigar factory. His business would eventually become the largest cigar and tobacco business in the state of Iowa. This photograph shows the store as it was on the southwest corner of Second and Perry Streets.

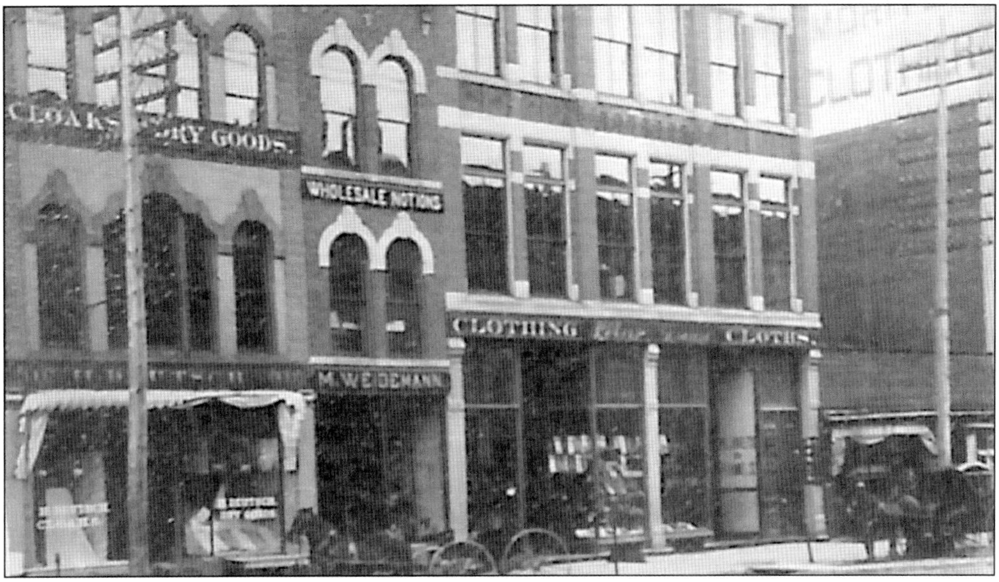

Robert Krause came to Davenport when he was only 18 years old. He worked at some local businesses before opening his own store in 1854. For the next several years, he successfully ran the store, seen here at 113 and 115 West Second Street. Eventually, Krause would branch out into other lines of business, including the Davenport Glucose Company.

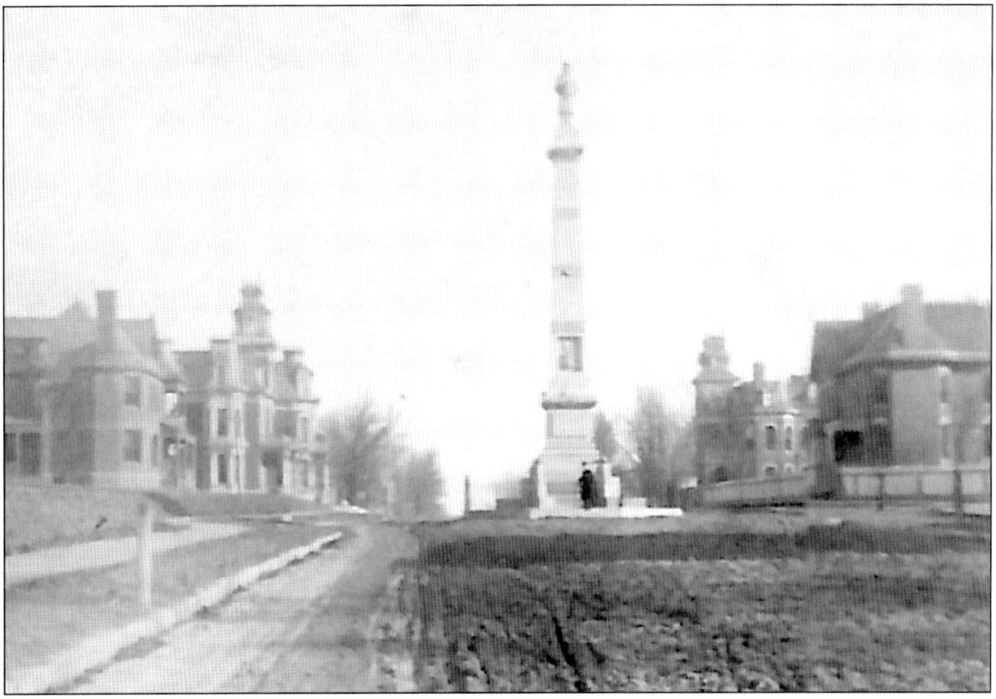

In this view of Main Street in Davenport, a monument dedicated to the soldiers of the Civil War is seen. In the left background is the mansion of Charles Ficke, a successful lawyer and former Davenport mayor who enjoyed traveling and donated his art collection to the city. In the background at the right is the home of James Thorington, who was also a successful lawyer and mayor of Davenport.

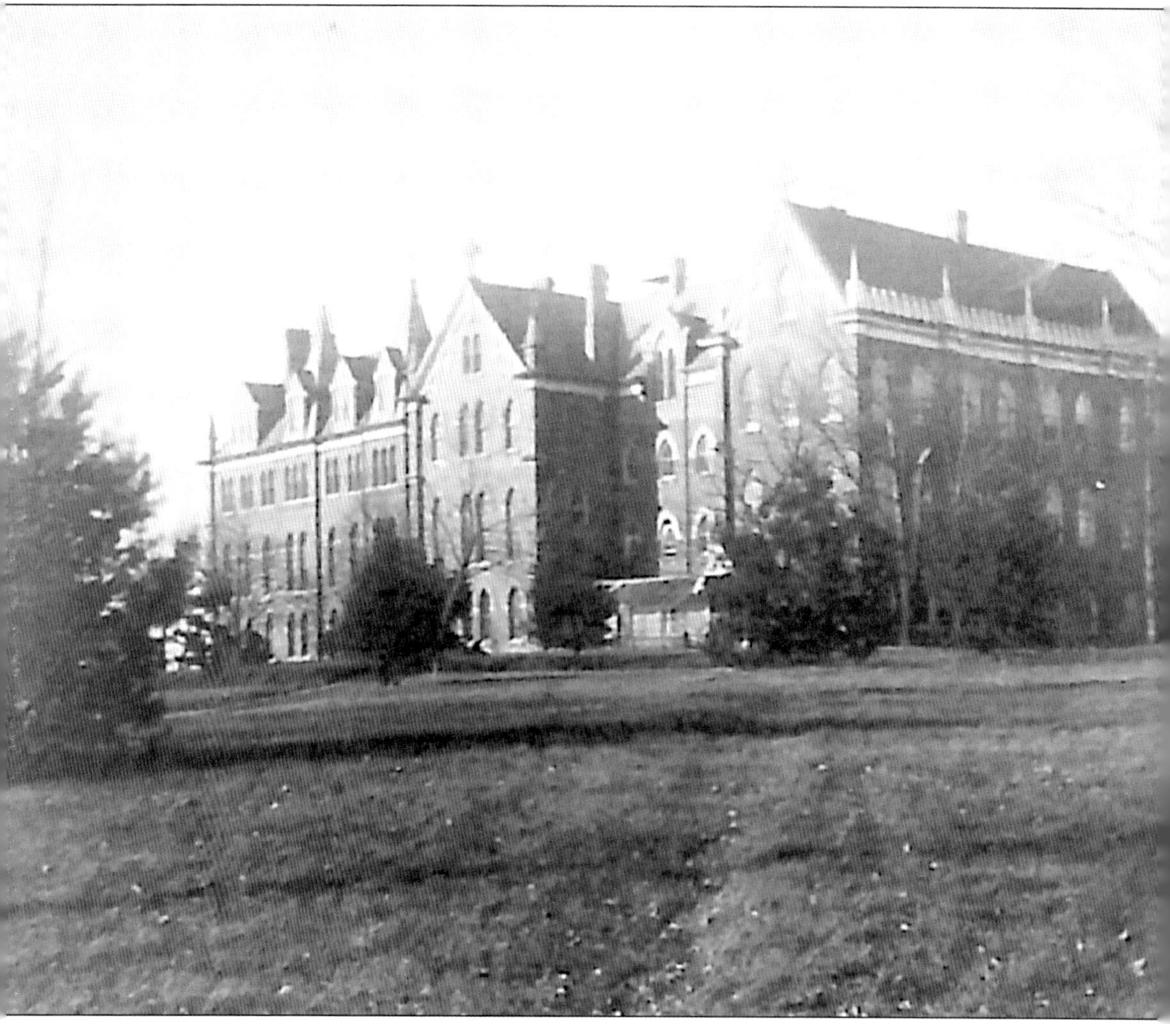

Mercy Hospital opened on December 8, 1868, under an arrangement between Scott County and the Sisters of Mercy that the county advance $2,000 for five years without interest. Ten insane paupers were, on the above date, at once transferred from the poor houses to the new hospital. The authorities guaranteed that there would constantly be at least that number of county patients in the care of the sisters.

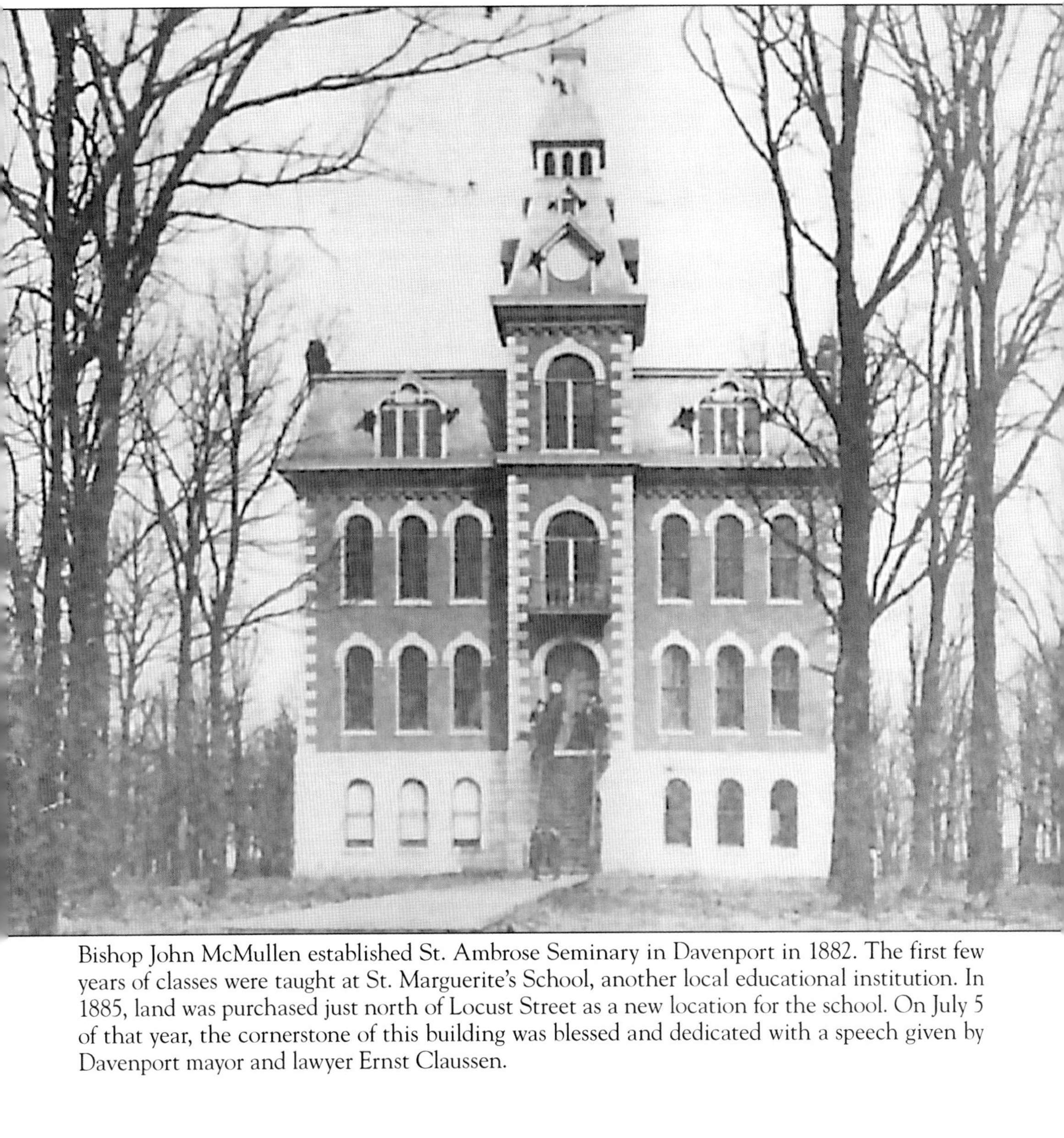

Bishop John McMullen established St. Ambrose Seminary in Davenport in 1882. The first few years of classes were taught at St. Marguerite's School, another local educational institution. In 1885, land was purchased just north of Locust Street as a new location for the school. On July 5 of that year, the cornerstone of this building was blessed and dedicated with a speech given by Davenport mayor and lawyer Ernst Claussen.

Consistent with our mission to preserve history on a local level, this book was printed in South Carolina on American-made paper and manufactured entirely in the United States. Products carrying the accredited Forest Stewardship Council (FSC) label are printed on 100 percent FSC-certified paper.

MADE IN THE USA